An Introduction to
DAOIST PHILOSOPHIES

An Introduction to
DAOIST PHILOSOPHIES

Steve Coutinho

Columbia University Press   New York

Columbia University Press
Publishers Since 1893
New York   Chichester, West Sussex
cup.columbia.edu
Copyright © 2014 Steve Coutinho
Library of Congress Cataloging-in-Publication Data
Coutinho, Steve.
An introduction to Daoist philosophies / Steve Coutinho.
   pages   cm
Includes bibliographical references and index.
ISBN 978-0-231-14338-7 (cloth) —
ISBN 978-0-231-14339-4 (pbk.) —
ISBN 978-0-231-51288-6 (electronic)
1. Taoist philosophy. I. Title.

B162.7.C68   2013
181'.114—dc23   2013003261

Cover design by Rebecca Lown

CONTENTS

Preface   *vii*

Acknowledgments   *xi*

1. Daoist Philosophies   1

2. Fundamental Concepts of Chinese Philosophy   19

3. The *Laozi*   45

4. The *Zhuangzi: Inner Chapters* and Zhuangzian Philosophy   78

5. The *Outer* and *Miscellaneous Chapters* of the *Zhuangzi*:
   From Anarchist Utopianism to Mystical Imperialism   126

6. The *Liezi*   145

7. Philosophy of Skill in the *Zhuangzi* and *Liezi*   168

Afterword: A Family of *Dao*   187

Notes   *191*

Bibliography   *217*

Index   *223*

PREFACE

The term "Daoism" is highly amorphous, as there is no unitary phenomenon to which it unambiguously refers. It may refer to the philosophical ideas advocated in early texts such as the *Laozi* and the *Zhuangzi*; to the syncretistic metapolitical thought of the Han dynasty; to systems of spiritual and meditative cultivation; to practices of alchemy and longevity; and to a number of institutional religious systems that have developed over the course of the last two millennia. This book does not pretend to be about all these forms of Daoism. Rather, it focuses specifically on the variety of philosophical ideas and viewpoints that are raised in three early Daoist texts.

Two texts in particular, the *Laozi* and the *Zhuangzi*, came to dominate the discourse and acquired the status of classics, at least in part because of the richness of their philosophical content. They are by no means the only early texts representative of Daoist philosophical thought. The *Huainanzi* and the *Lüshi Chunqiu*, for example, contain some material that resonates with Daoist sensibility. Roger Ames and D. C. Lau have produced a study and translation of "Yuan Dao," an essay from the *Huainanzi* that explicitly draws ideas from both the *Laozi* and the *Zhuangzi*. Harold Roth has recently produced a study of the "Nei Ye" chapter of the *Guanzi* and its possible relationship to early Daoist thought and practice. In this book, I have expanded the usual repertoire of the *Laozi* and the *Zhuangzi* with a study of the *Liezi*. Though it dates from a slightly later period, it is very similar to the *Zhuangzi* in style, spirit, and content, sharing and developing many concerns found in the earlier two texts.

Without denying the individuality of and distinctive differences among the three texts, or the plurality of voices and perspectives within each of them, they can be seen as sharing a distinctive philosophical sensibility that differentiates them from competing views of the time. Even if the authors, contributors, and commentators did not think of themselves as proponents of a single doctrine or as belonging to the same school, they are not unreasonably regarded as belonging to related traditions of thought. Broadly speaking, they each articulate a worldview that promotes a shift in emphasis from the human to the cosmic, or from the artificial to the natural. They also advocate ways of life in which we cultivate natural capacities, and modes of yielding, nurturing, nondeliberate interaction (*wuwei*) that have been overlooked or underdeveloped in our race to acquire culture and become civilized. Their concerns regarding humanity, technology, government, and nature are as relevant now as when they were written, and arguably more pressing than ever before. What the right name for this broad philosophical sensibility should be is a moot question. It has come to be known as "Daoism," and probably will be called that for a long time to come. But since it has multiple manifestations, I shall use the plural form, "Daoist *philosophies*."

This book provides a thorough scholarly introduction to the fundamental concepts of the various branches of Daoist thought represented in these three texts. It is written for two types of readers: those interested in philosophy who want to expand their range to include Daoism; and those interested in ancient China who wish to deepen their understanding of the philosophical issues raised by these texts.

It is first and foremost a work of comparative *philosophy*, using current concepts and methods of discourse: explication of philosophical concepts, articulation of philosophical theories, analysis of the philosophical problems that arise from them, and most importantly, exploration of attempts to solve those problems and thereby contribute to the development of those concepts and theories. It is thus the product of what Gadamer calls a "fusion of horizons": ancient Chinese discourse is used to aid our understanding of contemporary issues, and modern Western concepts and methods are used to read the ancient texts in a new light. Although it is an introduction, this study aims to stay true to the richness and complexity of the philosophical ideas without oversimplification.

Chapter One addresses the distinctive characteristics of and methodologies appropriate for ancient Chinese philosophical discourse, as these tend to be vastly different from those of Western philosophy. Chapter Two distinguishes a variety of basic worldviews and presuppositions and discusses some of the most fundamental concepts of ancient Chinese philosophies. Chapters Three to Six, after a brief discussion of each text and its authorship, proceed to elucidate the important concepts of the Daoist texts, noting deep differences from familiar Western concepts when appropriate. Generally speaking, these terms do not have direct equivalents in Western philosophy: resorting too quickly to familiar concepts results in common misunderstandings. Rather, the terms require extended explanations of their significances and associations in Daoist discourse. This constitutes a sort of "textual phenomenology": a mapping of concepts and conceptual differences by noting the associations, and consequent ranges of conceptual possibility, that are recorded in the texts. The ordering of concepts is significant: which are taken as central and which peripheral sets the tenor of the philosophy. For the most part, I begin with what I consider to be the most general concepts, the worldviews in terms of which the overall philosophy must be understood, and then work inward, as it were, from the cosmological and ontological to the existential, epistemological, and political.

My goal is to provide an interpretation of the early Daoist philosophies that respects their multiplicity and at the same time reveals their coherence as alternative developments of a distinctive philosophical sensibility. While there is no fixed essence of Daoist thought, I find several related notions close to its core: a shift in emphasis from the human to the cosmic, from the artificial to the natural; cultivation of natural life and tranquility; embodying natural spontaneity by diminishing artificial interference (*wuwei*); and an appreciation for the deeper productive value of emptiness, nothing, retreat, and reversal. I present and engage with traditional interpretations critically, and where I disagree I marshal arguments against them. It should go without saying that I do not present my views dogmatically, but in the spirit of continued open discourse.

Throughout the text, I draw attention to a recurring problem for Daoist philosophy: how can a philosophy that rejects humanistic values make sure it steers clear of inhumanity? The *Zhuangzi* text itself contains a formulation of this problem in chapter 23 (see pages 103–4 below). As I was finalizing the manuscript, I realized that the Utopian strand of Daoist thought might well have the conceptual resources for providing a naturalistic solution to this problem; I sketch the gist of the solution, but do not have the space here to develop it further.

In addition to the chapter on the *Liezi,* Chapters Five and Seven also present notable material. Chapter Five traces the development of Utopian and Syncretist thought in the *Outer* and *Miscellaneous Chapters.* Chapter Seven provides an analysis of the philosophy of skill in the *Zhuangzi* and *Liezi.* Through examination of the anecdotes of these texts, I articulate a coherent philosophy of the nature, acquisition, development, and performance of skill.

Translations are, for the most part, my own, but are sometimes based on Watson and Graham and modified for terminological and philosophical consistency. The references to Watson are to his translation, *The Complete Works of Chuang Tzu.*

A note on orthography: chapters in Daoist texts are referred to in the lower case with numerals: "chapter 6," for example. Chapters in this book are referred to in the upper case with numbers spelled in full, followed by the words "above" or "below": "Chapter Six below," for example. As with my first book, I sometimes make deliberate use of a new grammatical form, the "singular 'they'" to avoid sexist language.

ACKNOWLEDGMENTS

Every thought is nurtured in a history, a context of discourse, not only that of the academy, but also the experiences of a life, meditations on a text, and conversations with experts, students, and amateurs alike. To claim full 'authorship' of any thoughts without acknowledging the formative role of such contributors would be arrogant and inappropriate. I therefore extend my humble thanks to all my fellow travelers along the way. In particular, I would like to extend my profuse gratitude to Roger Ames, Hans-Georg Moeller, David McCraw, and Brian Hoffert for taking the time to review the entire manuscript and offer their invaluable thoughts and criticisms. Their suggestions have helped improve the text immeasurably, or at the very least remove a few traces of foolishness. I am also grateful to Brook Ziporyn, Jinmei Yuan, Geir Sigurdsson, Kurtis Hagen, Drew Leder, and Brian Lundberg for reviewing and commenting on parts of the manuscript.

Lastly, I would like to thank my students from Muhlenberg College and from Towson University for their conversation, discourse, and friendship. I have no doubt that their combined wisdom has shaped this text in ways that I could not hope to recount. I had intended to name students individually, but over the years the number has grown so large as to make an enumeration unfeasible. I therefore hope that they will accept my apologies for this omission.

An Introduction to
DAOIST PHILOSOPHIES

CHAPTER ONE

Daoist Philosophies

Daoism is often explained as the philosophy of The *Dao*—an absolute and transcendent substance, the utterly unspeakable ground of all existence that lies beyond the world of experience. Those who believe in a perennial philosophy—a single ultimate truth manifested to different cultures in different ways—take it to be the Chinese equivalent of Brahman in Vedanta philosophy, or of the Godhead in Christian mysticism. The *Laozi* says that there is something primordial and imperceptible; Vedanta says that Brahman is a ground of existence that transcends conceptual distinctions. Are these the same concept presented in superficially different ways, or are the similarities superficial and the differences so deep that the philosophies are actually in disagreement? From a philosophical point of view, the presupposition of identity is a little too hasty. Similarities can certainly be discerned, but there are also important differences. If we focus on the similarities we simply repeat the perennial doctrines of the perennial philosophy and deprive ourselves of the opportunity to learn what is distinctive about each. If, on the other hand, we pay closer attention to the differences, strive to interpret each tradition on its own terms, we open ourselves to the possibility of unanticipated insights. In fact, when the *Laozi* says that *dao* is primordial, this turns out to mean something radically different from the Vedanta proposition that Brahman is the ground of existence. The distinctive characteristics of this sort of worldview will emerge as the various Daoist philosophies are explored and developed throughout the course of this book.

While it is true that Daoist philosophies emphasize the fundamental importance of a subtle and expansive source of the world, there is a sense in which obsession with a transcendent and unspeakable *dao* is misguided. If we focus on *dao* only to say that it is ineffable, then we have understood nothing of Daoism, or *dao*, except perhaps that there is nothing to say about it. In fact, while it is true that Daoist texts emphasize the limitations of language, they notoriously do have a lot to say, not all of it empty and unintelligible, and not all of it saying, paradoxically if not incoherently, that nothing can be said. On the contrary, we are told that *dao* is vast, expansive, and cosmic. And to say this is, as we shall see, to say something profoundly significant.

Moreover, the single-minded concentration on *dao* draws attention away from several other concepts that are central to understanding Daoist thought, apart from which the significance of Daoist philosophy and indeed of *dao* itself cannot be understood. These include *tian* 天 "nature/cosmos," *wu* 無 "nothing," *de* 德 "potency," *fan* 反 "returning," and *zong* 宗 "the ancestral," among others.[1] What makes the Daoist *dao* distinctive is that it is the *dao* of nature, of absence, of potency, returning, and the ancestral. To locate the "essence" of Daoism in the concept of an unspeakable *dao* is, to borrow a popular slogan from Zen Buddhism, to mistake the finger for the moon.

Three names associated with the origins of this school of thought are Master Lao, Master Zhuang, and Master Lie: Laozi, Zhuangzi, and Liezi.[2] The term "*zi*" is difficult to render accurately in English: literally, it means "child," but is used as an honorific title for the teacher or proponent of a school of thought. The term "Master" is about the closest available term in English. Of these three, only Master Zhuang is taken to have been an actual person. The other two seem to be legendary characters who may or may not have been based on historical figures. Nevertheless, for ease of discussion, I shall follow the tradition in using the names as though referring to actual people. It should not be inferred that I believe that any of them actually existed. While the question of their existence might matter from a historical or religious perspective, nothing of consequence hinges on it from a philosophical point of view. Even if Masters Lao, Zhuang, and Lie did not exist, even if all three texts had multiple authors who did not intend to expound a unified philosophy, the texts still contain related philosophical material.[3] And it is the ideas, theories, and worldviews they present that are of primary interest to a philosopher. Furthermore, the *Laozi* and the *Liezi* certainly have sufficiently distinctive characters and styles of thought to warrant attribution of each text to a particular perspective, even if not to a single author. Variations and even inconsistencies can be found within each text, but these are not so widespread as to undermine their overall internal coherence. Moreover, even if the consistency within each text, or between them, was not explicitly intended as such by the various authors, this does not diminish its philosophical interest one iota.

Of the three, the *Zhuangzi* is most obviously an anthology of collected materials. A minimum of three related strands of thought can be discerned, each of which could be subdivided further. The first is composed of the first seven chapters, known as the *Inner Chapters*, generally attributed to Zhuangzi himself, together with an extensive collection of passages attributed to thinkers whose ideas resonate closely with those of the *Inner Chapters*. I call this strand "Zhuangzian" philosophy and discuss it in Chapter Four below. The second strand is a somewhat utopian set of chapters inspired largely by the more anarchistically inclined passages of the *Laozi*. The third strand lies at the other end of the political spectrum, advocating sagely rulership of a state, combining Mohist and Legalist political structures with the cultivation of Confucian virtues and Daoist meditative practices. This exemplifies the more eclectic spirit of the philosophy of the Han dynasty. The Utopian and Syncretist strands at first glance present wildly opposing social views, but on closer inspection they can be seen to share a philosophical heritage in the *Laozi* and the *Inner Chapters*. They are discussed in Chapter Five below.

The name "Daoism"—school of *dao*, or school of the way—is in one respect quite apt, yet in others somewhat misleading. It is apt insofar as it implies that one of the important features of this group of thinkers is their very distinctive conception of *dao*. However, if this is taken to mean that what distinguishes Daoism from other philosophies is that it alone is concerned with the *dao*, it is misleading. Most, if not all, early Chinese philosophies are concerned fundamentally with finding, explaining, teaching, and following the *dao*. That is, they are concerned with the *way*: the way to live a flourishing, harmonious life. Most of these schools share the sense that with the development of human society over the course of history, we have slowly lost our way, become increasingly out of attunement with what once must have been a naturally harmonious way of life.[4] The goal of the philosophers of each school is to understand the ways, *dao*, in which things function—whether human life, human values, social structures, or natural processes—and with this knowledge propose a way to bring us back to a state of harmonious flourishing.

But if all Chinese philosophical schools are concerned with the *dao*, why should this one in particular be singled out as the "school of *dao*"? There is no definitive answer to this question, but two possible reasons have to do with the breadth and inclusivity of the *dao* conceived by its proponents and a radical shift in perspective from that of other schools. Most of the pre-Qin thinkers were concerned with how to cultivate human order and flourishing in a social context. This was to be achieved by refining and developing the accoutrements of civilization: language, technology, regulations and measures, social hierarchies, laws and punishments, cultured behavior, cultivation of humanity, and ethical sophistication. Different schools emphasized different aspects in articulating their own preferred *dao*. For example, the Confucians emphasized social hierarchies and ethical cultivation; the Mohists and Legalists advocated clear laws, regulations, and standards; the Linguistic School engaged in the analysis and refinement of language and linguistic distinctions, whether for its own sake or for the purpose of achieving social order. According to the *Laozi* and the *Zhuangzi*, these philosophies had too narrow and shortsighted a focus. The Daoist texts demand instead that we broaden our perspective, expand our understanding of who and what we are as humans, our awareness of our existence in relation to all that surrounds us. We extend the boundaries of our self-identification until we encompass "heaven and earth" and "the ten thousand things." That is, our awareness must shift from the restricted perspective of the human point of view to the all-encompassing "nonperspective" of the whole cosmos.[5] Now the search for the way becomes a search for a cosmic way, whose significance extends far beyond the familiar boundaries of human life and human society.

While Confucius acknowledges that there is a cosmic aspect to the way, he warns us not to waste our time speculating about matters that lie outside ordinary human understanding. In *Analects* 11:12, when Jilu asked about serving the spirits, Confucius replied, "If you cannot yet serve people, how are you going to be able to serve the spirits?" When Jilu asked about death, Confucius replied: "You do not yet understand life; how will you understand death?" It is more important to attend to matters of social, ethical, and political concern, and more important still to tend constantly to the conditions that will promote a flourishing life.[6] The *Laozi* and the *Zhuangzi*, on the contrary, insist that it is possible to promote a flourishing life only by shifting our attention away from the focus to the periphery, from human concerns to *tiandao*, the way of the cosmos. Thus, although the Daoists were not the only thinkers to be concerned with following a *dao*, their conception of the *dao* to be practiced aimed to be the most cosmic and expansive.[7]

The second possible reason has to do with the apparent origins of the term "*daojia*." The first place we find the name "*Daojia*" is in the classification of the Grand Historian of the Han dynasty, Sima Tan. He grouped thinkers of the Warring States into six broadly conceived houses, families, or schools, *jia*:[8] *Yinyangjia* (the Yinyang school), *Rujia* (the Ruists, or Confucians), *Mojia* (the Mohists), *Fajia* (the Legalists), *Mingjia* (the Linguistic school),[9] and *Daojia* (the Daoists). His first reference to the school is in fact to *Daodejia*, the school of *dao* and *de* (the way and potency). Sima Tan's account of these schools is in terms of the kinds of *political* policies they promote, rather than religious doctrines. The goal of all these, he explains, is *zhi* 治, government, orderly administration or rule. He praises the Ruists for their emphasis on the relationships of propriety between ruler and minister, father and son, husband and wife, and elder and younger. The Yinyang thinkers, he tells us, correctly understand the importance of following the seasons, while the Mohists propose the strengthening of agriculture and economizing of expenditures. The Legalists promote the division of labor for distinct official duties and a hierarchical ordering that honors the ruler, while the Linguistic thinkers emphasize the importance of the correct adjustment of names and objects, and the tests of merit and blame. In the spirit of Xunzi's eclecticism,[10] Sima Tan acknowledges that while the ways proposed by the schools have undeniable virtues, they each have significant faults. The Confucians, for example, are "learned but lacking in what is essential, work laboriously and achieve little," while the Legalists are "strict, with scarcely any kindness."[11]

Of the six schools he names, only the last, *Daojia*, receives no criticism. This is the school to which Sima Tan himself subscribes. In fact, his purpose in listing and comparing the schools is to demonstrate its superiority over the others. It is superior because it adopts the excellences of the other schools, corrects their faults, and integrates them into a single practice. It thus displays the eclectic and syncretistic tendencies typical of Han dynasty thinking. Sima Tan lists among the virtues of *Daojia* that its policies are few, easy to adopt, and adaptable to changing circumstances. They go to the heart of the matter in the essentials of good government and waste no time with excessive detail and micromanagement. Sima Tan does not name the texts, but lists a few doctrines and concepts: "The Daoists do nothing, yet they also say that nothing is not done. Their substance is easy to practice, but their words are difficult to understand." They emphasize emptiness, *xu* 虚, and nothing, *wu* 無, as the root, and adaptation, *yin* 因, and following, *xun* 循, as the practice. The quotations and the concepts of emptiness and nothing appear to be references to the *Laozi*. The *Daojia* that Sima Tan describes is an eclectic theory of government quite different in spirit from most of the apolitical or antipolitical passages of the early Daoist texts. It does, however, resonate with a later stratum of the *Zhuangzi*, which Graham refers to as the Syncretist writings.[12]

Thus, the earliest recorded usage of the term *"Daojia"* that we have, from a self-professed adherent, refers primarily to this Han dynasty syncretistic school of sagely government. It would seem that the name "School of *Dao*" was appropriated to indicate its ideal of comprehensiveness: it is not just a partial way—Ruist, Mohist, or Legalist—but an all-inclusive way that incorporates the virtues of the others while avoiding their faults. As we shall see, the core metapolitical[13] principles of this school can be found in the *Laozi* and the *Zhuangzi*. The name eventually extended to these early texts themselves, the various philosophical ideas they express, and other philosophical offshoots that developed, such as the *Liezi* and the Utopian chapters in the *Zhuangzi*.

VARIETIES OF DAOISM AND THE PHILOSOPHICAL STUDY OF EARLY DAOIST TEXTS

The term "Daoism" is highly problematic, for at least the reason that its current meaning is not well defined. It seems to refer to a wide variety of cultural phenomena that developed over millennia and that are interconnected in complex ways: the ideas of the early texts, Han dynasty syncretism, systems of mind-body cultivation, and religious institutions, for example. Furthermore, the English term "Daoism" is ambiguous: it does double duty as a translation for two different Chinese words, "*daojia*" 道家 and "*daojiao*" 道教. The term "*daojiao*" (the doctrines of the way) refers to a group of institutional religious traditions that trace their lineages back to a distant past and include in their canon the *Laozi* and *Zhuangzi*, among many other texts. When the term began to be used in this way is unclear, but it is clear that the syncretist metapolitical movement to which Sima Tan belonged, *daojia*, and the religious institutions known as *daojiao* are significantly different.

"*Daojiao*" refers to a complex set of phenomena incorporating institutional structures, folk beliefs, rituals, spiritual practices, and sacred texts. It is a pluralistic amalgamation of rival sects and teachings that have developed in lineages over the centuries, such as the Taiping, Quan Zhen, and Celestial Masters. This last, perhaps the most ancient and influential, is traditionally said to have begun in 143 C.E. with the founding of a religious institution by Zhang Ling (or Zhang *Dao* Ling). He claimed to have been visited by the *dao*, in the person of Laozi himself, and instructed to establish an earthly institution whose political structure mirrored that of the celestial spirits. In addition to his personal revelatory experiences, he also drew from other sources, including popular religious beliefs and practices and early texts that explored natural and spiritual phenomena, especially the *Laozi*, which was subsequently bestowed the title "*Daodejing*," the "classical scripture" of *dao* and *de*.[14] The term "*jing*," previously used for Confucian classics and then for Buddhist sutras, thus endowed the text with an extra sense of scriptural authority. Scriptural titles were also eventually given to the *Zhuangzi* and the *Liezi*. The *Zhuangzi* acquired the reverential title "*Nan Hua Jing*," the *Scripture of the Southern Flower*, and the *Liezi* acquired the honorific title "*Chong Xu Zhen Jing*," the *Genuine Scripture of Overflowing Emptiness*. However, despite their honorific titles, neither of these two texts plays a central role in the practices and teachings of *Daojiao*.[15]

In recent years, some scholars have begun to challenge the distinction between Daoist philosophy and Daoist religion, and even question the legitimacy of the philosophical study of early Daoist texts. They may accept that there has been a traditional Chinese distinction between *daojia* and *daojiao*, but they correctly point out that this does not correspond to the Western distinction between philosophy and religion. The latter, they claim, is imposed by Western philosophers and favored by modern Chinese scholars, but has no genuine applicability to the cultural phenomena in question. The early Daoist texts, for example, involve essential references to psychophysical disciplines and "spiritual" or meditative practices; contemporary practitioners of Daoist religion claim a direct lineage to these texts.[16] They conclude that anything that might be called Daoist "philosophy" can only be understood as an integral part of the religious tradition.

Although it is true that the distinction between *daojia* and *daojiao* is not identical to the Western distinction between philosophy and religion, it does not follow that there is no way to understand the ancient Daoist texts independently of contemporary religious phenomena. In fact, *both* "philosophy" and "religion" as usually understood are concepts derived from Western cultural historical traditions, and *neither* maps easily onto the intellectual and spiritual traditions of China. It is true that the intellectual discourse of Confucianism and Daoism is very different from that of typical Western philosophical schools, such as Rationalism and Empiricism, but it is also true that the spiritual practices associated with Confucianism and Daoism are very different from Western religious phenomena such as Christianity and Islam.[17] If we conclude that we should not apply the term "philosophy" to these indigenous Chinese traditions on these sorts of grounds, then we must also conclude that the term "religion" has no applicability either.

If, on the other hand, *either* of these Western terms is to be of any use in the context of Chinese culture, they will have to be understood in a more flexible way. The question arises whether there is anything in the Chinese tradition to which the terms might reasonably be applied, with full understanding that they are not going to be exactly like their Western namesakes. There are early Chinese texts from the pre-Qin period classified as *zi* (texts attributed to "masters"), sometimes belonging to *jia* (loose groupings into schools). These texts recommend ways of life and disciplines of psychophysical cultivation grounded in a mutually critical, reflective analysis of ethical values, political structures, human psychology, the structure of the natural world, and so on. In this, they are not unlike the Hellenistic schools: holistic philosophies that recommend practices designed to promote a healthy, tranquil, and flourishing life given their understanding of the cosmos. The early Chinese thinkers and texts, then, can be reasonably compared with the Hellenistic philosophies, and thus can be understood as advocating a kind of philosophical discipline.[18] The pre-Qin texts were developed prior to the emergence of any form of Daoist religion, so scholars of religion sometimes refer to them as "proto-Daoist."

Now, *daojiao* in its several manifestations is centrally concerned with the regulation of human life through communication with a parallel world of gods and spirits, ghosts and demons. It has a highly structured hierarchical institution that mirrors the hierarchical powers of the spirit world, centered in temples and monasteries, whose practitioners are identified through their ceremonial garb. It is not unreasonable to use the adjective "religious" to discuss such cultural phenomena, provided we do not assume that what we are thus describing must share the same characteristics as typical Western religions. These religious institutions did not exist at the time of the *Laozi* and the *Zhuangzi*, so it makes no sense to insist that the early texts cannot be studied independently of them. Of course, describing early Daoist texts as "philosophical" and the later institutions as "religious" should not be taken to mean that there must be a sharp boundary between two mutually exclusive practices, or that there was no interaction and influence between them at all. But this does not warrant the conclusion that the texts lack a philosophical content that can be discussed independently of the later religious practices.[19]

Despite the historical connections and the areas of overlap, each of these cultural phenomena has central elements not characteristic of the other, and this is where the importance of the distinction lies. What is most distinctive about the religious traditions—a pantheon of spirits, generals, ghosts, and demons, arranged in a strict hierarchical order, whose authority and influence over the social world are mediated by a priesthood arranged in a parallel hierarchical order—has no relevance whatsoever to the philosophical discussions of the early Daoist texts.[20] Likewise, the philosophical content of those texts—their critique of the Confucian and Mohist understandings of government, ethics, and language, and their advocacy of a way of life free from institutional control—plays no significant role in the practices of the religious institutions.

In a more nuanced discussion of the issues, Livia Kohn criticizes the notion that a "pure" philosophy became "corrupted" in religious practice, but nevertheless recognizes *three* types of Daoists: "Literati Daoists," including the authors of the pre-Qin texts, *Laozi* and *Zhuangzi*, subsequent commentators, such as Wang Bi and Guo Xiang, and the political thought of *daojia*; "Communal Daoists," or practitioners of the various forms of *daojiao* or institutionalized religion; and those who cultivate health and longevity, as manifested in *taiji, qigong,* and traditional Chinese medicine.[21] The subject matter of this book would be classified under Kohn's first category.

HISTORICAL BACKGROUND

The origins of Chinese philosophy are traced to the period of the "Hundred Schools," toward the end of the Zhou dynasty. The rule of the house of Zhou lasted for approximately eight hundred years, beginning in the eleventh century B.C.E. and ending twenty-five years before the founding of the Qin Empire that unified "China" for the first time in 221 B.C.E. The ruling house was centered in the state of Zhou, and at its height maintained power over many other states across an area stretching approximately eight hundred miles from Xi'an in the west to the east coast, and over eight hundred miles from present-day Beijing in the north to Changsha in the south. Members of the royal household were set up in the various states, which owed the House of Zhou taxes, tributes, and labor. Around 771 B.C.E., the Zhou capital was attacked by so-called "barbarians" from the west. Land was ceded and the capital moved eastward, establishing the period of rule known as the Eastern Zhou (to distinguish it from the earlier period of the Western Zhou). For the next three centuries, known as the Spring and Autumn period, Zhou culture flourished and the civilization reached its peak. But this time of flourishing was also marked by a steady increase of internal battles.

According to the traditional Confucian telling of the history, political intrigues began as states turned against each other, though according to recent historical research, challenges to the authority of the ruling house were not unknown during the Western Zhou period.[22] Stronger states annexed weaker states, often under the guise of protecting them from their neighbors. States were also plagued internally by internecine battles. Over the decades the entire region became increasingly volatile. Although political instability began much earlier, the traditional starting date of the Warring States and end of the Spring and Autumn period is given as 475 B.C.E.[23] It ended in 221 B.C.E. with the founding of the Qin dynasty by the first Emperor, Qin Shi Huang Di.

It was during the Spring and Autumn period, at the height of cultural flourishing and as interstate warfare began to accelerate, that the so-called "Hundred Schools" of philosophical thought emerged. Perhaps as a result of being embedded in an ancient history and complex civilization, yet increasingly embroiled in aggression and its inevitable brutality and inhumanity, people began to reflect on the conditions of a harmonious society and what it even means to be human. Conflicting phenomena pulled thinkers in diverse directions. The cultures of the north, south, east, and west differed: some societies were complex, others were simple; customs and values varied dramatically from region to region. People were capable of living peacefully, acting out of compassion for others, and creating works of extraordinary artistry. The histories recorded the loftiest conduct of the most selfless rulers; yet they also recorded ample examples of so-called "nobles" who were motivated by power and acquisition of territory to commit acts of atrocity. The most virtuous societies were believed to have existed in a distant past, and in the *Analects*, the *Mencius*, the *Laozi*, and the *Zhuangzi*, we discern a poignant sense of having lost the way. Educators, thinkers, statesmen, and their advisors tried to understand the deeper causes of and possible solutions to this predicament. They articulated competing proposals, offered different *daos*: accounts of the "way" things should be, and means of practice that would facilitate a return to conditions of flourishing life and social harmony.

The first thinker and teacher to attain prominence was Confucius, with an almost impractically idealistic devotion to the cultivation of virtue. He found the *dao* in the processes of human cultivation and enculturation, particularized in his distinctive reinterpretation of the concepts of *ren*, *yi*, and *li*: humanity, rightness, and propriety. Subsequent thinkers either developed his way or reacted against it; almost none was not influenced either directly or indirectly by the *dao* proposed by Confucius. Mozi, who, according to traditional dates, was born after the death of Confucius, was the first critic of Confucianism. According to the Confucians, or "Ruists," our humanity begins in the family and extends slowly outward; as it does so, our ethical obligations must diminish by degrees. Mozi argued that ethical concepts require universality or impartiality.[24] Moreover, the boundaries of concepts must be kept precise, the correct application of terms must be carried out consistently, and evaluation of good and bad must be done clearly and without confusion. After the death of Mozi, Mencius followed the thought of Confucius along one course, seeing humans as naturally virtuous, and after him, Xunzi steered it along another, seeing virtue as needing to be artificially inculcated. Even Huizi and Gongsun Longzi, who appeared to have been concerned with purely theoretical paradoxes of language, were arguably influenced by Confucius' insistence on the correctness of linguistic terminology.

Much later, when the Warring States was about to come to its brutal end, Hanfeizi rejected the virtuous idealism of Confucius in favor of a realpolitik of universal laws enforced by strict punishments.

In this context, the authors of the Daoist texts formulate their critiques of the humanistic proposals and offer instead more expansive *daos* rooted in the natural, cosmic, or ancestral. If Zhuangzi's portrayal is a reliable guide, arguments between Ruists and Mohists dominated the ethical and political discussions of the time. The various Daoist traditions collected in the *Zhuangzi* anthology are, for the most part, highly critical of both doctrines. As in the *Laozi*, the Ruists appear to be criticized for the counterproductiveness of their ideals and their perceived hypocrisy; the Mohists are criticized for their overly simplistic view of linguistic and evaluative distinctions; both are criticized for short-sighted obsession with the artificial constructs of the human realm and neglect of our cosmic and ancestral context.

PHILOSOPHICAL AND HERMENEUTIC METHODOLOGY

Anyone familiar with typical Western philosophical discourse will be immediately struck by the apparently antithetical nature of Daoist texts. They tend to be jumbled anthologies of verse and narrative. Passages with different philosophical leanings are juxtaposed. Themes are not dealt with in a linear fashion, but are scattered throughout the texts; even individual paragraphs can contain a motley array of ideas. Reading them requires literary sensibility, time to ruminate imaginatively, and great patience. But the reader may still be at a loss as to how to extract their philosophical significances.

The *Laozi* is composed primarily of concise verse; the *Zhuangzi* and the *Liezi* are for the most part juxtapositions of narratives of varying length, not always obviously concerned with the same theme. They do not engage extensively in the articulation or refinement of definitions, and important terms are often used in different contexts that indicate more than one meaning. Perhaps most notably, there are relatively few explicit arguments whose purpose is to convince the reader of the truth of a conclusion. Western philosophers who identify the essence of philosophy as logical argument in defense of a position and in critique of opposing views are led to the conclusion that Daoist texts are not philosophical. Furthermore, Daoist texts are irregular in construction, contain multiple views that appear to be inconsistent, and are often written in a terse, imagistic style that seems far too vague and open to interpretation. It is also not always evident which voice, if any, is presenting the favored view. It is tempting to throw up one's hands and say that the texts are merely random anthologies with no single author, and therefore lacking philosophical cohesion altogether.

However, these conclusions are a little too easy and highly unproductive. Even in the West, logical argument has not been the defining essence of all philosophical thinking. Heraclitus, Kierkegaard, Nietzsche, Schopenhauer, Wittgenstein, Heidegger, Sartre, Deleuze, and Derrida have used imagery, poetry, paradox, metaphor, mythology, narrative, aphorism, and fiction to think philosophically, as well as phenomenological description and explicit experimentation with alternative styles and methods of conceptual exploration. The conclusion that Daoist texts that utilize such styles of discourse are not philosophical is therefore unwarranted.

Moreover, even granted that the texts are jumbled anthologies, it does not follow that we should not attempt to read them in an optimally cohesive way. It is always an advisable interpretive strategy to search for maximal cohesion where possible, and to distinguish inconsistent views only when absolutely necessary.[25] Indeed, the search for coherence and consistency, if successful, is profoundly satisfying, leads to new insights, and is of philosophical value regardless of the authors' intentions. This may irritate scholars who believe that they should do no more than uncover the original intentions of the various authors, but it is essential to the practice of hermeneutically minded philosophers and historians who recognize that there can be no such thing as reliable access to those original thoughts. Linguistically expressed theories always have implications that are not evident to those who formulate them, and the more complicated the theories, the less transparent and more surprising their implications. Moreover, meanings are always open, their boundaries receding vaguely into the distance; how we deal with those boundaries will depend to some extent on which paths we are inclined to follow once we get there.[26]

While ancient Chinese philosophical texts are certainly not lacking in arguments, Daoist discourse tends to function more hermeneutically by depicting worldviews in an attempt to make sense of the fundamental phenomena of existence, humanity, or society. Imagery and metaphor play an essential role in such explanations by overlaying patterns of similarity that help to shape understanding of the phenomena in question. When rational argument is employed, analogy again plays a central role. The phenomenon to be understood is compared to another one that is considered to be relevantly similar, then interpreted in terms of those similarities. Phenomenon A is like situation B; situation B has structure Φ ; therefore, phenomenon A can be understood through structure Φ. Notice that such hermeneutic explanations do not presuppose a "realist" conception of "truth": one does not necessarily take A to *have* the structure Φ, but to be interpretable through it.

It is the mark of a philosophical reader, whether Western or Chinese, ancient or modern, to be interested not only in understanding the ideas expressed in these texts but also in making a critical evaluation of their plausibility.[27] The philosophical study of ancient texts is thus dramatically different from the approaches of other disciplines: the historian or scholar of religion does not usually take the claims of the ancient texts seriously or attempt to critique the relative plausibility of the various views. But the highest respect a philosopher can give to a philosophical position is to take it seriously, engage with its ideas, challenge, question, ask for clarification. Besides, arguing against a position and defending a view against criticisms have always been at least part of philosophical activity in China. The *Zhuangzi*, for example, criticizes the philosophies of the Ruists and the Mohists; the Mohists criticize the Ruists; Mencius argues with the Mohists; Xunzi criticizes Zhuangzi. Even if it were to be shown that this sort of analysis was not typical of the subsequent tradition of Chinese philosophical discourse, it would not mean that contemporary philosophers ought not to engage in it. On the contrary, we should be celebrating the production of new philosophical activity through such cross-cultural fusions of horizons.[28]

When one takes an idea seriously, questions inevitably arise: some things may not be clear, others may not seem consistent. A major component of philosophical method is attempting to construct clarifications and definitions when these are not explicitly given in the text. A historian or expert on religions may not be interested in addressing such questions, but a philosopher's calling is to identify such problems, and where possible, to solve them. That is part of the goal of this book: not only to explicate Daoist philosophical concepts, worldviews, and methods of thinking but also to encourage the reader to notice problems in the articulation of these concepts and in the relationships between them, identify objections to a philosophical view that must be answered if it is to be taken seriously, and provide arguments in favor of the position when convinced of its plausibility.[29]

To do this in a responsible way, one must be careful not to assume naïvely that terms that initially sound familiar have the same significance as their Western counterparts. We should instead aim to explicate their significance by noting carefully how they function in their own context and how they relate to other significant terms. Chinese texts often include glosses, brief characterizations of how a word is understood. These are not intended as precise definitions of the kind expected by a Western philosopher. We know this because one and the same text can give different glosses, in the full awareness that different instances will require them; these are not taken as refutations of the original gloss. Hence, the original cannot have been intended as a universally applicable definition. In the absence of explicit definitions, one must look for associations of important terms; this method can be thought of as a kind of "textual phenomenology." The associations of terms give hints regarding what is thinkable and not thinkable in the original language: they help us plot the conceptual or semantic boundaries, which may be more or less clear depending on the concept and on the amount of context and associations available in the texts.

Of course, attempting to understand these linguistic associations does not mean that we are recovering the original intentions of the ancient writers. As Gadamer has pointed out, it is simply not possible to extricate ourselves from our own social and historical contexts and unproblematically adopt the discourse of the ancient texts. We cannot avoid imposing our own presuppositions or interpreting the texts through our own contexts. But we can aim to interpret as responsibly as possible, that is, to approach the ancient concepts open to the possibility of deep and philosophically significant differences, and to struggle to identify and think through concepts from our own discourse that impose what appear, in our best and evolving judgment, to be the *least inappropriate* of available meanings. This is precisely the kind of hermeneutic methodology that Roger Ames and David Hall argue for extensively throughout their books. The concepts and arguments in this book represent the current results in the ongoing evolution of my own understanding and are offered not as the last word, but in the full expectation that they need further argument, refinement, and improvement.

HOW TO READ DAOIST
TEXTS PHILOSOPHICALLY

The *Laozi* is a collection of dense, minimalistic verses: it strikes the reader as a gossamer of obscure images reflecting one another through an almost contextless semantic darkness. Its philosophical methodology might be described as structuralist: meaning is conveyed through the juxtaposition and contraposition of ideas. In ancient Chinese texts, meaning is often encoded in sentences with parallel structures, arranged in couplets, triplets, or larger groupings. This is especially so in the *Laozi*. Philosophical claims are made through comparison and contrast. When they are compared with surrounding sentences that contain explicitly evaluative terms, it often becomes clearer what is being promoted and what is being criticized.[30] Hans-Georg Moeller demonstrates how metaphors and images that recur through the text have structural significance; they allude to one another, creating epicenters of resonance.[31] Though arguments can sometimes be discerned and reconstructed, they are not the primary means of philosophical persuasion; rather, there is a network of images and ideas with explicit and implicit parallel structures of significance. Interconnections build and shift as one develops familiarity with the verses, but the meaning never crystallizes into a final form. Despite its popularity, this methodology makes the *Laozi* one of the most difficult texts to interpret in a responsible manner.

The primary mode of philosophical discourse in the *Zhuangzi* and the *Liezi* is literary: they philosophize through literature, especially narrative. Philosophical ideas and worldviews are sometimes expressed literally, but this is not the favored method. More commonly, ideas are *exemplified* in stories. This is especially appropriate for discussions of pragmatic and existential concern. The purpose of the stories is often to challenge conventional wisdom by exploring anomalous cases: unfamiliar things, people, and circumstances that complicate our naïve presuppositions. But the existential significance of the anomalous cases can rarely, if ever, be expressed as a straightforward universal "moral."

The method of narrative is also used to explore Daoist views of the world. This can be thought of as a kind of phenomenological discourse: the narrative passages encode philosophical presuppositions, and analysis of the unfolding of events yields an understanding of the worldview behind the narrative. The presuppositions of any worldview allow for certain kinds of possibilities, limiting what may or may not happen; what occurs in the stories will therefore exemplify those possibilities, and thereby help to reveal those presuppositions. Each element of the story has a philosophical function in relation to other elements. A specific character who is able to perform certain tasks, for example, is being used to make a general point about the conditions and possibilities of human action. The unfolding of events, and relevant evidence from other stories, texts, and contexts provides further evidence for either the development or the correction of philosophical interpretations.

Discussions between interlocutors provide a more familiar source of philosophical discourse. Aside from the explicit statements of philosophical views, analysis of the discussions can also uncover deeply held convictions, styles of argument, and the means through which ideas may appropriately be challenged. The narratives and discussions are sometimes interspersed with highly abstract discourses about fundamental concepts, such as existing and not existing, right and wrong, things and boundaries. This method is used when considering issues of ontological, epistemological, and cosmological significance. It can be understood as a type of phenomenological explication: a reflection on our most fundamental concepts, the relations between them, and how they function to construct our understanding of the world as we engage with it. Unfortunately for the reader, these explicit passages tend to be dense, expressed with obscure vocabulary, paradoxical, and lacking sufficient context for clear and straightforward interpretation. But active interpretation is also part of the pleasure of engaging philosophically with ancient Daoist texts.

The elements of Daoist narrative often include fantastic beings and events that cannot be interpreted literally. The narrator of the first chapter of the *Zhuangzi* is not literally claiming that there exists a fish the size of a continent. One must extract the salient characteristics of the image, metaphor, or fictitious entity and identify what philosophical concepts it is being used to explore. There may, of course, be more than one. The size of the fish may represent vastness as that which goes beyond our ordinary understanding, as well as the vastness of the cosmos, while the fish, the darkness, and the ocean represent the *yin* phases in the transformations of things.

The myths and narratives that exemplify a general point should not be treated as articulating a strictly universal claim, unless the text explicitly says so. Rather, there is a general 'maxim' exemplified by the particular story: that is, a contextualized generalization. When similar stories are contrasted, it is the differences in detail and in context that are significant. Thus, one should refrain from explaining the ideas as absolutely fixed structures that describe an independent reality. The very choice of narrative as a philosophical medium should call into question such realist presuppositions. The hermeneutic techniques required for reading fiction would be an odd choice for someone intending to describe literally the structures of an independent world. On the contrary, this method of writing, thinking, and reading requires the reader actively to interpret and reinterpret the structures of the world represented.

Lastly, Chinese philosophy does not divide into separate areas in the way that Western philosophy does. All texts have multiple layers of significance. Images, metaphors, and narratives may have linguistic, epistemological, cosmological, ethical, and political implications simultaneously. Even the most abstruse arguments are rarely far from having a pragmatic application. When the *Zhuangzi* investigates the nature of linguistic judgment, the possibilities of knowledge, or the ontological generation and determination of existing things, the context of the discussion is existential: how to live wisely in the face of the uncertainties of life and the inevitability of death.

CHAPTER TWO

Fundamental Concepts of Chinese Philosophy

Some terms play a foundational role in the philosophical discourse of a culture and get passed down as continuing themes, either presupposed by the tradition or made the explicit object of discussion and argument. In the West, these have included "truth," "reality," "illusion," "beauty," "justice," "mind," "essence," and "God," among others. These concepts are widespread, and although they are explained differently by different thinkers, they are foundational to much Western philosophical discourse. Indeed, the words are often capitalized to indicate that what they refer to has an ultimate, transcendent, or absolute status. They do not, however, generally play a central role in the early Chinese philosophical tradition, and what appear at first glance to be Chinese equivalents turn out to have significantly different meanings in the Chinese context. The most important concepts presupposed, or explicitly discussed, by Chinese philosophers include "*dao*" (way), "*tian*" (the natural world, the cosmos, the heavens), "*ren*" (human), "*wen*" (culture), "*wei*" (artifice), "*yan*" (language), "*wu*" (nothing, absence), "*qi*" (energy, mass-energy), "*yinyang*" (complementary contrasts), "*xing*" (natural tendencies), and "*zhen*" (genuineness). These can be considered fundamental insofar as they tend to be presupposed in some form or another by early Chinese thinkers and writers. Their importance largely remains unquestioned, and though they may be explained in different ways, the manner in which they are used retains a distinctive core, suggesting something fundamental to early Chinese worldviews.

But there are also fundamental *modes* of thinking: modes of discourse and practice through which we attempt to understand the world. These fall into four broadly conceived kinds: the rational, the empirical, the pragmatic, and the hermeneutic. Rational discourse emphasizes reflection on the meanings of concepts to discover the essential structures and properties of anything to which they could possibly refer, and attempts to refine arguments to demonstrate the truth of one theory by eliminating all other hypotheses as impossible. Empirical discourse emphasizes the senses and controlled experiments: our observations provide data to be explained in terms of mathematical patterns described by natural laws. Pragmatic discourse emphasizes concepts and practices whose primary purpose is to enable us to solve problems and live flourishing lives. And hermeneutic discourse emphasizes making sense of the world, our lives, and our multifaceted forms of significant experience, giving them meaning and value through interpretation. Versions of all of these can be found throughout the history of Western culture; some have emerged as privileged over others by what have arguably become the dominant modes of discourse of Western culture in general and Anglo-American philosophy in particular. The rational and the empirical have primacy, with the pragmatic taking second place and the hermeneutic relegated to a lower status in terms of its capacity to yield a reliable understanding of the world and our experience. The Chinese cultural tradition has followed a different tendency, with the pragmatic and hermeneutic being valued as the primary modes of understanding and the rational and empirical falling to second place.[1]

In this chapter, I shall discuss the fundamental Chinese concepts "*dao*," "*de*," "*tian*," "*ren*," "*yan*," "*wei*," "*wen*," and "*yinyang*," in light of these cross-cultural considerations, highlighting important differences in category, worldview, and modes of discourse, especially as exemplified in the various ways "*dao*" has been understood.[2] What will emerge most distinctively are the pragmatic, processive, hermeneutic, and naturalistic tendencies of early Chinese philosophical thinking.

DAO 道

The word "*dao*" is often said to be the most basic concept of Chinese philosophy. It might be thought of as having the same philosophical status as "Truth" or "Reality" in Western philosophy. Literally, it means "path" or "road." Etymologically, it consists of the radical for "walk" on the left hand side, 辶, and the graph for "head" on the right, 首. The "walking" radical under which the word is classified in the modern dictionary once took the form of a foot taking a step on a path.[3] A *dao* is the path one takes, the path one makes, and the path as it guides those to follow. Many words contain this component; notably, it is used almost exclusively for verbs related to movement of some kind.[4] By extension it takes on the abstract sense of "way" or "ways": *how* processes occur or how things ought to be done. Thus, even as a noun its connotations are processive and adverbial. A *dao* might be social, political, personal, or natural. Confucius and Mozi, for example, advocate ways that are simultaneously social, political, and personal; Zhuangzi and Liezi, ways that are both cosmic and personal but with social consequences; the syncretist Daoists combine this with a way to govern a state.

The philosophical use of the term contains an evaluative element; it implies not only the way the world is but also the way it should be. There is thus a source of tension in the use of the word. There is not just one way the world is, but many; some result in flourishing, some result in destructiveness. The task of the sage or philosophical master is to identify which ways lead to flourishing and which do not: to forge a more fruitful path and show us how best to negotiate it. The Confucians, Mohists, and Legalists believed that it was the wisest of the leaders who were able to discern, chart out, and implement those ways. In contrast, the Daoists believed that we once conformed to those ways naturally, until we began to follow artificial procedures and social conventions.

Dao as Pragmatic

Traditionally, "*dao*" has been rendered in English as "The Way" or "The *Dao*," with its importance and uniqueness emphasized by capitalization and use of the definite article. It appears to name a unique thing, often described as static, unchanging, and eternal: the underlying ground or Substance, the ultimate Reality behind the appearances. However, this conception of *dao* as transcendent turns out to be a presupposition of the reader or translator rather than implicit in the text. The concept of strict transcendence is highly artificial and attempts to outreach the limits of ordinary language. It may be defined as that which goes beyond the world of experience and must be posited as necessary for its existence.

Throughout the history of Western philosophy, concepts intended as metaphysically transcendent have invariably been accompanied by extensive discussions and arguments distinguishing them from naturalistic and pragmatic impostors. Thus, the concept of metaphysical substance as the logical condition of the possibility of change or as the necessary substrate in which qualities inhere is distinguished from material or physical substance; the concept of a transcendental self as the condition of the possibility of unified consciousness is distinguished from any concept of a natural self that can be empirically experienced; and the metaphysical distinction between the world of mere Appearance and the ultimate Reality that underlies it is differentiated from the everyday practical distinctions we make regarding what things are and how they appear. That is to say, the everyday concepts, meanings, and distinctions that are pragmatically encoded into our ordinary language must be artificially, and therefore explicitly, refined into their idealized or absolutized counterparts.

It is significant that Daoist texts do not contain such discussions. When we read early Daoist texts more neutrally to discover whether they express views that are more consistent with metaphysical or pragmatic presuppositions, the evidence appears to favor the latter. The fundamental tendency of Chinese philosophy, even at its most rarified intellectual heights, remains grounded in pragmatic concerns and hermeneutic methodology. That is, Chinese philosophers attempt first and foremost to interpret the world and thereby investigate its significance for us, our lives, and our behavior. To say that the discourse of *dao* is pragmatic is to say, in part, that the context of even the most theoretical questioning is always how it works, and how we might learn from it. Philosophers such as Huizi, who had a tendency to get lost in abstract paradoxes and contradictions, were criticized dismissively and remained relatively uninfluential precisely because their philosophies lacked, or were believed to lack, pragmatic relevance.[5] To say that a methodology is hermeneutic is to say, in part, that it uses meanings, images, narratives, and metaphors to interpret and make sense of our experience of the world. Hermeneutic methodology makes extensive use of what Pierce calls "abduction"—

interpretations of scant evidence that fill in the blanks, as it were, painting a picture, telling a story, or articulating a theory that thereby makes sense of our limited experience (whether perceptual, aesthetic, or linguistic) in more or less plausible ways.[6]

Dao as Holistic and Immanent[7] Source of Things

The *Laozi* articulates a conception of *dao* that is understood to be originating, mothering, beginning. This deep, generative aspect is often understood in the strongest sense of metaphysical "transcendence," utterly beyond the empirical world of which we are aware and in which we engage, and in some sense prior to and responsible for it. Now, originary questions and answers should not strictly be taken to be metaphysical unless they explicitly reject the adequacy of naturalistic explanation: they become metaphysical when, and only when, the necessity of something utterly beyond the natural world is either explicitly argued for or can be demonstrably shown to be presupposed. The development of originary questions from the naturalistic to the metaphysical can be traced through a certain kind of logical procedure. A fundamental question is raised about all natural phenomena, but any answer given in terms of natural phenomena is regarded as insufficient, on the grounds, implicit or explicit, that nothing can explain itself.

Western texts that articulate a conception of a transcendent origin go to great lengths to provide extensive arguments of this nature.[8] They try to show explicitly that holistic, naturalistic accounts cannot succeed, because they result in contradictions. Of course, transcendent accounts of the origin of the world are riddled with logical problems of their own, but those who articulate them appear to do so from a conviction that holistic accounts should be shown to be impossible. To confidently attribute a conception of a nonempirical beginning or origin, that is, an origin beyond the natural world, to Daoist thinkers, we would need to find extensive argument showing that anything worldly will not suffice as an explanation. However, in the *Laozi* and the *Zhuangzi*, there is no unambiguously explicit articulation of an ultimate reality that is different from and superior to the realm of practical experience. In the absence of such an explicit argument, it is unwise to simply assume that the authors of the *Laozi* and the *Zhuangzi* shared these convictions.[9]

On the contrary, a fundamental theme of early Daoist philosophy, the holistic interdependence of opposites,[10] even of something and nothing, existence and nonexistence, suggests a thoroughgoing naturalism: a conception of the world as a self-generating organic whole. It did not have a transcendent origin; both existence and nonexistence are worldly processes that emerge from each other. Certainly, *dao* plays a role as source, but it is understood as immanently involved in and inseparable from what it produces. Thus, the natural world is understood as a whole with two integrated types of aspects, one subtle and one manifest. The subtle aspects are deep and generative, but nevertheless thoroughly contained holistically and inseparably within the natural whole. They are intangible, but ubiquitously present in the functioning of the natural processes that make up the whole. Within such a worldview, the fundamental status of *dao* cannot be taken to be that of a ground or substance beyond the world of appearance. It is an integral aspect of the way the world is that remains firmly embedded within those natural processes themselves, not standing mysteriously aloof and beyond them as an absolute ground of Being.[11]

I shall reserve the term "metaphysics" for theoretical discourses that aim to articulate the nature of a reality that transcends appearances, and "cosmology" for discourses that are superficially similar but do not presuppose the necessity of such a transcendent origin, and that use hermeneutic methodologies to interpret the world ultimately for the pragmatic purpose of living well, that is, in accordance with its *dao*.

Dao as Processive

If we interpret the term "*dao*" in the light of these observations, we can take it as gesturing at the deep and elusive aspects of the *manner* of development of actions and processes. With regard to nature, it would refer to *how* the processes of transformation take place. When applied to humans, it refers to how a flourishing life should unfold and develop. "*Dao*" functions metaphorically to highlight the patterns traced out, as it were, as processes develop over time. The passing of time must be envisaged spatially in order to imagine the manners of unfolding as patterns or paths. But we must take care not to be misled into substantializing the abstract pattern when it is spatially "frozen" in this manner.

The word "*dao*" was not often used verbally in ancient Chinese, but it is used as a verb in the very first line of the *Laozi*. This verbal sense is often interpreted as meaning "to speak," which is not altogether implausible. However, the word is rarely, if ever used unambiguously in this sense in ancient Chinese philosophical texts. I suggest that, since the term is of such fundamental significance, it is better to preserve and verbalize its primary philosophical meaning. While this might seem difficult at first, it becomes easier once we realize that a way is already processive: the formation of a way and the process of walking a path are already temporal activities. Moreover, when "*dao*" is used verbally in early texts, it is more often used to mean "to guide" and "to lead." Chapter 2 of the *Zhuangzi* says that the way is formed by being walked: the process of walking the way is the coming into being of the way itself, suggesting that the way is understood not as a static object but as a process.

Dao as Discourse

Verbally the word "*dao*" means to guide, to lead, to show the way. By extension it can refer to an explicit explanation or statement of the way, and eventually even takes on the meaning "to say." Indeed, Chad Hansen takes *dao* to be primarily linguistic. *Dao* is guiding discourse:[12] a way of understanding the world, of dividing, characterizing, and evaluating it that will function as a guide for our behavior. Different *daos* make competing claims about the best way to divide the world and the best way to engage in it successfully. According to Hansen, then, Daoist philosophy is first and foremost a philosophy of language, and claims about *dao* are actually claims about the ability of different systems of distinctions to capture the way the world is and function as guides for behavior.

Dao as Indeterminate

We should be careful not to be misled by the quirks of translation into English. In classical Chinese there is no distinction between singular and plural, no definite article "the," and no indefinite article "a"; terms are most commonly used indeterminately with regard to number, unless the context allows us to interpret more specifically. Thus, "*dao*" can mean "way," "a way," "the way," and "ways," and need not be used with unitary reference unless the context requires it. When a philosophical text articulates an understanding of its preferred way, the reference is specifically to its own preferred *dao*, but not necessarily in terms of number. Thus, its *dao* may have several aspects, several possibilities of manifestation, several ways it may be followed. It may thus be understood as having an integrity that is indeterminately plural, manifested simultaneously as a way to cultivate oneself, a way to interact with others, a way to govern a state, and not necessarily as a single unity that is uniquely individuated with precise boundaries. This is especially true of the term "*dao*" as it is used in the *Laozi*. Indeed, in this text, *dao* seems to be essentially indeterminate,[13] resisting definition and determination at every turn.

As we shall see, even in the most metaphysical-sounding passages of the *Laozi*, *dao* is always described as supremely subtle, escaping the limits of discernibility. It is a deep-rooted and potent source of the production of existing things and the particular manners in which they are produced and develop. Thus, *dao* is not one among the many particular things in the world; it lacks the determinacy and definition of an individual thing, and as such cannot be observed or manipulated in the same way. It is subtle and intangible, but this does not mean that it escapes all observation. If that were the case, it would never be possible for us to learn from it or put it into practice.

POTENCY[14]   *DE*   德

A counterpart of *dao*, *de* can be thought of as the distinctive potency or efficacy of each thing, each creature or person. It can be understood as an inner source of power that expands outwardly as a kind of charismatic influence. Some people have magnetic personalities: others are drawn to them, admire them for their excellence. Entertainers and sports people in particular attract followers and fanatics. This fascination may be rooted in something as superficial as their physical beauty and charm, in their fluency with words, or more deeply in the qualities of their character and their capacity to excel at what they do.

Such charisma is also manifested in the realm of politics: there are those who have a gift for leadership. "*De*" is used in this sense by the Ruists to refer to the ethical virtues of an excellent ruler, that is, one in whom the *dao* is manifested. Their personality and strength of character inspire others to follow them: not only are their words persuasive, but their actions are exemplary. They inspire trust and respect, are able to govern wisely, and influence others effortlessly through the power of their charismatic character alone. They are thus able to bring people to a state of flourishing without actively taking control of them, without the need to articulate laws and impose punishments. The Confucian understanding of *de* is intrinsically ethical: it does not describe a ruler who has a gift for exploiting the people or attacking and annexing neighboring states, and who incites others to wicked behavior, no matter how influential and successful. *De* is simultaneously the inner *potency* that gives rise to ethical character, the power of *influence* that follows from exhibiting virtuous behavior, and by extension the *virtue itself* that manifests in one's bearing. The abilities attributed to *de* are natural and intuitive; they arise from our natural tendencies, and although they can be cultivated, they are not simply the product of training.

In Daoist texts, the term takes on a more extended sense. It still indicates the influential capacity of a person, but when it is applied to natural phenomena its ties to humanity become diminished and its ethical sense becomes more ambiguous. It becomes the natural potencies of any creature or person, thing, or phenomenon, especially those that affect whatever lies within its sphere of influence. This is still thought of as an admirable quality, to be nurtured if possible, and in that sense has a normative force. But it is less clearly an ethical force. It is possible for there to be *de* or potency that is ethically neutral, and perhaps even, as Robber Zhi argues in the *Zhuangzi*, for *de* to be unethical.[15]

NATURE, COSMOS *TIAN* 天

According to Xunzi, Zhuangzi was obsessed with *tian* and lost sight of the importance of *ren*, humanity. Although Xunzi does not explicitly discuss the *Laozi*, nature or the cosmos can also be seen as fundamental to its worldview, but expressed with the term "*tiandi*" 天地 ("heaven and earth"). Pinpointing the exact significance of the Chinese word "*tian*," however, is not easy. It is semantically complex, and while it shares much with each of its traditional English dictionary entries, "nature" and "heaven," it also differs from each of them in important ways. Moreover, these two English words themselves have a diverse array of meanings and associations. Not only are nature and heaven vastly different, their philosophical significances, as we shall see, are diametrically opposed. All this combines to make translation of the term deeply problematic.

Both translations, "nature" and "heaven," have cultural connotations and philosophical histories that can cause misunderstanding if taken to apply to the Chinese word "*tian*." The word "nature," for example, might be taken to imply a physical world in which the mental or spiritual has no place. The term "heaven" might likewise be taken to refer to a realm of paradise where a personal God dwells, or to imply a metaphysically transcendent power.[16] Of course, there is no single, monolithic "Western" concept of "heaven" or of "nature." Each term has many facets of meaning and may be understood differently by different thinkers, or when used in different contexts. Moreover, from a philosophical point of view, these terms have fundamentally opposed significances, and we can only use them comfortably and without fear of misunderstanding when these differences are made explicit. In the following sections, I highlight typical Western cultural associations and compare them with Daoist ideas, especially as developed in the *Laozi* and *Zhuangzi*.

"Nature" and "Heaven": Comparative Differences and Difficulties

Philosophically speaking, the natural world is understood as the empirical world: the world that we observe through sensory experience. Scientifically, the natural world is one whose causal connections and inner workings are governed by natural laws, the patterns and regularities of which can be discovered experimentally and expressed, or approximated, in scientific theories. This is the physical, material world that we come into contact with every day, that is studied by astronomy, geology, physics, and chemistry and often understood in largely mechanistic terms.[17] But the word also has organic connotations: the domain of nature is the domain of ecology, environmental science, zoology, and botany. This is the biosphere, the world of intricate processes that function holistically in evolving systems that continuously balance, sustain, and rebalance themselves in response to complex conditions that change on multiple levels. Although an organic view can be found philosophically articulated in Chinese cosmological texts that discuss the complexity of transformations, and practically in the development, for example, of Chinese medicine, the mechanistic view was not prevalent in early Chinese thinking.

The natural world has often been thought of as a resource, at our disposal, for human consumption. This can be seen in the biblical conception of "man" as the culmination and caretaker of "creation." It is also present in Bacon's conception of nature as a resource to be controlled and manipulated according to our needs and desires, and it is abundantly evident in the way we relentlessly exploit natural resources for our ever-increasing comfort and convenience. By contrast, in early Daoist texts, nature is not thought of as a resource provided for human consumption, but as the context within which humanity finds its place, nurtured and sustained along with all other things.

Nature is sometimes equated with that which is wild and untamed, that which encroaches on civilization and must be held at bay. In the popular imagination, the thought of the natural world often evokes images of animal behavior, especially predatory behavior, and even social Darwinist conceptions, or misconceptions, of the survival of the "fittest." Conversely, it is sometimes held up as a romantic ideal of harmony and perfection. The latter can be seen in the political views of utopian philosophers such as Rousseau and is also present in some ecological responses to a technologically driven, consumerist society. Xunzi saw nature as an unruly force that needs to be controlled by humans in order to flourish to its maximum potential, while the Daoists maintained something of a utopian conception of nature and natural life as idyllic. The early Daoists saw nature as untamed, but not wild and dangerous; in contrast with civilization, but not necessarily destructive. Rather, civilization was perceived as invading and harming nature. While the early Daoist view of the world is consistent with that of evolution—complex processes that mutually fit and adjust, allowing things to grow and transform in new ways in different contexts—natural creatures are not defined as predatory or self-interested.

On another level, we can also talk about the natures of things. What happens naturally is also what happens spontaneously, following the inner tendencies of things. The inner makeup of each thing makes it the kind of thing that it is and shapes how it ordinarily behaves. The early atomistic philosophers, such as Democritus, appealed to the inner structures of things, too minute to be perceivable, to account for differences in kind. A comparable concept can be found in Chinese, "*xing*," though it is not explained mechanistically and is considered to be beyond the capacity of conceptual understanding; it is sometimes discussed so as to include its attendant processes of growth and transformation.

The word "heaven," on the other hand, has very strong religious connotations. Literally, it can refer to the sky, but more usually, it refers to a spiritual realm beyond the physical world, a paradise in which the highest Divinity dwells, a place of eternal bliss that is a reward for the souls of those who have lived a good life. It is often contrasted with hell, a realm of eternal punishment. These are conceived of in some sense as places, but they are not necessarily physically located in some stretch of the universe, and can only be reached after death. They are thus said, in a metaphorical sense, to be "beyond" the world: heaven is "above" and hell "below." Heaven is a realm of purity, light, and peace, its value expressed through the metaphor of height; hell is a place of darkness and suffering. "Heaven" can also be used metonymically to refer to God as the ultimate power. In contrast, notions of celestial and infernal dimensions are alien to early Daoist thinking: they entered the Chinese worldview only with the entry of Buddhism into China through Central Asia, sometime during the Han dynasty.

In the plural, "the heavens" refers to the sky, distant and superior, an ultimate power responsible for our lives and our circumstances, though not in complete control of them. It is not necessarily conceived of as a personal force, but neither is it simply as impersonal as the forces of nature. As we shall see below, "*tian*" does indeed have great affinities with this usage of the term.

Most notably, in Western philosophical discourse, heaven and God are not merely supernatural entities that are somehow in the world but not bound by the laws of nature; they are metaphysically *transcendent*. That is, they lie utterly beyond the empirical world and are not accessible to experience in the way that the natural world is. Indeed, they constitute the conditions of the possibility of existence of the empirical world, which is, in some sense, their "creation." Thus, not only are the meanings and connotations of "heaven" and "nature" entirely different, the philosophical connotations of the two terms are entirely distinct: heaven *transcends* nature.[18]

Tian: The Heavens as Nature, Transcendence Naturalized

Thus, while the early Chinese understanding of "*tian*" has much in common with each of the Western notions of heaven and nature, there are also significant differences of emphasis and association. Most importantly, early Chinese cosmology lacks any strong conception of a dualism between heaven and the natural world. In fact, by not distinguishing them, early Chinese cosmology might be thought of as naturalizing the transcendent.

Like the word "heaven," the word "*tian*" translated most literally means "sky." It also implies the sky as a natural force that oversees all, a vast, overarching, expansive, and ubiquitous power responsible for things; in this sense it might be thought of as "the heavens," or at its most expansive, "cosmic forces." As the heavens, it is constant or regular, *chang* 常, in its functioning, overseeing everything below, throughout all seasons. Indeed, the constancy of *tian* is precisely the regularity of the seasons, the regularity of organic processes in general, especially the cyclic processes of living and dying through which what we would call the biosphere sustains itself. Thus, while it refers to the heavens above, it does not necessarily exclude the world below. In an extended sense, it refers to the cosmos as a whole. Even as the ultimate power that sets the conditions for things, *tian* cannot sensibly be described as "beyond" the natural world. Indeed, as natural powers they are manifested *in* natural phenomena.

In both Daoist and Confucian texts, the heavens or forces of nature, *tian*, are the powers that produce things, give life to them, impelling their growth and development and enabling them to be what they are. *Tian* is also manifested internally within things. That wood should be hard and strong, that water should be clear when pure and level when unmoved: these are tendencies that arise within the natural world itself. But we should not assume that these phenomena are understood purely mechanistically or in purely physical terms. The naturalness of *tian* does not exclude its being spiritual. That is to say, phenomena not ordinarily thought of in purely mechanical terms—life, heart, mind, spirit—are not understood as "supernatural." However, although *tian* is also spiritual, it is not thought of as a single spirit, a single divinity, a single consciousness. Nor is it a realm in which such spirits live. *Tian*, in its most philosophical sense, is not a person or a place, but the productive power of the natural world imbued with the accumulated potency of everything ancestral.

Of course, humans are also products of nature, produced by *tian*. *Tian* gives birth to us, makes us what we are, gives rise to our inner tendencies and powers, and impels our life processes, our living tendencies. In this way, *tian* sets the conditions for flourishing and "healthy" lives. Our natural tendencies propel us from birth to maturity and eventually through the phases of dying. If they are allowed to function well, without constraint, we will flourish; if they are interfered with, the processes will be unable to function in a manner conducive to health and longevity.

The Daoist conception of the natural is of what spontaneously follows when inner tendencies are allowed to manifest. Natural events are those that are not deliberately controlled or prevented from developing in accordance with their inner dispositions. Things naturally flow where and how they will. From a civilized point of view, such spontaneity might appear unruly, chaotic, and complicated. But nature has its own means of flourishing; it does not rely on thinking, conceiving, using language to understand things and control them. Its patterns and regularities are complex and seemingly irregular. But if we can expand our viewpoint, see the natural world without such humanistic preconceptions, then we will see that it has an orderliness of its own that does not require human interference to function smoothly and successfully.

THE NATURAL AND THE HUMAN

The relation between the natural and the human is one of the most fundamental issues addressed by Chinese philosophy. In the crudest of brush-strokes, the Confucians emphasize the importance of what is distinctively human, while the Daoists deflect our attention toward the background of natural conditions within which the human is able to flourish. But the very attempt to distinguish the human from the natural world gets us entangled in a philosophical problem: it seems to imply a distinction between what is natural and what is not. How can anything that exists in the natural world not itself be natural? If it is produced by natural things and has natural tendencies of its own, on what grounds can we distinguish it from what is natural? In the following, I discuss some of the characteristics of the counterpart to *tian*—the human, language, artifice, and culture—before returning to consider this problem.

Human   *Ren*   人

The word "*ren*" means human, or person; it is gender neutral and indeterminate with regard to number. So it is misleading to translate it as "man" or "a man." Rather, it means human and humans, person and people. Thus, "*ren*" does not primarily denote an individual, but includes both the singular person and people as a whole. The word "*ren*" 人 is also etymologically related to the word "*ren*" 仁, an ethical concept of fundamental concern to Confucius and his students. The *Shuo Wen*[19] explains the structure of the character as being composed of the graphs for "human" 人 and "two" 二, thereby indicating how humans interact when they come together. Its ordinary meaning includes "kindness" or "benevolence," but the Confucian understanding deepens its significance to reflect its etymological heritage. As Confucius responds to his students' questions about *ren*, it gradually emerges as a virtue that lies at the very heart of being human, indeed, the virtue of being human itself. The Confucian classic *Zhong Yong* goes so far as to define "*ren*" 仁 as "being human," *ren* 人.[20] It is the quality that constitutes our being human, in virtue of which we deserve to be called "human." For this reason, I prefer the translation "humanity."

In its sustained meditations on humanity, the early Confucian perspective manifests its humanistic orientation. The goal of Confucianism is to cultivate what invests human life with deep significance: virtue and culture. Humans are capable of acting with ceremonious respect, *li* 禮, and of doing what is right, *yi* 義, in preference to what is of personal benefit. This ethical understanding of humanity is the precursor to Mencius' and Xunzi's interest in human nature: whether it spontaneously tends toward or away from being good; whether the goodness we observe in people is inherent or must be cultivated.[21] Either way, our humanity is not only our starting point but also an achievement: we construct our humanity. Human cultivation is a never-ending process; humanity is always a work in progress. The ideal is not a perfected end point, but something more beautiful that precedes and exceeds us, is always ahead of us and out of our reach.

The Daoists consider human-oriented endeavor of such a magnitude to be counterproductive and disastrous, an artificial fabrication at odds with the natural way. As we shall see below, they account for our deviation from a more primordially natural way with our predilection for linguistic activity and manipulative transformation of our environment in accordance with artificially induced dissatisfactions. But this leads to a problem that recurs throughout the Daoist texts. This critique of humanity is not to be taken lightly: as one moves from a human to a cosmic perspective, ethical concepts lose their grip; one cannot judge actions to be good or bad. Is there anything in this philosophy to prevent a person who thinks this way from acting in a manner that ordinary people would consider inhumane? This concern is not just a Western philosophical imposition: chapter 23 of the *Zhuangzi* contains an articulation of the problem.[22] As we shall see in Chapter Five below, the utopian Daoists may have the means to solve it.

Language   *Yan*   言

Humans speak, think, write books, give advice; we describe things, put them into words, in an attempt to understand what they are and to communicate our understanding. We live through language; it is an inescapable medium through which we understand our world and in which we coexist. As children, we learn in part by acquiring and developing linguistic skill: we divide and categorize all phenomena through terminology, *ming* 名, into such and such objects, such and such processes and events, such and such kinds. Insofar as we live through language, we certainly notice its ubiquity but do not ordinarily sense its depth. We take the things we know and name to be real, existing independently in the way that we understand them even if we had never used concepts to categorize them. Red would be red even if humans never verbally articulated the concept; a book will continue to be a book even after the last human ceases to think of it that way.

With language we communicate our understanding of the world to each other and pass it down to future generations. It encapsulates and transmits the understandings of the past, but is also flexible enough to enable new ideas to be formulated and old concepts to be modified, replaced, or corrected. But words are not just descriptive, they are also normative: we evaluate the groups of things we have described and categorized as better or worse. We encode our worldviews and their inherent values through linguistic systems, and we make judgments through criteria that express our values. We persuade others, approve and disapprove of them, praise them when they conform to our demands and expectations, and blame them when they fall short. Thus, in early Chinese philosophy, language is understood to have three basic pragmatic functions: to organize and classify into kinds, to evaluate into hierarchies, and to communicate those classifications and evaluations to cohorts and descendants, in order to both pass on the accumulated wisdom of the past and exhort them to strive to live up to our ideals.

Activity and Artifice   *Wei*   為, 偽

Sometimes, the deepest and most abstruse philosophical issues are concealed in the simplest of everyday words: "be," "must," and "not," for example, give rise to the philosophical concepts of Being, necessity, and negation. In classical Chinese, "*wei*" 為 is one of these extraordinary words, revealing a deep-rooted pragmatist ontology. It means "to do," "to act," "to make," "to become," and "as," and can also function nominally to refer to doing, acting, and making. It can often be translated with the copula, "to be," suggesting that the equivalent of "being" in ancient Chinese was conceived with pragmatic significance as a kind of acting or *functioning*. Things *are* what they *do*, what they act *as*. It is also sometimes used in the sense of the word "*wei*" 謂, meaning "to call" or "to deem as." This suggests a close conceptual connection between how something functions (what something is) and how it is understood to be (what it is called). Humans act in accordance with an understanding of how things function, and what things are is in part a matter of how we understand and interact with them. We deem things useful, beautiful, valuable; we interact with them as such, manipulate them as such, and that is what they become—they function as useful, beautiful, and valuable things.

Its philosophical significance for Daoism can be further understood by examining the etymologically related term "*wei*" 偽, where 爲 is combined with the "human" radical 亻 and means "artificial activity." This is contrasted with *zhen* 真, genuineness, what is so without being forced or contrived. "*Zhen*" can refer to what a thing is in its innermost nature, and also has connotations of truth: being true to oneself, or authenticity, and being true to others, or sincerity. In modern Chinese it refers to what is true or real, but in ancient Chinese its ethical senses take priority. "*Wei*" as the opposite of "*zhen*" can thus also imply lacking sincerity or being disingenuous. Xunzi, however, uses the term in a positive way. He regards the human additions to the world as essential to good order.

We transform the world to suit our purposes, and thus create artificial things and structures in an effort to improve on nature: this is the activity of technology. We have reached the point where we make dwellings that are almost impervious to wind and rain, clothes that imitate the softness and warmth of fur, vehicles that move faster than the speed of sound. We prefer these additions and improvements to coping with natural circumstances on their own terms. We do not like to trust the accidents of nature, but prefer to be in control of our environmental conditions. The word "*wei*" thus connotes human *artifice* in all its senses, positive and negative.

Culture   *Wen*   文

Human transformative activity is not random, but accords with artificial structures, patterns, and values, and these function to transform not only our environments but also ourselves. Everything we do is imbued with a sense of proper form, a right way to be performed, which is transmitted from generation to generation. The right way to eat, to sleep, to communicate are all clothed in a particular style of a particular community, passed down from its predecessors. The forms we imitate and embody from the very first moments of our lives eventually become transparent, seem effortless and natural. It is usually not until we come face to face with cultural difference, with people whose behaviors we find odd, surprising, and even unnatural, that we realize the contingency of culture: that it is artificial, its particularities and peculiarities highly variable, and must be inculcated and cultivated over many years. The combined product of all this transforming activity, linguistic and performative, is the human world in all its multiple manifestations. The social patterns, the physical tools and machines we use, the abstract constructs through which our lives are given significance, and the values by which they are judged are all constitutive of culture, *wen*. The most complex societies with the most highly developed technological constructs we deem to be "civilizations."

Confucians in the tradition of Xunzi recognize and emphasize both the contingency and the necessity of culture. Though the forms that particular cultures take may vary radically, some form of enculturation[23] is necessary to ensure human flourishing. The natural is merely raw material in need of completion: human cultivation is required to enable not only ourselves but also our environments to function well. The best structures and patterns, even if they are rooted in what is natural to us, cannot appear by themselves but must be first discovered and then passed on to future generations. Human life is optimal when our relations are regulated by values and ideals; nature functions optimally when humans cultivate it in accordance with those same ideals. Weeds and jungles grow naturally; gardens, orchards, and crop fields must be cultivated. Caves occur naturally; homes must be designed and constructed. What is natural respects no stipulated regulations, appears wild and unruly, and if left to its own devices will tend to disorder. For things to flourish harmoniously, an artificial systematic order must be imposed to guide their growth and development.[24] We thereby not only construct things that are useful and beautiful but also create the very standards of beauty and usefulness by which to judge them.

Daoist Critique and Recommendation

The Daoists have a surprising and paradoxical critique of the Confucian view: it is precisely the effort to add to and improve upon nature to make it orderly and harmonious that leads to disorder and disaster. Nature is seen as ancient and awe inspiring, its inner workings utterly beyond our limited understanding, and not to be trifled with. We believe that we can improve on the very world that has produced us only because we fail to appreciate it on its own terms. In fact, the achievements of humanity pale in comparison with the magnificence and intricacy of the natural world. We must instead be willing to undo our artificial social structures, let go of our need to control our lives, and return to a simpler, more natural mode of existence. As we shall see, this returning is not a single achievement but a process, a turning around, a change of course.

However, reversing direction and setting out on a path away from artifice and toward simplicity can be no simple task. We have been enculturated since the day of our birth, and humanity as a whole has been immersed in complex cultural systems for millennia. This enculturation shapes, informs, and civilizes our natural selves. It is not just that our naturalness is hidden, covered over with the superficial appurtenances of culture; it has been transformed into something new by unceasing processes of molding and forming, carving and polishing. To return to a more natural way of life, we need to find it first, to reclaim and nurture it. But how is it even possible to know what our natural impulses would have been if we had not been socialized? If we have been so thoroughly transformed by language and culture, we cannot simply relinquish them. Instead, we would have to actively investigate, discover, understand, practice, and embody more natural functions and modes of behavior. If such a thing is even possible, it can be no easy matter. Daoist practice is thus emphatically not simply letting it all hang out and "going with the flow," as is often claimed in the popular literature. On the contrary, the return to natural simplicity is, paradoxically, for most practitioners a tough life demanding years of discipline.

Challenge to Distinction

The distinction between the natural and the artificial is one of the most fundamental of Daoist philosophy, and at the same time, difficult to pin down. How can anything that exists in the natural world not be natural itself? Humans are not unnatural; hair and toenails, secretions and excretions are human products, and are all entirely natural, as are the additions of any other creature. Also, products of human artifice are products of natural creatures, and themselves are made of materials that have natural tendencies. In what sense is artifice not natural? Moreover, aren't language, society, and technology themselves natural? Don't animals also communicate, live in social groups, use tools, build nests, and have hierarchies?

The Daoists nevertheless presuppose that there is an important distinction to be made, and their way of life depends on successfully making such a distinction. Moreover, in preferring the natural to the artificial, they are making a recommendation that requires real and dramatic changes in lifestyle.

Defense of Distinction

The distinction in question is not a mutually exclusive dichotomy between what is purely natural and what is purely unnatural. Rather, it is a complementary contrast between phenomena that we identify in practice as "natural" and those that we call "artificial," and this contrast is a matter of degree.[25] That is, when we classify some things and processes as more natural than others, we are really classifying not their degree of naturalness, but their degree of artificiality. While everything is natural and nothing can be purely artificial, some things are clearly more artificial than others. It is the absence of artificiality that is informally, but misleadingly, described as "purely natural."

The purely natural, in this loose sense, might be glossed as whatever occurs by itself, unaltered by human purposes. Paradigmatic examples would include the sun emitting radiation, the displacement of leaves by the wind, the sprouting of a windblown seed in a forest. It is understood in contrast to artifice: the transformation of something natural according to human purposes. Tools, technology, culture, and civilization are products of such human transformative activity. We manipulate material to create something designed to meet our needs, something that would not otherwise have existed. We use rocks to create a dam: the rock is natural and its blockage of the water is natural, but our deliberately placing the rock in the stream so that we may block the water from reaching a particular area of land or save the water for future use—that is artifice. It is not only physical objects that we manipulate in this way. We may manipulate our own behavior: moving, walking, and touching are natural. But shaking someone's hand in conformity with social etiquette to demonstrate our respect and good will is artifice. The degree to which we interfere with or transform something natural according to our designs is the degree to which we create an artificial environment. Constructing a skyscraper requires more artifice than building a hut, which in turn involves more artifice than hollowing out a cave. The degree to which we transform our own behaviors to conform to culturally imposed standards of acceptability and meaningfulness is the degree to which we turn our own lives into products of artifice.

In fact, this applies to any purposive creature. Although everything remains natural, there is always for any creature also some degree to which its environment may be modified according to its purposes. Thus, animals that engage deliberately with the world cannot eliminate artifice altogether: a macaque that sits in a hot pool turns it into a bath; a wolf snarls to frighten away a challenger and has communicated successfully its position in a social hierarchy. These are natural behaviors, yet they can all correctly be understood as involving minimal degrees of artifice. Moreover, to the extent that the capacity to transform the world purposively is natural (insofar as it arises without our deliberately creating it), artifice itself is natural. However, this does not entail that the concept of artificiality is meaningless: it would only be meaningless if the artificial had to be radically distinct from the natural.

The difference between human and animal artifice is that humans have the capacity to deliberate and transform the world to an unlimited degree, and are also capable of choosing not to exercise this capacity. Birds build nests, but they do not erect skyscrapers; apes make use of a hot spring, but they do not construct Jacuzzis; wolves howl and live in packs, but they do not write novels or legal codes defining the proceedings of a representative parliament. More importantly, these creatures are not capable of any further development of their artifice: nor are they capable of controlling the degree to which they engage in it. Only humans have the exponentially unlimited capacity to plan and transform our worlds in this way, and the capacity to refrain from doing so. The more immersed in artifice our lives become, the further we drift from our natural moorings. The significance of the distinction then lies not in the mere fact that humans create products, but in that they create products of a very distinctive kind: cities and circuses, wheels and crossbows, books and theories, skyscrapers, computers, satellites, nation states, legal codes. There is a clearly recognizable sense in which these constructs are additions to and distinctively different from what is produced by the rest of the natural world.

Thus, although the humanity with which the Confucians are concerned, our being cultured and civilized, is indeed a natural part of us, a problem arises when we see its value but fail to see its limitations—when we pursue the deliberate and artificial construction of our lives and our environments at the expense of our natural simplicity. Ironically, it is the path of control that the Daoists see as spiraling out of control. It may be natural for humans to be artificial, but the degree to which we choose to pursue artificially constructed lives and an artificially constructed environment at the expense of other natural capacities is problematic.[26] Social structures thereby become increasingly intricate, and the more complex the structures, the knottier the webs that tie us in. Cities, states, laws, institutions take on lives of their own and make it increasingly difficult for us to dissolve them for a life of unstructured simplicity.[27]

Complementary Contrasts   *Yinyang*   陰陽[28]

"*Yin*" and "*yang*" are certainly not uniquely Daoist concepts. In fact, the terms occur only once in the *Laozi*, in chapter 42, and are only explicitly mentioned in passing in the *Zhuangzi*. Nevertheless, these metaphors embody a way of understanding change that pervades these texts and is central to their understanding of *dao*.[29] In a similar way, the concepts "*dao*," "*de*," and "*wuwei*" were not invented by the Daoists, yet are still taken to be distinctive of Daoist philosophy.

When the natural world is observed as a holistic system of interconnected processes undergoing constant change, some salient patterns begin to emerge. Perhaps the first among these is seasonal transformation—not just the exchange of seasons themselves, but more generally the relationship of celestial phenomena to those of the earth, and the resulting cycles followed by both living and nonliving things. This understanding of natural change is embodied in the traditional Chinese metaphors of "*yin*" and "*yang*," the names for the northern and southern slopes of a mountain. Those who are in the habit of retreating to the mountains, observing the climate and the terrain, may notice two distinctive characteristics: the parts that face the sun often tend to be brighter, warmer, and drier than those that face the other way. This is certainly not universal to all mountain slopes, but is a general characteristic that becomes pronounced in certain geographical locations. In this basic sense, "*yang*" can be translated as "sunny side" and "*yin*" as "shady side."[30] Adjectivally, the words can mean simply "shady" and "bright" respectively, but they eventually came to express a host of qualities directly or indirectly associated with these sides of the mountain.

In the northern hemisphere, the *yin* side of a mountain tends to be cooler, darker, cloudier: morning mists collect along the northern slopes, while the rays of the rising sun disperse the moisture along the southern peaks. The mists become rain, which produces rivulets, streams, and waterfalls. The moisture enables plant life to grow, which in turn provides a habitat for other creatures. The combined activities of precipitation and biological activity keep the soil soft and fertile. In contrast, the *yang* side tends to be warmer, brighter, clearer, and therefore drier, with firmer soil. By extension, *yang* becomes associated with the sun, *yin* with the moon, and hence also day and night, summer and winter. If *yang* connotes the sky, and rising, then *yin* connotes the earth, the streams, and descending. More abstractly still, if *yang* is firm and bright, then it is also forceful, energetic, progressing, strong, and filling, and if *yin* is soft and dark, then it is also yielding, resting, retreating, gentler, emptying, and returning. Culturally, they also are associated with male and female, or rather qualities associated with masculine and feminine roles: *yang* connotes leading while *yin* connotes following; *yang* implies strength and force, *yin* is associated with yielding and nurturing. These are not strictly biological gender terms, since all things and all people are supposed to have both qualities in an appropriate balance.[31]

Notice that extending the metaphorical associations still further can yield different classifications for some of these: following the model of dark and light, we get dying as *yin* and growing as *yang*; fall as *yin* and spring as *yang*. But following the model of the fertile and barren we would get the opposite: the alive and supple as *yin*, the dead and dry as *yang*; spring as *yin* and fall as *yang*. Thus, *yin* and *yang* are complex enough for each to contain elements of the other. Notice also that while the moon is *yin* when compared with the sun, it is *yang* when compared with the surrounding night sky. Again, the sky is *yang* when compared to the earth, but *yin* when compared to the sun or the moon. This, however, does not mean that *yin* and *yang* are completely relative. The sun, for example, has the greatest degree of *yang*, followed by the daytime sky, the moon, the night sky, and the earth, least *yang* of these four. Indeed, this must be the case if the concepts of balance and excess of *yin* or *yang* are to be meaningful. Thus, in their most general sense, they are not understood as essentialized forces of nature but as multifaceted characteristics of the phases of natural processes. However, while they are complex, contextual, and matters of degree, they are not completely relative.

In contrast, in typical Western discourse, pairs of concepts tend to be understood as opposites: opposed to each other, mutually antagonistic, and often mutually exclusive. Truth is opposed to falsehood; being excludes nonbeing; death is the enemy of life. Each element is self-contained and sharply defined, distinguished completely from its opposite. They may be *conceptually* dependent on each other, but they are defined by mutual *exclusion*. Truth and falsehood, being and nonbeing mutually *negate* each other. While relational terms ("big" and "small," "more" and "less," for example) and vague boundaries (between red and orange, or between childhood and adulthood) are recognized by logicians, they have been considered to have a subordinate status: a perfect language would eliminate them in favor of terms that are neither relational nor vague.

A reader who approaches Chinese texts with such presuppositions is likely to misinterpret their philosophical significance. In Chinese thinking, pairs of concepts are more likely to be presented as what I call *complementary contrasts*.[32] The structural characteristics of complementary contrasts are exemplified in *yinyang* pairings. Neither phase of the pair is ever static, but always in the process of transforming to some degree into or from its complement. This view is sometimes compared to that of Heraclitus, but for Heraclitus the ruling principle is agonistic: opposites are at war; the fires of becoming are kept burning by tension between the enemies. The Daoist view, however, is that contrasts do not conflict but rather mutually complement each other. That is, each is incomplete without the other, and the momentum of transformation between *yin* and *yang* phases is kept going by mutual yielding, not mutual aggression. Lastly, between *yin* and *yang* lies not a sharp and precisely defined boundary, but an extended phase of *yin*-becoming-*yang*, and between *yang* and *yin* is a phase of *yang*-becoming-*yin*. There is no single precise point at which one can be said to begin and the other end; each blends smoothly into the other across a penumbra of vagueness.[33]

Thus, *yin* and *yang* cannot be essentialized in a simplistic way as "forces of nature." But they are sometimes used, especially in later texts, to classify types of energy, *qi* 氣.[34] The word "*qi*" means "vapor," "air," "atmospheric phenomena," or "breath," and philosophically connotes a tenuous energy from which all things are formed. It is thus perhaps a kind of stuff not understood substantially, but processively as energetic condensation into *yin qi* or rarefaction into *yang qi*.

Dynamic Balance and Priority of *Yin*

While *yin* and *yang* are mutually productive and yielding, they are not necessarily equal at all times. There is, or should be, an appropriate balance between them. Exactly where that balance lies depends on the specific details of any particular process. Our first reaction may be that balance requires equality, but in fact, the Daoist conception of natural balance is complex and dynamic. Imbalance is not merely inequality, but is heading toward one extreme to an excessive degree. Equality presupposes a static conception of balance that would not allow for natural cycles of change. *Dynamic* balance requires leaving the center and constantly returning; only through such mutually balancing *processes* can organic phenomena thrive. Walking and running, for example, are types of controlled falling: we propel ourselves forward and throw ourselves off balance, each foot falling forward in time to redirect the fall to the other side. The sort of balance that allows organic phenomena to flourish is likewise maintained over time, but it is not just a matter of eventually equalizing extremes. Oscillation between extremes might occur naturally, but it does not usually promote organic flourishing. Likewise, throwing ourselves over and falling down to the left and then to the right achieves equality between the two sides, but it is not the kind of movement that Daoists would consider to exemplify natural balance.

Paradoxically, if there is any recurring insight at the heart of Daoist thought, it is that *yin* phases are in some sense more primordial. Throughout Daoist texts, the productivity of darkness, confusion, emptiness, and indeterminacy is presupposed. But this gives rise to a conceptual problem: can it coherently be maintained that *yin* and *yang* are in a mutually productive and balanced relationship, and yet that *yin* is in some sense more fundamental and therefore to be preferred? I suggest that the answer is yes. Productive balance between *yin* and *yang* requires that *yin* be central. *Yin* is a phase of rest and indeterminacy that provides the conditions for regeneration. We shall see the same issue in relation to something and nothing, *you* and *wu*, in the next chapter. Each gives rise to the other, and yet *wu* plays a more productive role without being transcendent.

CHAPTER THREE

The *Laozi*

AUTHORSHIP

The *Laozi* is traditionally attributed to an elder to Confucius, known as Laozi, or Master Lao.[1] There is an ancient mythology surrounding this venerable name, but no indisputable historical evidence to corroborate his existence. Modern scholars regard the text as a collection of aphorisms accumulated over time, generally associated with a distinctive philosophical and literary sensibility but not composed as a single coherent theory by any one person. I nevertheless briefly recount the traditional "biography," as it provides the narrative background against which the text has been interpreted.

The evidence collected by the Grand Historian of the Han dynasty, Sima Qian,[2] consists of inconsistent hearsay and legend. He says that Laozi was born in the hamlet of Quren in Li village, Ku county, in the southern state of Chu. Since he is taken to be older than Confucius, the story implies that he would have been born sometime before 551 B.C.E. According to Sima Qian, his family name was Li 李 and his personal name Er 耳, but he went by the adopted name ("style") of Dan 聃.[3] Already the names do not inspire much confidence in the historical accuracy of this information: "Lao" 老 is not a family name at all, but means "old"; it appears to be used as a title for anonymous sages respected by Daoist writers. "Li," although a family name, does not seem to have been in existence at the time of Confucius and was not common until after the Warring States period.[4] Furthermore, Csikszentmihalyi and Ivanhoe note the colorful meanings of these place names ("*quren*" 曲仁 means "twisted humanity," "*li*" 厲 means "cruel," and "*ku*" 苦 means "bitter"), which strongly suggest that they were literary inventions rather than actual places.[5] Sima Qian himself acknowledges his own uncertainty when he notes that some people say that he was the author known as Lao Laizi, while others say that he was the archivist Taishi Dan (儋), the Grand Historian of Zhou; that some say he lived to the age of 160 and others that he lived to the age of 200. Quotations in the *Zhuangzi* attributed to Lao Dan (聃) either can be found in the *Laozi* or have close affinities with the ideas expressed in the text, but it is unclear whether this Lao Dan is being identified with Taishi Dan, the historian.

Sima Qian recounts a story in which Confucius consulted Laozi about *li* 禮, the traditional rites or propriety. This is extraordinarily unlikely: Confucius, the champion of *li*, would hardly consult his arch-critic about his own ideal. Laozi brusquely dismisses Confucius' question and reproaches him, urging him to be less haughty and avaricious in his aspirations. Confucius, oddly enough, is profoundly impressed and leaves describing Laozi as a dragon, an unearthly creature capable of extraordinary transformations. This is reminiscent of similar stories from the *Zhuangzi*, in which Confucius visits Lao Dan and is chided for worrying about controlling the affairs of the world, rather than trusting the tendencies of natural processes. There are several other stories in which a Confucian scholar consults a recluse, only to be criticized for being concerned about trifling matters or for being overbearingly self-righteous; sometimes the Confucian leaves having been humbled by the otherworldly wisdom of the recluse. Such accounts serve the rhetorical function of criticizing the Confucian way while teaching a moral in keeping with that of the utopian Daoists.

TEXT[6]

The *Laozi* is a very short text, consisting of a mere 81 sections, traditionally called "chapters" or "verses," expressed in some 5,000 words.[7] The religious tradition of Daoism has endowed it with the title "*Daodejing*," the "Classic of *Dao* and *De*." The term "*jing*" had been used for the Confucian classics[8] and was later adopted to translate the Buddhist term "sutra." Its use in the title thus serves to bestow upon this text the rank of a Confucian classic and the aura of a Buddhist scripture. Despite the popularity of this honorific, I shall continue to refer to it as the *Laozi*. It has traditionally been divided into two sections, chapters 1 to 37, known as the *Daojing*, or "Classic of *Dao*," and chapters 38 to 81, known as the *Dejing*, or "Classic of *De*." Until recent times there have been two principal versions of the text, the He Shang Gong and the Wang Bi, both dating to around the middle of the third century C.E. The two versions do not differ greatly, but contain commentaries written from two very different perspectives. The first is attributed to a commentator known as He Shang Gong and has been associated with the practices of the religious tradition of Daoism; the second was written by Wang Bi, a Confucian scholar of the Wei-Jin dynasties.[9] Wang Bi's commentary takes *wu* 無, "nothing," as the most fundamental ontological concept.

In 1972, excavations at tombs in Ma Wang Dui in present-day Hunan province uncovered a collection of silk manuscripts dating to 168 B.C.E. or earlier. There are two versions of the Ma Wang Dui *Laozi*, called the A and B versions. They are significant because they attest to the remarkable coherence of the text, despite its ostensibly random appearance. They contain all 81 chapters, though arranged in a slightly different order and without explicit chapter divisions. There are some minor variations of characters and some differences in grammar, but most notably, very few differences of meaning. Apart from the placement of the *Dejing* before the *Daojing* and some shuffling of chapters, the differences in arrangement from the received text are not significant. Lines within chapters follow the same order, and the series of chapters is more or less the same.[10] Because the B version juxtaposes the *Laozi* text with passages attributed to the mythological figure of the Yellow Emperor (Huang Di), scholars believe that this version probably belongs to the eclectic Han dynasty school known as "Huang-Lao."[11]

In 1993, excavations at tombs in Guodian, a village in present-day Hubei province, unearthed bamboo manuscripts dating to approximately 300 B.C.E. Included among these texts are three bundles of chapters also found in the received *Laozi*. These bamboo slips contain material from 31 chapters—roughly 40 percent of the standard text—but arranged in a completely different order. Of the 31 chapters, only 16 are complete—that is, the same length as their counterparts in the received text. There are a few differences from the received version, but most are minor from a philosophical point of view. One line in chapter 19 contains a difference in terminology—"humanity" and "rightness" are replaced with "artifice" and "craftiness"—which has the overall effect of appearing less anti-Confucian. There is much less emphasis on cosmology and more on self-cultivation. The third bundle, however, also includes an extended passage, very unlike the *Laozi* in style, called "The Great One Gives Birth to the Waters," providing a type of *yinyang* cosmology that is not usually associated with the *Laozi*.

Most scholars now regard the received *Laozi* not as a treatise on a unified philosophy but as a collection of passages broadly coherent in style. According to D. C. Lau,[12] it is an anthology of sayings written in the style of a distinctive literary genre associated with a hermitic way of life that was critical of Confucianism.

PHILOSOPHY OF THE *LAOZI*

The *Laozi* contains some of the most abstruse material in the early Chinese philosophical tradition and belongs to an immediately recognizable genre of dense philosophical verse. Despite its appearance, its philosophical ideas have a significant degree of coherence; some are influential in both the Utopian and the Syncretist strands of the *Zhuangzi*,[13] others in the *Liezi*. There are two broad themes: as a political treatise, it espouses a view that may perhaps be classified as a species of moderate anarchism; as a cosmological treatise, it articulates a distinctive way of understanding the mysterious natural processes of the cosmos. The cosmological ideas undergird its political recommendations, in what Hans-Georg Moeller calls a "metapolitical" philosophy.[14] These two concerns are also unified in a similar way in the Syncretist passages of the *Zhuangzi*. The text seems to be associated with techniques of psychophysical discipline, but the extent to which it articulates those practices explicitly is a matter of some disagreement. It has also been interpreted as a mystical treatise espousing a version of the perennial philosophy, according to which there is an absolute ground of Being that cannot be cognitively grasped, expressed linguistically, or experienced through the senses, but can nevertheless be encountered through some form of meditative practice. Again, the extent to which this reading can be sustained by the text remains in dispute.[15]

The *Laozi* ponders the types of question that certainly have the *potential* to lead us to the concept of the transcendent, as they did in ancient Greek thought. This has been the most common account, especially in popular Western commentaries and books on Daoist religion.[16] The *Laozi* is said to posit a primordial and transcendent origin of the empirical world, one that is ineffable and beyond perception. After all, anything like an ancestral origin or a wellspring of existence could not appear as just another entity. It could not be a visible, perceptible thing, for how could a mere thing play such a primordial role? As a thing, its own existence would also need to be accounted for. This kind of reasoning about the issues raised by the text leads interpreters, not unreasonably, to understand this imperceptibility as indicative of transcendence. We are, it would seem, talking about an ultimate origin, beyond all existence and beyond the empirical world. However, while the text does have the potential to steer our thinking in this direction, its overall coherence should make us wary about accepting this interpretation too hastily.

Adopting a more cautious cosmological interpretation, I maintain, yields a more consistent reading and avoids inappropriately imposing metaphysical presuppositions.[17] In fact, since the text contains no unambiguous and explicit arguments in favor of a transcendent origin, we are methodologically obliged to strive to articulate as coherent a conception as we can of an immanent cosmological source. My sense is that such a notion can indeed be articulated coherently: at the very least, any logical problems faced by the notion of an immanent source are matched by corresponding problems with the concept of a transcendent origin.

Numerical references in the following are to the traditional chapter divisions. Readers are encouraged to use several translations and compare them with my own. This exercise should offer some insight into the linguistic difficulties of grappling with this text.

COSMOLOGICAL CONCEPTS

Way[18]   *Dao*   道

Although *dao* is often said to be ineffable, the *Laozi* does not shy away from discussing it and explicitly describing its characteristics. The descriptions are mysterious, to be sure, and often hard to interpret, but they succeed not just in evoking an image but also in conveying several interesting philosophical claims.[19] Most references are simply to *dao*, but some are to *tiandao* 天道, the way of *tian*; *dadao* 大道, the vast way; and the ancient *gu* 古 way.

The first line of the *Laozi* is probably the most famous quotation from the entire history of Chinese philosophy and yet, despite its succinctness and apparent simplicity, one of the most intractable to interpret. Phrased as sparsely and literally as possible, it says, "*Dao* can be *dao*-ed; it is not a *chang dao*." Traditionally, the second instance of "*dao*" has been taken to mean "be spoken," and "*chang*" to mean "eternal," and the grammar is interpreted to produce the following familiar doctrine: "The *Dao* that can be spoken is not the eternal *Dao*." The intention behind this translation is clear: there is one, unique, eternal *Dao*; it cannot be put into words because it transcends the natural world that it creates.

Despite the popularity and pedigree of this interpretation, there are several problems that it would be remiss not to consider in detail. First, while the word "*dao*" can mean "to say" and is often used to introduce quotations in nonphilosophical texts from later periods, it is rarely, if ever used unambiguously in this sense in pre-Qin philosophical texts. Moreover, the *Laozi* does indeed have much to say about *dao*. Chapter 4, for example, tells us that *dao* is deep and inexhaustible, and chapter 25 says that *dao* goes around tirelessly, can be the mother of the world, and models itself on *ziran* (natural spontaneity). While a claim is being made about the difficulty of describing *dao*, it cannot be that nothing can be said about it.[20] Fortunately, however, it is not necessary to interpret the text in such an inconsistent manner. Given that *dao* has such an important role, it would be wise to find a verbal meaning reflecting its primary sense of a *way*. Verbally it can mean "to be considered as a way," "to be taken as the way," "to lead or guide the way"; by extension it can also mean "to make a way" or "to follow a way." These, I believe, should be our first choices in interpretation, which might yield something like "*dao* can be followed," or "*dao* can be taken as a guide," or even "*dao* can be forged."

Second, the word "*chang*" does not mean "eternal" in Zhou dynasty Chinese: it means "regular" or "ordinary." It can be translated as "constant," not meaning static and unchanging, but in the sense of that which constantly recurs.[21] Thus, the second half of the sentence becomes "It is not a regular *dao*." Third, the surface grammar of the sentence is of the following form: "*Dao* can be followed; it is not a regular *dao*." It appears to make two assertions: *dao* can be followed, and it is not a regular *dao*. Classical Chinese grammar allows us to interpret this as an "if . . . then" sentence: "If *dao* can be followed, then it is not a regular *dao*," or "A *dao* that can be followed is not a regular *dao*." What determines which is to be preferred is the context: if the text as a whole justifies the "if . . . then" interpretation, then that is the most likely meaning. The traditional mystical interpretation of *dao* as that which lies beyond the world would require this "if . . . then" construction. However, as we have seen, this requires stretching the meanings of "*dao*" and "*chang*" beyond their Eastern Zhou ranges of significance. Besides, whether or not this is the case, my goal is not to repeat yet another account of the same trite philosophical dogma, but to bring to life a different textual philosophical possibility that I hope will at least yield a richer and more plausible understanding of this all too familiar text.

I shall therefore attempt to interpret the sentence in its most literal sense, to mean that *dao* can be forged and followed, and yet it is no ordinary *dao*. That is to say, even though this cosmic way is not an ordinary way, it nevertheless guides us and can be followed. Its all-encompassing status makes it an extraordinary phenomenon, but does not prevent it from being accessible. Following this interpretation, the second line would be claiming that *dao* can be discussed, but not in any ordinary sense of naming and describing. Thus, the first two lines of the *Laozi* affirm a special role for *dao* without requiring that it transcend language or worldly existence altogether.

This role of *dao* as a phenomenon so deep that it lies at the limits of discernibility is described through metaphors of depth *yuan* 淵, obscurity *hu huang* 惚恍, mystery *xuan* 玄, and formlessness *wuzhuang* 無狀, *wuxing* 無形.[22] Chapter 21 says that *dao* "as a thing" is quiet and confused; chapter 14 says that when you look it does not appear, and when you listen, it is unheard. That is to say, *dao* is not an object that has a clearly delineable form, and so cannot be known or understood as an ordinary perceptual object. This might, with good reason, be taken to suggest that *dao* is something altogether transcendent and otherworldly. But it does not have to be interpreted this way. There are worldly phenomena that can aptly be described as subtle, mysterious, and not observable as things: the fragility of a sheet of ice, the trustworthiness of a friend, the imaginative genius of an artist. There are even perceptible phenomena that are not well-defined entities: the shadow of a tree, for example, or the reflection of the shadow in a lake, or even the absence of detail in the reflection of the shadow. All these are empirical phenomena yet are not distinct or determinate objects. They can be observed, but on closer inspection they dissolve into nothing: a shadow is not a presence, but the absence of light; a reflection, though observable, is not itself an entity. In chapter 14, the terms used to describe the imperceptibility of *dao* refer to its subtlety *xi* 希 and minuteness *wei* 微. Subtlety and minuteness are worldly qualities. *Dao* is able to extend everywhere and pervades all things only because it is so tenuous and rarified, that is, only because it is not a delineable entity. Metaphorically speaking, it is so fine and refined that, like water or air, it penetrates to the depth of the most impenetrable places. As the deepest and most long-standing tendencies of natural processes, those hidden within the natural workings of all things, *dao* is not accessible as an ordinary sensory object.

According to chapter 25, *dao* does not alter, and yet it is described in dynamic, processive terms: it spreads into the distance, reaches all things, and returns. The constancy of *dao* thus cannot be that it is a static substance underlying change. Rather, the way never swerves from its course, but is neither static nor ordinary and totally predictable. Its movement is ubiquitous, as the way of nature: there is no thing or event in the natural world that does not follow its propensities. According to chapter 37, *dao*, like nature, does not engage in deliberate actions, does not control what happens, and yet is somehow responsible for all things that happen;[23] it endows them with the natural tendencies through which they spontaneously develop. It enables natural phenomena to grow and flourish as their inner potential comes to fruition. It would seem then that when people are allowed to follow their natural tendencies, human life will also flourish. This idea, as we shall see, forms the root of Daoist metapolitics. In chapter 4, *dao* is described as vast, deep, and inexhaustible; in chapter 2, it is said to produce all things, to benefit them, and yet not to claim possession or demand gratitude. *Dao* is thus thought of as a mother to all things: it gives birth to or generates them and continues to nurture them as they develop. It is an unlimited wellspring that appears from the human perspective as inexhaustible generosity, and at the same time the "mother" to which all things return.

The Ancestral[24]   *Zong* 宗

Like the ancient Greek cosmologists, the *Laozi* expresses a fascination with the mysteries of existence: the origins of things, their emergence, their sustenance, their maturation, and their return. What explains their inexhaustible variety, what they are, where they come from, how they grow, and why they are the way they are? The *Laozi* might thus be said to be concerned with the sources and natures of things. It does not, however, attempt any kind of scientific investigation of these questions; nor does it articulate a metaphysical proof of the necessity of a transcendent origin. Rather, it attempts, as a phenomenologist would say, to "describe the phenomena" of emergence by clustering together a network of metaphors through which to understand them: *shi* 始, literally meaning "beginning" but etymologically suggesting giving birth; *mu* 母, meaning "mother," and *zong* 宗, "ancestor." The botanical metaphor *gen* 根, "root," appears to refer to the particular origins of particular things. The word *men* 門 means "gateway," but although the metaphor is derived from a socially constructed artifact, it is used to refer to the birth of living creatures from the womb. The sense behind all these terms is that of a vast, deep, and indeterminate productive power.

Our first tendency might be to think that "*mu*" refers to a human mother, but the word itself is more general. Literally, it refers to the female of any creature that produces and nourishes its offspring. The mothering metaphor also implies the continued sustenance of existing phenomena, the nurturing conditions that allow them to flourish to their greatest potential. Although the term "*shi*" seems least metaphorical in its significance, being equivalent to the words "beginning" and "origin," etymologically it also appears to refer to birth from a female. The term "*zong*," ancestral, emphasizes the historicity of production: the mother from which a creature arises itself has a mother, and thus begins a regress. The concept of the ancestral thus turns our attention away from the immediate production of a particular phenomenon to its deepest origins. The further one looks into the past, the more universal the ancestors become: the further back we trace our ancestries, the more people to whom we find ourselves related.[25] The *Laozi* follows such ancestral lines into the murkiest distance, beyond our human predecessors to the most distant ancestor, not only of all animals but also of all life, and indeed of all things. That which is most ancient, from which all things spring, and through which all things are continuously nourished can be identified with nature or the cosmos itself. When the ancestral is understood as nature itself, it cannot be thought of as confined to the past. Nature as ancestral source then is the ever-present productive potency through which the cosmos continually reproduces and sustains itself.

"*Gen*" and "*ben*" as root metaphors evoke the richness of the soil, a source that is itself a product of the decomposition of organic and inorganic matter. The soil may be understood metaphorically as a womb within which the seeds of things are nurtured and through which they are eventually brought to life. The root is the locus connecting the plant to the earth, the product to its source. The roots draw from the indeterminate richness of the soil and provide a pathway through which the determinate and specific complexity of the particular plant becomes integrated, emerges, and comes to light. This, of course, applies not just to plants but metaphorically to all emerging phenomena: the root represents that by which the indeterminate in general is channeled into a determinate form.

The concept of a primordial source of all phenomena might well be thought to suggest a transcendent origin, perhaps even a primordial Creator. It is true that the metaphors discussed above are fiercely naturalistic, but that does not preclude their being used with transcendent significance. Indeed, transcendence can only ever be articulated through concepts describing natural phenomena, and therefore can only ever be articulated through metaphor. The term "transcendence" itself, for example, etymologically means "rising beyond"; and "substance," sometimes used to discuss the metaphysical ground that lies beyond experience, etymologically means "standing under." "Rising beyond" and "standing under" are metaphors drawn from empirical phenomena. Nevertheless, and more importantly from a comparative philosophical point of view, the notion of a primordial origin does not *need* to be interpreted as transcendent. We have models for understanding origins that are naturalistic. Natural science, for example, attempts to provide ultimate explanations of the origins of the cosmos without ever invoking the existence of anything that transcends the natural world. Natural cosmology attempts to explain the origin of the empirical world using only empirical science; evolutionary biology attempts to explain the origins of life using only natural scientific explanations; psychology attempts to explain the mind without appealing to any phenomena that are not part of the natural world. The principles that account for the production of the natural world are found within that world itself: the Big Bang from which the universe explodes, the primordial sludge from which life was once thought to have emerged, or the inorganic elements on which organic compounds depend.

Of course, there is an inescapable circularity involved in attempting to account for natural phenomena by appealing only to natural phenomena. Creationists[26] believe that this circularity is a serious logical flaw and argue that a transcendent origin is therefore logically necessary. Naturalists point out that this appeal to a transcendent origin beyond the world doesn't avoid the problem of circularity, but only defers it to the transcendent origin. The question then is not whether the circularity can be avoided, but whether a meaningful sense can be given to the notion of a natural origin. Can there be some fundamental ground of productivity *within* the universe that accounts for the continued arising and dissolution of all natural phenomena? This, I believe, is the least intrusive way of interpreting the cosmology of the mutual production of absence and presence that is evoked in the *Laozi*.[27]

Absence and Presence[28] *Wu You* 無有

Wu and *you*, nothing and something, not being there and being there, not having and having, not existing and existing: this pair of concepts indicates the central role of ontology (theories of existence) and cosmology (theories about the existence and nature of the cosmos) in Daoist philosophy.[29] "*You*" 有, not unlike the French "*il y a*" or the Spanish "*hay*," literally means "to have" or "it has," is used to assert that something exists or is present, and can be translated "there is" or "there are." "*Wu*" 無, which literally means "to lack" or "it does not have," is used to deny the existence of something or to assert that something is not present, and in nonphilosophical texts and contexts can often be translated as "no," "not," and "nothing." In philosophical contexts, the terms are used as nouns and take on a more complex range of meanings. The primary senses of "*you*" are of things that exist, or the presence of existing things, or the world insofar as it contains existing things. The primary senses of "*wu*" are of the absence of things that once existed, or the conditions prior to the existence of something, or the absence in a particular place of something that exists elsewhere. Juxtaposed, "*wuyou*" connotes the processes of coming into and going out of existence of the myriad phenomena that make up the natural world. It is tempting to assume that such a cosmological concern with existing and not existing must be identical to Western *metaphysical* concerns with "Being" and "Non-being." That, however, would be a hasty and problematic assumption.

Western metaphysical interest in Being can be traced to the philosophies of Parmenides and Aristotle. Parmenides argues that Being, as the totality of existence, must be a single, eternal, unchanging, undivided substance. It must have all these properties or it would not be the totality of all existence. More generally, the philosophical term "Being" is not necessarily synonymous with "existence." Insofar as it derives from Aristotle's metaphysics, it is considered to be the most general of words and combines three distinct senses: existence, identity, and predication of an essence. In European languages such as Greek, German, and English, the verb for "to be" is used not only to assert that something is (its existential use) but also to identify which thing it is (the "is" of identity) and to explain what it is, or to describe or define it (its predicative use as a copula).[30] Aristotle's "Being" appears to combines these three logically distinct functions: the concept of the Being of something includes not only its existence (*on, estin, ousia*), but also its identity, and its essence (*to ti esti, to ti ein einai*). The Chinese word "*you*," however, can only be used existentially, not as a copula or to assert identity. It therefore cannot be identical to the Aristotelian concept of "Being."[31]

Not until the mid-twentieth century, with Heidegger's phenomenological ontology, do we find a conception of Being that provides a more serviceable equivalent to the term "*you*." Heidegger is critical of the entire tradition of Western ontology and seeks to investigate phenomena afresh in order to come to a new understanding of the meaning of "Being." He rejects the theoretical, substantialist, essentialist concepts that have molded Western metaphysics since Parmenides and Aristotle as failing to express our most primordial relationship with Being, and attempts to rethink the manner in which Being is manifested to us, independently of the history of metaphysics. Of course, this is a monumental foundational task, and as such, it begins without a clear method or criteria of success. Is it even possible to rethink Being independently of a tradition of philosophical investigation? What method could possibly be employed? By what criteria do we judge our phenomenological explorations? In *Being and Time*, Heidegger attempts to answer these questions and articulates his phenomenological conception of

Being. It is a complex analysis, but essentially involves rethinking Being as the temporal manifesting of phenomena to us as engaged beings ("*dasein*") intimately incorporated into the world through our concerns and projects. This more pragmatic, temporalized, and phenomenological-hermeneutic understanding of Being certainly seems to have more in common with the ancient Chinese worldview and philosophical methodology, and so might provide a more appropriate way to understand "*you*" than the Aristotelian or Parmenidean concepts.

The philosophical term "Non-being" is used only to negate the existential use of the word "Being." It is rarely, if ever, used to discuss the nonidentity of two things or what something is not. Nevertheless, there are still problems with taking it as the equivalent of the Daoist negative existential, "*wu*." For example, the Parmenidean concept of "Non-being" is understood to be the absolute negation of Being. That is, Non-being, or nonexistence, is the absolute absence of all existence. Non-being does not and cannot exist, because existence is what all beings have in common. If Non-being existed it would have existence and therefore would be a being and not Non-being. In the *Laozi*, the term "*wu*," however, is not the absolute contradictory of the term "*you*." According to chapter 2, "*you* and *wu* mutually produce each other," and they are listed alongside the contrasts "beautiful" and "ugly," "high" and "low." *You* and *wu* are thus understood as like other worldly opposites: *yin-yang* contrasts that complete each other, produce each other, yield to each other, and are necessary for each other. It is not that *you* is worldly and *wu* transcendent: neither is the absolute origin of the other,[32] and both are manifested in the world of experience. *You* and *wu*, then, are the presences and absences that manifest as a result of the cycles of production and dissolution, integration and disintegration, that make up the world. Nevertheless, just as with *yin* and *yang*, the two are not of equal value: *wu* and *you* are mutually producing, yet somehow *wu* is of greater cosmological significance than *you*.

Although the term "*wu*" does not often occur by itself in the *Laozi*, it is one of the most important conceptual devices of the text, and indeed of Daoist philosophies in general. Used as a noun, it can be translated as "nothing," "absence," or "lack," but when used philosophically it takes on a very distinctive sense, not easily translatable into English. There are two fundamental connotations: emptiness and indeterminacy. In the *Laozi*, *wu* functions to reverse the priority of significance of the positive and negative through a kind of *gestalt* inversion. Ordinarily we pay attention to clear, determinate, nameable things. In advocating *wu* forms of negation, the *Laozi* dissolves the focus of our concentration and draws our attention toward the indeterminacy that lies at the periphery of our awareness, the emptiness that surrounds, defines, and makes possible determinate things. This form of negation might be thought of as a function that discloses an indeterminate "space" that allows for many uses and possibilities to manifest within it. According to chapter 11, the reason that doors, windows, cups, and wheels are useful is because of what is not there. *Wu* is the empty space that is the condition of the possibility of the functioning of what is present. By emphasizing the importance of such a space, whether physical, psychological, or phenomenological, the *Laozi* encourages an attitude in which we refrain from imposing our plans and preconceptions and thereby allow the phenomena to develop according to their own potential, modified minimally by our intentions.

In practical application in the *Laozi*, the term "*wu*" often takes an object such as knowledge, action, or desire. Reflecting on its general use as a modifier in early Daoist texts suggests that rather than simply negating these concepts to get their contradictories ("ignorance," "inactivity," "desirelessness") or negating a sentence to get its denial ("there is no knowledge"), it has a distinctively Daoist function of *optimal* minimizing. The semantic function of "*wu*" is to optimally minimize the clarity and determinacy of the concept it modifies. This is not unrestricted lessening, but presupposes a specific kind of function: a minimal amount necessary to cooperate symbiotically with our environments. All references to the "minimal" or to "minimizing" below should be understood in this way. To be effective, the process requires maximal efficiency through embodied understanding of natural tendencies. If this is right, then the *Laozi* does not advocate complete avoidance of action, knowledge, or desire. If *wei* is action that is deliberate, then *wuwei* is action that is minimally active and controlling; it is a way of engaging that allows the phenomena to develop in accordance with their own proclivities. If *yu* 欲 is desire for sensory gratification and objects of acquisition, then *wuyu* involves minimizing such desires in favor of more natural needs and propensities. It may be interpreted as a reduction of determinate sensory and acquisitive desires and a nurturing of natural processes so as to allow them to take their own course (see "Desire" in the second part of this chapter). To put it paradoxically, *wuyu* is a desire that is satisfied with nothing more than natural simplicity.

The World and Myriad Things[33] *Tiandi Wanwu* 天地萬物

Reflections on the "world" play a central role in the *Laozi*. Several concepts are used: *tiandi*, "heaven and earth"; *tianxia*, "all under the heavens"; *wanwu*, "the myriad things." Literally "heaven and earth," "*tiandi*" refers to the natural world as a whole, or the cosmos, in terms of its integration or wholeness. It thus has the same significance as the more general sense of "*tian* 天." In the *Laozi*, "*tian*" is often used in its more restricted sense to refer to the heavens.[34] The earth models itself on *tian*, and *tian* models itself on *dao*, which in turn models itself on *ziran*, natural spontaneity (see below). The heavens are said to be great or vast *da* 大 (chapter 25); they oversee everything. The net of *tian* is cast so wide that everything on earth falls under the purview of the heavens. The use of the more general sense of "*tian*" also occurs in the *Laozi*, though less often. For example, the term "*tiandao*" 天道[35] refers to the way of the cosmos or nature as a whole, and is contrasted with the way of humans.

The term "*tianxia*" 天下 literally means "all under (*xia* 下) the heavens," but several different senses can be discerned in the *Laozi*. Most often the word has the sense of "the whole world"[36] as the all-encompassing realm of *social* concern, the whole kingdom, or possibly even the whole empire,[37] that is governed by the ruler. Sometimes it refers to all people in the world, or just "everyone."[38] Occasionally it refers to the realm in which all things exist,[39] and can be thought of as almost synonymous with *tiandi* or even *wanwu*, "everything." For example, chapters 43 and 78 refer to water as the gentlest thing in the natural world.

While natural events and the myriad things that arise and decompose do not last forever (chapter 23), the cosmos, *tiandi*, itself is enduring. According to chapter 7, this is because it does not produce itself (*zisheng* 自生, "self-producing/self-living"). This might seem to contradict the naturalistic view of the world, but the rest of the chapter indicates a different moral. What is at stake here is not whether the cosmos is self-originating, but how it is able to sustain itself. The claim that the cosmos does not produce itself means that it does not live for its own existence: it exists only in producing the myriad things; it is able to bring itself to completion only by being without self-concern. That is, the enduring of the cosmos *is* the production and dissolution of the myriad things. Thus, the key to longevity lies not in self-preservation but in cultivating productive connections with all things.[40]

Literally, "*wanwu*" 萬物 means "the ten thousand things." It refers to the cosmos not in terms of its integration but in terms of its multiplicity. "Myriad things" is a good equivalent, insofar as "*wan*" and "myriad" both mean "ten thousand" and both have a general sense of "innumerably many." The word "*wu*" 物 originally meant "cattle" and became extended to mean animals or creatures in general. The things might be understood as creatures, not in the etymological sense of objects that have been created, but insofar as the term carries connotations of having been brought to life or having been produced naturally. The metaphor of birth is applied to the production, or coming into existence, of all things, whether living or not. The term "*wanwu*" also has connotations of bustling activity, the emerging and dissolving of the full panoply of ordinary and extraordinary phenomena that make up the world. From the perspective of the universe as a whole, the difference between things that emerge through biological processes and those that emerge in other ways becomes less salient. Organic processes are, after all, a subset of chemical processes. The difference does not vanish altogether, but it becomes less prominent when viewed from the perspective of the grand scheme of things. Nevertheless, a major concern is to enable life to flourish to its fullest natural potential, so while all natural processes are important, biological processes retain a special role.

Interestingly, the text has no unified statement regarding what exactly produces the many things. In chapter 1, for example, it is *ming*, naming, that mothers them; in chapter 2, it is implied that they arise from *wuwei* (see "*wu*" above and "*wuwei*" below); in chapters 4 and 34, their ancestral dependence on *dao* is implied; in 39, they are produced through *yi*, unity or integration; in 42, they are produced after *san*, three; and in 40, they are produced from *you*, something, which in turn comes from *wu*, nothing. This surely indicates that any attempt to find a unified cosmological theory in the *Laozi* is misguided. The most we can say is that the many things are produced or born, and that this engendering of things is attributed variously to productive ancestral processes of integration and distinction. *Dao* the way, *wuwei* minimal action, *you* something, *wu* nothing, *yi* integration, and *ming* naming all have some role to play in this productive process. Beyond that, the text is not specific.[41]

Regularity[42]   *Chang*   常

The myriad things are varied and spontaneous, but in their transformations they can also be seen to manifest regularities. The ordinary sense of "*chang*" is "regular," "common," even "ordinary." It also has a sense of constancy, not in the sense of stillness or endurance of some unchanging thing, but in the sense of patterns that recur. Most straightforwardly, it is the constancy of the seasons and of the natural cycles of birth, growth, age, death, decomposition, and recomposition into new organisms. It refers especially to cyclical regularities, the cyclical changes of production of dissolution that can be discerned throughout nature and characterized through the complementary contrasts *yin* and *yang*. But it need not refer only to patterns that are obvious. Although the ways of natural transformation are everywhere, the regularities do not necessarily occur as evenly as the seasons. The patterns in which the surface of a waterfall disintegrates, the swirling of eddies in the mist, the darting of a school of fish, the formation of a flock of birds—these display a kind of natural regularity, but not one that is even, symmetrical, or predictable in any simple way. *Chang* might be thought of as the consistency of natural transformations that is hidden beneath any apparent disorderliness. To understand a phenomenon is to have recognized the patterns through which it recurs, either explicitly through being able to describe it or intuitively through being able to recognize it again, anticipate a future occurrence, or embody it in one's own behavior.[43]

Chapter 40 says, "the movement of *dao* is reversal." This passage, I believe, provides a key to understanding the processes of *dao* as understood in the *Laozi*. It specifies the most basic tendency of the way: reversal or returning, *fan* 反. All natural processes, insofar as they are regular and cyclical, intimately involve oscillation.[44] The process of circling or cycling is one of continuous turning, and therefore in some sense of constant *re*turning. For a vast array of natural phenomena, we perceive this as a continuous exchange between contrasting pairs that become salient from the perceptual perspective of the human organism: heating and cooling, becoming light and dark; day returning to night, which in turn returns to day. The same applies to the seasons, as plants return to life in the spring and return to the soil in the fall. Moreover, modern science continues to furnish us with endless examples of cyclical patterns: the nucleus and satellite structure of atoms, solar systems, and galaxies; the rotations and revolutions of subatomic particles, stars, and planets; the life cycles of stars, galaxies, and the cosmos as a whole. The ubiquity of revolutions, rotations, and cycles of activity throughout the physical universe, at microscopic and macroscopic levels, is quite startling.

But, as noted above, regularities do not always follow simple circular patterns. Mathematically, the process of circling can be manifested in several ways: rotating about an axis, revolving around a center, spiraling toward a focal point; cycles of oscillation, expansion and contraction, can also be mapped as forms of circling or constant returning. Moreover, they need not always be describable through such simple mathematical functions. They may involve complex overlays of cyclical changes, with phases not always obvious or equally balanced; they may, in a fuguelike manner, be extended or expanded, and modify each other through mutual interference. The intricate interweavings of cycles may result in patterns whose cyclical structures are thus hidden: weather patterns, ocean currents, evolutions of environments and species. The fact that we may not immediately see them does not mean that they are not there.

If nature does indeed conceal deeper uniformities and regularities, then all natural developments ultimately share similar propensities. If there is a central insight in the cosmology of the *Laozi*, it is perhaps that the way of all natural phenomena is guided at several levels by centripetal tendencies: gravitational or magnetic tendencies, as it were, that keep us on our path by constantly pulling us back.[45] Regular return can be thought of as the result of attraction toward the lower of two contrastive energy states: to the earth, to the night, to the soil, to the winter. In general, it might be thought of as the attractive force of *yin*. The momentum created by this pull through any movement creates the torque or swing that turns the movement back on itself, and by acting continuously allows it to continue reproducing itself indefinitely. A finite line can be made infinite by uniting its beginning and end points into a circle. Organic processes of disintegration create the conditions that enable the productive stages of growth to begin once again. This principle of constant return would have the same status as the principle of conservation of mass-energy in modern science: it is not a law that has been proven, but a guideline by which to judge and understand all the cyclical transformations of natural phenomena.

In terms of pragmatic application, *fan* is interpreted as a method of reversing priorities. According to the *Laozi*, reversal is the kind of activity we must understand and embody if we are to be as successful as nature in our lives and daily activities. We usually seek to progress, but the advice of the *Laozi* is to retreat. To dismiss and reject softness, darkness, yielding, resting, emptiness, absence, and *yin* is to overlook their regenerative value. The *dao* of the *Laozi* is thus a gentle way, the way not of strength but of weakness. We sustain our energy by resting; we overcome obstacles by yielding to them; we progress by retreating. In general, we are able to continue indefinitely by slowing, subsiding, and starting over, using the momentum of the fall to propel the next rise.[46]

A problematic conclusion might seem to follow from the Daoist concept of contrastive balance and of the mutuality of loss and gain. One might think that if all phenomena inevitably follow cyclical patterns, then there is no such thing as loss. Anything that we perceive as loss is necessary for the production of something new. Therefore, we need never worry about destruction. Exploitation is natural and will lead to the annihilation of some species, perhaps including ourselves, but also to the emergence of something new. As we shall see in the second part of this chapter, this sort of consequence, though not necessarily embraced, is symptomatic of the move from the human to a cosmic perspective.

Continuity and Integration[47] *Yi* —

Complementing the multiplicity of the world is its integration. Literally, "*yi*" is the number one, in one way, the simplest and most familiar of concepts. Yet familiarity conceals the possibility of deep misunderstanding. In the *Laozi*, *yi* is extraordinarily difficult to interpret, since so little is said of it. How we interpret it leads to vastly divergent understandings of the text. In Western philosophy the concept of the "one" connotes unity, identity, wholeness, and universality. Parmenides' Being is the One: the single, unchanging, undifferentiated whole. Reading "*yi*" as the "One," as is often done, leads to interpreting Laozi as a neo-Platonist. It might also be taken as a reference to the problem of the One and the Many, and thus as an attempt to articulate a concept of an abstract realm of universal essence. However, since there is no background of Platonism whatsoever in early China, and since it appears to be inconsistent with the naturalistic tendencies of Daoist thought in particular, it would be wise to resist translating "*yi*" as "the One" and thus inadvertently imposing such culturally inappropriate philosophical presuppositions.

But this is far from the only significance of the number one. A modest stretch of the imagination yields the following array of significances that differ quite dramatically in their philosophical implications: sameness, continuity, coherence, singularity, uniqueness, aloneness, delineation, determination, integrity, and integration. In early Chinese philosophy and history, the term "*yi*" generally has a different set of connotations from those of Western philosophy: it often has a temporalized sense, referring to the continuity between past and present; it also has psychological or phenomenological significance and connotes concentration of intention. This suggests that the concepts of continuity, concentration, and integration are more consistent with the worldview of the *Laozi* as a whole. Reading *yi* as "wholeness or integrity" leads to an interpretation consistent with naturalism, according to which the world is integrated and continuous, not requiring anything other than itself in order to be explained and understood. On this reading, *yi* is not an abstract entity distinct from the natural world but the wholeness, continuity, and integration of the cosmos itself.

ETHICO-POLITICAL CONCEPTS

Critique of Humanist Virtues

State authorities generally use regulations and punishments as the means to attain a harmoniously functioning society free of crime, but Confucius argues that this falls far from the ideal of an ethically flourishing society.[48] Enforcing laws and punishments is at best a superficial solution to deep-rooted social problems; it indicates that people are not authentically motivated by ethical considerations. Moreover, laws and punishments cannot make people virtuous: they may refrain from selfish and harmful behavior, but insofar as their motivation is to avoid punishment or gain a reward, it will not be ethical. What is needed is the cultivation of ethical virtues—humanity (*ren* 仁), rightness (*yi* 義), and propriety (*li* 禮)—for their own sake, and this is achieved not through rewards or punishments, but by setting an example for others to imitate. According to Confucian psychology, people may be motivated by fear and pleasure, but they also admire charisma and excellence of character: they cultivate their own character by imitating and embodying the qualities of those they admire. When values are internalized in this way, people will eventually want to do what is right, *yi*, because they are spontaneously moved by the beauty of what is right, and for no other reason.

According to the *Laozi*, however, such an emphasis on humanistic virtues is not only shortsighted but also misguided, hypocritical, and counterproductive. Daoism and Confucianism should not be construed as espousing philosophies that are entirely antagonistic,[49] but the *Laozi* does launch an attack on virtues such as humanity, *ren*, and rightness, *yi*.[50] Any philosophy that promotes these sorts of virtues, as do Confucianism and Mohism, will thereby be open to its critique. Perhaps with a deliberate sense of irony, one of the criticisms of humanist virtues echoes the Confucian criticism of laws and punishments mentioned above. According to chapters 18 and 38, the need to cultivate virtues artificially is merely a sign that people have already lost their natural sense of virtue. A society that needs to promote the cultivation of virtue is one whose members are not genuinely ethical. However, while this may be an interesting rhetorical flourish, it does not succeed as a persuasive criticism. That the times are out of joint and people are no longer virtuous is a presupposition of the Confucian *dao*. Indeed, if that were not the case, there would be no need for the Confucian prescription. At any rate, more must be said to show that once genuine virtues are lost, they cannot be recultivated.

A stronger line of criticism can be found in chapter 19, and also in 38. In promoting a human way that requires the cultivation of humanity and rightness, the Ruists are worsening the very problems they are trying to solve. Get rid of humanity and rightness and the people will flourish of themselves; propriety is itself the beginning of disorder. Unlike the first criticism, this one presents a serious challenge. The cultivation of virtue itself prevents people from flourishing, precisely because the virtues are valued. The *Laozi*'s diagnosis of social ills is that artificial objects of desire fuel greed and competition (see "Desire" below). Humanistic virtues become objects of desire even if they are pursued for their own sake. People compete for goods, power, prestige, and renown, and adding *ren* and *yi* to the list only makes things worse.

Whether or not the criticism succeeds, such an attack on the cultivation of ethical virtues might well seem a little disturbing. It is not obvious why rejecting humanity and rightness would not result in inhumanity. The question would be easy to answer if the text were more direct, but while there are passages that presuppose recognizably ethical values, others remain stubbornly vague and deliberately paradoxical.

Certainly, much of the text seems to presuppose a recognizable sense of ethical value. Chapters 31 and 46, for example, criticize warfare, and thereby recognize the value of life; chapters 53, 72, and 75 criticize exploitation and oppression of the people, and thereby display a sensitivity to injustice and recognize that causing suffering is wrong. Most importantly, chapter 60 explicitly says that the sage does not harm people. However, this is in stark contrast to the most disturbing passage of the collection, chapter 5, which says explicitly that both the cosmos and the sage are not humane, *bu ren* 不仁. Moreover, the text is also replete with paradoxical passages that multiply the interpretive difficulties. In a kind of Nietzschean transvaluation of values, chapter 38 tells us "the highest virtue is not virtuous"; in the same vein, chapter 41 says that ample virtue seems defective and plain virtue seems soiled; chapter 2 literally says that to recognize the good is itself bad. In chapter 15, those who have the way are described in a manner hard to empathize with. They seem to lack the warmth of full humanity: they are cautious as though fording a stream in the winter, fearful of their neighbors, like melting ice, solemn and robust, vast and confused. Many interpreters take these ethical conundrums in their stride: the paradoxes are tamed and defanged, and made to mean something quite safe and comfortable. These overly kind interpretations strike me as a little too hasty, as they do not do adequate justice to the philosophical problems that arise. Indeed, as we shall see below, the paradoxical passages derive from a displacement of humanistic concerns and thereby, whether intentionally or not, open up the possibility for anti-humanist tendencies to develop.

Perhaps the most common solution is to interpret the ethically ambiguous and paradoxical passages as rhetorical overstatements that merely reject a particular manner of embodying virtues. It is not that we give up humanity altogether, only the humanity that is too pleased with itself. We do not announce our virtuosity. Such interpretations, however, seem ad hoc, and more importantly, do not succeed in distinguishing Daoist virtues from their Confucian counterparts: genuine Confucian virtue is not self-important, but is manifested in humility. If that really is the core of the criticism, there is no significant difference between the Ruists and Daoists on *ren* and *yi*.

A more promising way to defuse the explosive potency of the dangerous passages is to take them as challenging the humanistic orientation of Confucian ethics. True humanity is not humanistic; genuine humanity is not contrived. We should not impose artificial rules, structures, desires, and values, but rather return to a simplicity that is naturally harmonious.[51] We should refrain from *cultivating* artificial virtues and instead concentrate on *nurturing* natural excellences. The *Laozi* would thus replace the old ethical virtues with a new set of nonhumanistic virtues. This seems to be a plausible direction of interpretation, but now the problem is that it is not clear what kind of behavior would result from putting those new virtues into practice.[52] We can certainly reject traditional values, provided that we have a deeper set of ethical values by which we judge them. But if we reject *all* ethical values as artificial, any virtues that remain will by definition not be ethical. Only if we can find recognizably ethical values rooted in the natural way can we be confident that natural virtues will be ethical. It is far from clear, however, what in the *Laozi* can justify such confidence.[53]

From the perspective of the whole, none of the myriad things is favored by the forces of nature. They certainly have no partiality for human concerns. As we have seen, chapter 5 tells us that the natural world does not exhibit humanity: "The cosmos is not humane: it treats the myriad things as straw dogs."[54] Nature follows its course without regard for our hopes; natural disasters occur without taking account of human suffering. Generations replace one another like the seasonal changes of the forest leaves. When stated descriptively, there is nothing problematic about this insight. The problem arises insofar as the *Laozi* implies that we too must shift to this perspective. This reminder of our insignificance encourages us to view human concerns not as interested participants, but from the perspective of an indifferent observer—not just a different but equal bystander, but a witness whose perspective is broader and more inclusive. Indeed, the same chapter explicitly goes on to recommend this: "Sages are not humane: they treat the people as straw dogs."

The process of ethical maturation is the process of expanding the boundaries of our concern. As children, we act sometimes selfishly and sometimes out of concern for others. The extent to which we learn to care about the needs of others is the extent to which we grow as ethical beings. As we gradually become more aware of the suffering that human activity causes animals, we come to recognize the ethical demands made on us by other creatures. In contemporary terms, as the effect of human action on the balance of the natural environment spirals out of control, "deep ecologists" argue that we must struggle to expand the purview of our ethical considerations still further. Can we continue to exploit the environment for our own temporary benefit, or do we need to balance our interests with those of our descendants and of other creatures, and perhaps even, if this makes sense, of the earth or the cosmos itself?

Chapter 49 says that the sage accepts all people and does not distinguish between the good and bad. In chapter 27, we learn that the sage extends this concern to all the myriad creatures. But the more we expand our ethical concern, the more diluted it must inevitably become. Should all creatures really have equal concern? Is the suffering of dogs and cats as important as that of humans? Are the interests of cockroaches and centipedes as important as those of dogs and cats? How about bacteria and viruses? Cancer cells? What about blades of grass? Drops of rain? The further we extend our concern, the less meaningful that concern becomes. When we include everything as equally important, the ethical demand made by each thing loses its impact. When the interests of all creatures are equally valued, the suffering of any one of them becomes insignificant. We either end up, like the devoted Jain ascetic, barely able to breathe, eat, or move, or we give up all hope of making any ethical judgment whatsoever. At best, even if there is such a thing as action that will further the interests of all things equally, it becomes impossible to say what that action is. Arguably, some later Daoist philosophers and interpreters seem to edge in the direction of abandoning ethical judgments altogether. Indeed, one popular interpretation of Daoist philosophy is precisely that it equalizes and thereby abandons all ethical judgments.[55] This is surely a consequence that should not be accepted lightly. If there is a way of saving the trajectory of Laozian philosophy from such a nihilistic fate, it is certainly worth pondering.

Moreover, the ethically ambiguous passages appear to be engaging in precisely the kind of intellectual *craftiness* that is criticized elsewhere in the text. (See "Natural Simplicity" below.) While dense and impenetrable poetry is a powerful and appropriate linguistic device for phenomenological explorations of ontology and cosmology, it leaves a lot to be desired when discussing ethical concepts. It seems clear that the paradoxes are not intended to lead to a position that justifies cruel and unethical behavior, but they unfortunately do not contain sufficient philosophical resources to circumvent such an interpretation. If there were no ethically ambiguous or paradoxical passages, or passages rejecting humanity or asserting that the sage is not humane, this would be less of a pressing problem. Even the statement in chapter 60 that the sage does not harm people is insufficient. For example, natural disasters do not deliberately harm people; they just happen. That we take them to be harms arises from a human perspective. In the same way, the sage who governs from a natural perspective does not deliberately harm people, does not distinguish those who deserve to be harmed from those who deserve to be rewarded. But this is because the sage does not recognize anything he or she does as causing harm. This does not rule out the possibility that the people affected might perceive it as a harm. The parent who sees from a vaster perspective sometimes says that we have to be cruel to be kind: the child who is deprived of a toy perceives this as great injustice and does not see the broader lesson of generosity that is being taught. The situation works in that case because the parent is inculcating a broader ethical, but still humanist value. But the sage who transcends all humanistic values by definition cannot be teaching from a broader ethical standpoint.

Nevertheless, in the following analysis, I shall present what I understand to be the implied positive ethico-political program of the *Laozi*, always aware that the text's philosophical resources are insufficient to prevent the possibility of development in an unsavory direction.

Desire[56] *Yu* 欲

The ethical and political criticisms and recommendations of the *Laozi* appear to be grounded in a psychology of desire. We might understand the *Laozi*'s concept of desire by distinguishing it from needs and wants. Some conditions are necessary for being able to live with minimal standards of comfort and decency: food and shelter, for example. These might be thought of as natural needs. But there are also conditions whose presence leads to higher levels of comfort or well-being: condiments to add flavor to our meals; a beautiful view from a vantage point; a brief rest in the middle of a busy day. They might be classified as wants. These may not be necessary for survival, but they increase our quality of life and are still quite obviously natural.[57]

Desires, as understood in the *Laozi*, however, seem to refer to something that is inconsistent with a natural life. They appear to be constructed by human artifice, and thereby also essentially involved in insatiable cycles of acquisition. In chapter 12, it is not colors and sounds per se that blind and deafen us, but the *five* colors and the *five* sounds: that is, colors and sounds as construed within a system of artificial classification. The linguistic terms through which we understand our social structures create divisions: we contrast the good with the bad, the beautiful with the ugly, the noble with the mean. The contrasts are hierarchical and set up objects of desire: things that are valued, the acquisition of which increases our social standing—virtue, beauty, nobility, honor, wealth. Objects of desire are thus constructed goods, whether material or social, and desires themselves are understood as artificially inculcated products of socialization. All we need are coverings to protect us from the elements; we want clothes that are comfortable and fit well. But we desire fashionable name brands produced by highly skilled artisans and made of high-quality imported fabrics. Such "additions" to our nature distract us from what is sufficient for our natural flourishing.

Moreover, the cultivation of desire leads to a cycle of self-propelling excess. If something is desirable, then more of it is better. A system based on acquisitive desire encourages greed (chapters 3, 12, 19). This fuels a cycle of acquisitiveness that leads to extravagantly wasteful levels of excess and luxury. The desire for property, wealth, territory, or power, once encouraged, becomes impossible to restrain. Even encouraging virtue and the acquisition of honor and status opens the way for competition and contention, and thereby for theft and corruption. As we shall see in the next chapter, this line of thinking is taken up by the utopian Daoists of the *Zhuangzi*.

Natural Simplicity[58]   *Pu*   樸

The natural way, by contrast, is one of simplicity. To embrace simplicity is also to return to a more childlike state, unpretentious and lacking sophistication. According to chapter 37, "When things transform, should desires arise, I shall subdue them with the simplicity of namelessness," that is, with the simplicity that arises when the evaluations and preferences grounded in linguistic distinctions are minimized (*wuming zhi pu* 無名之樸). A simple, natural life is one that minimizes contrivance, busyness, and shrewdness. Chapter 65 says that a state governed by the crafty will fall prey to theft and exploitation.[59] The cultivation of naturalness thus becomes the deconstruction of desires for such goods, *wuyu* 無欲: the cultivation of satisfaction with natural simplicity. And this is achieved by curtailing our tendency to use evaluative labels *ming* 名 to distinguish some objects as more desirable than others. The reduction of artificially induced aspirations leads to a corresponding reduction of competition and conflict. When people are not confused by cravings for luxury and excess, they know sufficiency; they are able to sustain themselves, control themselves, and pacify themselves.[60]

A common objection to this sort of primitivist vision is that it is naïve and idealistic, and ultimately impractical. People will always be motivated by desire, will always compete for luxury and excess, and will never return to such a state of natural simplicity. It is hard to argue with this empirical claim, which does appear to be borne out by the evidence (though this by no means implies that all people will only be motivated by these things). However, even if it should be true, philosophically speaking, this remains a weak criticism. The claim of the *Laozi* is not that this is an easily practicable solution to the ills of a complex society, but that this is the only feasible solution. If one agrees with the solution in principle but objects that it is not practicable, then the *Laozi* has won the argument.

State[61]   *Guo*   國

While the *Laozi* has a reputation for being an otherworldly "mystical" text, in fact more than half is devoted to issues of rulership, or governing *zhi* 治, and makes direct reference to the sage or wise ruler *shengren* 聖人, the empire *tianxia* 天下, the people *min* 民, or the state *guo* 國, or expresses ideals of effective rulership.[62] Indeed, Sima Tan describes the school of *dao* as a theory of government. This might seem surprising, since we have seen that the *Laozi* criticizes the humanistic *daos* devoted to cultivating social harmony and advocates instead a return to a natural simplicity. But the two are not inconsistent. They might seem so if we consider the natural and the social as mutually exclusive categories, and especially if we contrast the social with the individual. The rejection of a humanistic focus on society would then entail concentration on oneself as an individual apart from social relations. But we have seen that Daoist thinking, and indeed Chinese thinking in general, tends not to view contrasts in such a dichotomous way. Thus, the natural and the social, or the natural and the human, (and also the social and the individual) are not antagonistic but complementary, and cannot be completely at odds. If we as humans are to recover our naturalness, we must do so as the social creatures that we are.

Indeed, the *Laozi* presupposes the existence of some kind of social structure, often referred to as the state *guo* 國. The question, then, is not "How do we give up being social beings and return to nature?" but "How do we as social beings live in greatest harmony with the natural way?" Two opposing types of answers can be found in the text. There is a utopian strand that idealizes small-scale social groups and another strand that advocates ruling a large state by a paradoxical method of not ruling. Some characteristics seem to follow from the desire to imitate nature and minimize artificial structures. If nature has no ruler, no laws, and no punishments, would we not also flourish by having no ruler, laws, or punishments? Shouldn't we all just be free to do whatever we would do naturally? Indeed, the people should be able to lead contented lives without the ravages of state control and battles with neighboring states, without fear of death, and even oblivious to the very existence of power, law, and punishment. The people should be encouraged to appreciate what they have, not endlessly pursue acquisitions (chapter 12). The governing structures should be kept simple and unoppressive, with few laws and regulations (or prohibitions, *ji* 忌), and without robbing ordinary people of the wealth they produce. Taken to its logical conclusion, this would lead to a form of anarchism: a utopian theory that an ideal society can only be created without the oppressive demands, laws, and orders of a ruler. There should be no government, no hegemonic positions of authority, no external control of people's lives. People flourish best when they are free to live naturally and govern themselves as they please. The vision of the *Laozi* is thus not antisocial, but has anarchistic or social libertarian[63] tendencies.

Like most forms of anarchism, the *Laozi* does not go to the extreme of rejecting all government. In fact, the political passages of the text take the form of advice for successful rulership. The behavior of the sagely ruler is described as the ideal, but the description of this sagely behavior is paradoxical and abstruse. The concept of leadership that emerges is quite distinctive, if not unique. It is not simply that there is no ruler, but that ruling is the province of rulers who are not rulers, and that ruling is the activity of ruling by not ruling, administering by not administering, controlling by not controlling. How these paradoxes are resolved leads to different understandings of Daoist society. Some strands of the *Laozi* text insist on a small-scale utopia; others presuppose the possibility of effortless rule of an entire empire. As we shall see in Chapter Five below, these two distinct tendencies will emerge again in the Utopian and Syncretist strands of the *Zhuangzi*.

According to chapter 80, the society most in tune with nature would consist of small communities. The larger the social group, the greater the necessity to create and implement structures of monitoring and control.[64] The only way to avoid imposing complex artificial structures that interfere with our daily activities would be to avoid large-scale social organizations altogether.

At the other end of the political spectrum, some chapters of the *Laozi* even allow for rule of the whole world *tianxia* by following similar types of rulership strategy, and chapter 62 refers explicitly to the Emperor, *tianzi*.[65] Chapters 63 and 64 give the clue as to how this can be achieved. The sage has focused attention on what is present on a small scale, and is concerned only about the immediate situation. It is precisely because of this small-scale concern that the larger projects, built out of the smaller ones, are able to take care of themselves.[66] Thus, if a large-scale anarchist-type society is to be workable at all, it cannot take the form of a top-down structure but must begin from the ground up; it must emerge from the smallest interactions and expand outward. In effect, there can be a successful empire only if there is no empire as such to be controlled. In the famous quotation of chapter 64, the journey of a thousand miles begins with a footfall. And, it might be added, it is only ever accomplished with each single footfall. Thus, the business of the whole is taken care of not by taking care of the whole, but by taking care of the parts.

Minimal Artifice and Naturalness[67] *Wuwei, Ziran* 無爲,自然

According to chapter 37, *dao* does not make anything happen, yet nothing remains undone. Nature does not force natural phenomena to occur, but simply allows them to grow and flourish in accordance with their natures.[68] Though nature may in some sense be ultimately responsible for all things, it does not micromanage affairs. Indeed, that is why the extraordinarily complex natural world is able to exist: if it had to be controlled and manipulated deliberately, it would not be possible at all.

It might seem that this description is based on a category mistake. It treats Nature, or *dao*, as though it is a thing, a caretaker responsible for the world, but recognizes that it cannot be understood as a thing that acts and creates. Instead of drawing the simple conclusion that Nature is not a thing at all, it draws the paradoxical conclusion that it is a thing that is not a thing, and acts by not acting. Why take this convoluted route to mystify what might seem to be a simple point? I think there is good reason. The point of observing and understanding natural functioning is not just theoretical, but to provide a model for how we ourselves should behave or act. If it is possible for us to modify our behavior to imitate and embody how natural phenomena occur, this is best done by analogizing ourselves to Nature as that which is responsible for what happens, and this requires at least attempting to reify Nature as though it were a thing. That attempt results in thinking of it as an extraordinary kind of thing.[69] If we rest content with the claim that Nature is not a thing and so does not do anything, there is nothing for us to learn. The application of the human model of action is then not a category mistake, but a deliberate deployment of an appropriate metaphor for a specific pragmatic purpose. This also, incidentally, shows that paradoxes need not always be meaningless; they may sometimes have practical significance.

Thus, humans should also refrain from such action, *wei*: that is, we should not impose artificial structures in an attempt to control and manipulate things. We must first appreciate the natural tendencies of the circumstances, of our surroundings, of other people, and of ourselves. We should then explore the most efficient way of dealing with things, one that accords closely with their immediate natural tendencies. Rather than planning for all contingencies in advance, we should wait to observe how things develop, sense how they tend to move themselves, and then move with them, redirecting them with minimal effort. According to chapters 63 and 64, the sage concentrates on the task at hand, and thereby anticipates and averts all disasters before they even have a chance to arise. It is not that we cease to plan, think, and control, or attempt to leave no footprints whatsoever. The only way we could do that would be to disentangle ourselves from the natural world altogether, and to do that we would have to cease to exist. Rather, we optimally minimize our intention to control according to artificially inculcated desires, and instead seek to fulfill our wants and needs with the least interference possible. In this way, we watch how nature flourishes and find a symbiotic place in its pattern, enabling both it and us to flourish to our natural potential.

The result of acting with optimally minimal artifice is optimally maximal naturalness *ziran* 自然, "what is so of itself." Liu Xiaogan goes so far as to claim that *ziran* is indeed the most fundamental value of the *Laozi*.[70] If *wuwei* is a form of interaction that optimally minimizes interference and allows phenomena to manifest in accordance with their natural tendencies, then *ziran* is the spontaneous manifesting of those natural tendencies themselves, whether in the natural world, in human life, or in social interactions. Politically, if *wuwei* is the minimal interference of the sagely ruler, then the resulting natural state, *ziran*, can be interpreted as expressing the ideal of democracy in its purest form: people should be free to govern themselves, *zizheng* 自正 (chapter 57).

Sagely Ruler[71]   *Shengren*   聖人

As with nature, the best ruling takes place when there is no ruling. If the ruler does not actively rule, then effectively there is no ruler as such. The sagely ruler does not show himself, does not contend, and rather than taking a position of authority, adopts an inferior position. The ruler does not control the people but serves them; he or she has no concern for his or her own success, but only for the comfort, security, health, and well-being of the people. The sage thus takes on what would be considered in ancient Chinese society, just as in modern Western culture, a maternal role: to care for the people, to enable them, nurture them, to stand back and provide a space that allows them to grow and thrive.[72] Ideally, the work of the ruler, like that of nature, must be so surreptitious that the people are barely aware that there might be a ruler, or if there is one, who it might be. It should appear that social flourishing is something that simply happens by itself, *ziran* (17).

But when the ruler truly becomes one of the people, one with the people, all people become equal to him or her. In fact, if each and every person ensures not their own well-being but the well-being of others, enabling others to thrive and achieve success; if no one takes charge, but is concerned only with nurturing others and allowing them to flourish, then effectively everyone is playing the maternal role of the Daoist "ruler." This ideal is consistent with both anarchism and the most radical of democracies: when everyone is responsible for the well-being of the whole, then no single person is in charge. To be sure, this has never been a standard interpretation of the text, but it emerges quite smoothly and effortlessly from the paradoxical characteristics of the ruler. In fact, although the advice for rulership appears to be addressed to only one person, there is nothing in the text to limit how many may follow it.

But what happens when the people do not flourish? What happens if the people do not live up to the trust placed in them? What if, instead of acting for the well-being of others, they act only out of greed, oblivious to the suffering their actions will cause? Is this simply to be allowed, on the grounds that they should never be oppressed by regulations? One Laozian response might be that this would only ever happen in situations where regulations have already developed and the people are not trusted to look after themselves. We should therefore abandon all regulations and simply go back to trusting the people. This, however, is a dogmatic answer and is disturbingly overoptimistic. It is hard to see how abandoning laws and regulations can by itself change the hearts of people determined to exploit others.[73] Empirical experience strongly suggests that this is thoroughly mistaken.

A more plausible answer is that, while the ruler should refrain from active interference with people's lives, there might be times when more or less activity is advisable. Chapter 60 says that ruling a large state is like cooking a small fish. In cooking a small fish, one must not push or prod; there cannot be too much heat or too little; the smallest variations can make the difference between overcooked and undercooked, too rare and too dry, evenly cooked and unevenly cooked. Rather, one must develop a deep sensitivity to its texture, decide what to cover and what to expose to more heat, sense when it is about to be perfectly cooked, and refrain from further involvement. Moreover, catastrophic events are often the macroscopic result of small-scale phenomena: a trigger event leads to the undermining of the whole. If one develops a deep, embodied understanding of a medium, one may sense what causes trigger events to arise and what kinds of catastrophes they may cause. The deeper one's intuitive insight, the more likely that one will be able to sense the development of these triggers and to redirect the course of phenomena away from them. In this way, disasters may be prevented before they ever have a chance to develop.

This sort of skill arises only with the deepest familiarity born of extensive experience. Only then can one guide with minimal interference: allow circumstances to follow their natural course, and gently redirect when absolutely necessary. One can do so only by being sensitive to the inner tendencies; one must understand the smallest constituent events before one can take charge of things on a larger scale. The excellent ruler thus has a deep sympathetic understanding of the needs of the people and also the remarkable skill of being able to redirect their behavior with minimal and ideally undetectable interference. But even then, there should be no single individual who takes charge of the whole. By understanding only the most immediate phenomena and distributing partial responsibility to each member of a whole, the whole will inevitably take care of itself.

This ideal, however, depends on the assumption that large-scale problems can always be dealt with, and can best be dealt with, only by focusing on adjusting the immediate situation at hand. This seems clearly to be false. Certainly it is a wise and productive mode of action, and admirable when successful. But its efficacy cannot be guaranteed in *all* cases. Long-term consequences are not always traceable from immediately detectable tendencies. The development of a system is only partly determined by its internal tendencies; it is also dependent on external factors that are not available to reflection on the task at hand. Indeed, the only way to deal successfully with many such external factors is to have an explicit and artificially constructed plan of action. By failing to account for such factors, *wuwei* and *ziran* can inadvertently lead to the accumulation of injustice and to the undermining of a society that has no other mechanism of social growth. The accumulation of small changes can lead to the evolution of predators or the development of a plutocratic power base. Through small and insignificant exchanges, the wealth generated by the people can be siphoned upward to a small elite class, who thereby own and redistribute resources unjustly.[74] They effectively become equivalent to the oppressive state structures of which the anarchist or libertarian disapproves, not by manipulative interference and control but surreptitiously, through the very means of noninterference that the *Laozi* recommends. The *Laozi* has undoubtedly identified one important mechanism necessary for a flourishing life, but it certainly is not sufficient to ensure its utopia.

CHAPTER FOUR

The *Zhuangzi*

Inner Chapters *and Zhuangzian Philosophy*

AUTHORSHIP

Unlike Laozi and Liezi, Zhuangzi, or Master Zhuang,[1] is the one early Daoist thinker whose existence few scholars have doubted, though the evidence regarding his life is neither extensive nor indisputably reliable. He appears to have flourished during the reign of King Hui of the state of Liang, who lived from 370 to 319 B.C.E., and King Xuan of the state of Qi, who lived from 319 to 301 B.C.E. According to Sima Qian, he was born in the village of Meng, in a contested territory in the southernmost part of Song and the northernmost part of Chu, and worked as a minor official at a place called Qi Yuan (Lacquer Garden). One set of traditional dates places his birth and death between 369 and 298 B.C.E.

There are stories scattered through the text in which Zhuangzi appears as a protagonist. Some of them are in the *Inner Chapters*, but most are in later strata of the book. They are largely consistent in style and content, portraying Zhuangzi as a recluse, living in poverty and shunning the offers of political employment made by the rulers of his time. This last element of the stories, while rhetorically effective, is doubtful: rulers greedy for power and territory would hardly be likely to court the services of a Daoist recluse who considers governing to be beneath contempt. It is, however, in keeping with the iconoclastic spirit of the utopian Daoists, and the allegories of recluses who refuse to sully themselves with political office.

In the *Inner Chapters* are many stories involving Ruists and Mohists, including Confucius himself. That they are allegorical is evident from the very beginning of the collection, where we read about a fish the size of a continent that turns into a bird with a wingspan that stretches across the entire sky. Indeed, one of the major methods of the philosophical discourse of the *Zhuangzi* is allegory. The purpose is to present a 'model': an actual concrete circumstance, through whose structures and elements one may explore the consequences of various philosophical positions. The stories about historical characters lend themselves readily to such interpretation, and there is no reason to believe that they were intended as factual records.

Some version of the ideas associated with the *Laozi*, if not the *Laozi* text itself, was probably in circulation when the *Zhuangzi* was composed. The discovery in 1993 of the bamboo manuscripts at Guodian dating to sometime before 300 B.C.E. indicates that a collection of passages that can also be found in the received *Laozi* was in existence by the end of Zhuangzi's life, and therefore was compiled either during his life or before. Although the *Inner Chapters* do not contain direct quotations from the *Laozi*, passages that echo its ideas and linguistic style suggest its possible influence. Zhuangzi would have been a contemporary of the Confucian thinker Mencius, who, unlike Zhuangzi, did serve as an advisor to both King Hui of Liang and King Xuan of Qi. According to Mencius, the greatest threats to Confucianism at the time came not only from Mohism but also from the ideas of Yang Zhu. Mencius presents Yang's philosophy as a form of radical egoism, the diametrical opposite of Mohist impartial concern for all people. Whether this is a correct depiction of Yang Zhu is controversial. Although the "Yang Zhu" chapter in the *Liezi* largely corroborates Mencius' account, A. C. Graham believes that it is not accurate and finds less egotistical passages in the *Outer Chapters* of the *Zhuangzi* that he believes give a more plausible and less biased portrayal of Yang's ethico-political theory.[2] Zhuangzi and Mencius were contemporaries, but neither gives any clear indication that he was aware of the philosophical views of the other.[3]

The traditional dates would also make Zhuangzi a contemporary of Hui Shi, or Huizi, with whom he is said to have shared a profound, if unlikely friendship, as each seems to have been critical of the other's intellectual competence: Huizi regularly chides Zhuangzi for talking nonsense, big talk not relevant to human lives; Zhuangzi, in response, ridicules Huizi for his shortsightedness, his analytical obsession, and his inability to see beyond his immediate political interests.[4] And yet, when Zhuangzi passes Huizi's grave, he stops to lament the death of the one person with whom he could communicate (269). Perhaps for this reason, the problem of communicating and making judgments across deep differences of perspective is a theme that Zhuangzi takes up explicitly at the end of the second chapter, the *"Qi Wu Lun."*

TEXT

The *Zhuangzi* text is an anthology of philosophical essays, aphorisms, and allegories of varying length written by many authors with different philosophical views, dating from least the late fourth century B.C.E. and compiled possibly during the second century B.C.E. It stands among the literary masterpieces of the Chinese tradition. One can discern series of family resemblances between the various views throughout the text: sometimes the similarities, and perhaps even the lines of descent, are clear; at other times it takes a monumental effort of intellect to see any resemblance whatsoever. But distinctive clusterings of characteristics can be found throughout the text, crisscrossing and overlapping[5] between the related philosophical positions. One senses the historical development of a Daoist sensibility as schools branch off in several directions. The vast majority of the passages that made their way into the anthology have recognizably Daoist themes among their most basic concepts. This is true even of the Syncretistic passages that date to the early Han dynasty, which are the most distant in philosophical spirit from the *Inner Chapters.*[6]

A fifty-two-chapter edition of the text was edited down to thirty-three chapters by the Jin dynasty thinker Guo Xiang (d. 312 C.E.),[7] whose commentary has had a profound impact on subsequent interpretations. The chapters were written and collected over several centuries, and the anthology has traditionally been divided into three parts: the *Inner Chapters* (chapters 1 to 7), the *Outer Chapters* (chapters 8 to 22), and the *Miscellaneous Chapters* (chapters 23 to 33). The *Inner Chapters* are generally thought to be the work of Zhuangzi himself, though recently scholars have begun to question the extent to which even they can or should be considered the work of a single writer.[8]

Each of the *Inner Chapters* is a collection of passages of varying length, and each tends to be centered on a particular theme, though some are more miscellaneous than others.[9] The chapters are written in a similar array of literary styles and appear to express several aspects of a broadly coherent philosophical view of the world, language, nature, life, death, action, and humanity. Each chapter has a three-character title that expresses at least one central aspect of the philosophical content. Indeed, the interpretation of the chapter title has become an important part of interpreting the philosophical significance of the text.

Several of the *Outer* and *Miscellaneous Chapters* (11 to 27 and 32, but most notably, 17 to 20 and 22), contain discussions of the same themes as the *Inner Chapters*; they use similar stories and are written in a comparable style. Graham classifies chapters 17 to 27 and 32 as belonging to a "school" of Zhuangzi. Chapter 17, "*Qiu Shui*," "Autumn Floods," is noteworthy for developing the theme of vastness from chapter 1. Several philosophical possibilities are explored here in an extended narrative: these include skepticism, relativism, absolutism, and a situated pragmatism. Chapter 18, "*Zhi Le*," "Ultimate Happiness," echoes the theme of life and death from chapter 6. Chapter 19, "*Da Sheng*," "Penetrating Life," explores in greater depth the cultivation of natural embodied skill. When themes are taken up directly from the *Inner Chapters*, they are often accompanied by explanations of statements that were originally asserted without context and left unexplained; they also sometimes integrate themes not explicitly related in other chapters, confirming the holistic texture of the philosophy. They are therefore usually taken to be representative of the discourse of early thinkers who were deeply influenced by Zhuangzi.[10] However, we cannot be absolutely sure which passages constitute the earliest strata of the text; in particular, we cannot be sure that all the passages of the *Inner Chapters* were written prior to all the passages of these chapters. In the course of editing, some of them may have been moved to the *Outer Chapters* and vice versa. For this reason, I interpret them together under the rubric of "Zhuangzian" philosophy,[11] though for convenience of discussion, I sometimes attribute the ideas to Zhuangzi or to the *Inner Chapters*.

Variations on Zhuangzian thought, as well as permutations, hybrids, and intermediate philosophical positions, can also be found in the *Outer* and *Miscellaneous Chapters*. There are, for example, passages that have much in common with the cosmological passages of the *Laozi*, others that resonate with the Utopian strand of Daoism (see Chapter Five below), and some that follow up ideas developed in a more metaphysical direction in the *Liezi*. For example, chapter 20 contrasts the simplicity of a natural life with a life devoted to profit and desire, and in so doing echoes the *Laozi* and paves the way for the development of the primitivist ideals of the Utopian chapters. Chapter 22 is an extraordinary chapter ostensibly eulogizing ignorance, stupidity, and speechlessnes, and filled with riddles and paradoxes that anticipate Zen *koans*. Graham goes so far as to describe it as a form of antirationalism.

ZHUANGZIAN PHILOSOPHY

Zhuangzian philosophy is hard to classify in Western terms. It is certainly existential in spirit, dwelling on the significance of life and the inevitability of death. It advocates a way of life that is at once thoroughly, joyfully engaged and dispassionately tranquil. This way is rooted in a deep and paradoxical understanding of our place in the world: that we are both an integral part of the processes of nature and only a minuscule constituent of a vast and disinterested cosmos; that we are thoroughly at home in the world and yet only temporary guests. From our ordinary everyday perspective, we take the dramas of our social lives very seriously. We judge the value of our existence according to the standards of success that have been ingrained in us since childhood. But are these values genuine? Do they really represent who we are and what we have the potential to become? Or are they superficial distractions, drawing us away from something deeper, more natural, more genuine? While Zhuangzi raises many questions and often expresses an attitude of epistemic humility—"How should I know that?"—his skepticism is not universal. It is quite clearly directed against thinkers who place an artificial humanistic *dao* above that of nature.

Compared with the *Laozi*, the style of the *Zhuangzi* is more personal, stopping to marvel at the magnificence of nature, the variety of creatures, the diversity of humanity, and the significance of the events that fill a human life. It never loses its cosmological concerns and remains largely aloof from politics. Still, even in the *Inner Chapters* we see the sprouts of ideas that will eventually grow into the metapolitical theory of the Syncretist passages.[12]

Traditionally, two interpretations have been influential. From a religious point of view, the text has been treated as espousing a mystical doctrine of an absolute, metaphysical *Dao* that lies beyond the reach of language. From a philosophical point of view (not only modern, but extending as far back as Guo Xiang in the Jin dynasty), the text has been treated as an exercise in relativistic epistemology, ontology, and ethics. More recently, some scholars have constructed an interpretation that is comparable with the way of life recommended by the ancient Skeptics. My own preference is to steer clear of all three, to avoid absolutism, relativism, and Skepticism. Instead, I see the Zhuangzian worldview and way of life as a nature-oriented form of pragmatism involving mind-body discipline and cultivation of tranquility; it is existential in spirit and comparable, but not identifiable, with the way of life recommended by the ancient Stoics.[13] For this reason, I begin with the concepts of Circumstance, transformation, and vastness and defer the complex discussion of evaluative judgments until the end of the chapter. The linguistic and epistemological claims must be situated within this overall existential-stoic context for their full significance to emerge. As I see it, the abstruse discussion of *shifei* judgment is deployed in service of a more practical philosophy that enables us to find our home in an unfathomably vast and infinitely varied world whose endless changes seem indifferent to human fortune.

The translations below are based on Watson's, but modified for consistency with my terminology. Again, readers are encouraged to compare translations for a fuller sense of the linguistic efforts involved in interpreting the text. Page references are to Watson's *The Complete Works of Chuang Tzu*.

CONCEPTS

Circumstance[14]   *Ming*   命

To tend to your heart-mind so that sadness and joy do not sway or move it; to understand what you can do nothing about and to rest content with it as Circumstance, this is the height of potency. (60)

We cannot choose our parents or our birthplace; we cannot change past conditions or the natures of things. These are the great circumstances, *ming* 命,

that we have no choice but to deal with. The term *"ming"* has an intricately related set of meanings that have no clear connections in English: "command," "call," "name," "life," "fate." As a verb, it can mean "to call" or "to ordain." In political contexts, it refers to the commands or edicts of a ruler. What the ruler has ordained must then be realized: a ruler can only rule by authority, which in turn requires that their commands be obeyed. It is this authority that enables the pronouncements of a ruler to become what Austin calls "performative utterances."[15] In the act of issuing an edict, it is thereby already law; in pronouncing a couple married, they are thereby married; in the act of bestowing a peerage on a commoner, they thereby become a knight. The act of naming a thing or an event as of a certain kind is precisely what turns it into a thing or event of that kind. This metaphor of ordination gets applied also to the activity of *tian*: *tian* also *mings*, but what it calls into being are the circumstances of nature and the particular circumstances of our lives. *Tian* thereby produces things, gives them life or existence as the kinds of things they are, with their particular tendencies and conditions. This metaphor is deeply ingrained in the language, but the imperialist tone is absent in Zhuangzi's usage.

By extension, *"ming"* also refers to whatever has been made so, whatever has been called into being: the circumstances of nature, the circumstances into which we are thrown, which in turn provide the conditions that make us what we are. This is the way things are independently of us, the circumstances of the world that we have no choice but to deal with. *"Ming"* thus names the conditions, both internal and external, under which things emerge and within the particularities of which they must coexist. Existentially, it is "what is allotted" to each of us: the background circumstances into which we are born, our life conditions, and the resulting lifespan. It refers to any and all circumstances outside one's control: the changes of the seasons, the political situation and material conditions into which one is born, and propensities from birth for distinctive abilities or particular illnesses. Different responses to these will result in different courses of life and different possible lifespans. Thus, appealing to the concept of *ming* is not necessarily a form of determinism, according to which everything that happens was destined to happen. Nor is it a form of fatalism, according to which some specific future events (our fate or destiny) cannot be avoided no matter what we might do.[16] Rather, like the Stoic concept of *fortuna*, it is simply a recognition that we do not set the terms and conditions of the cosmos, but have to work with them as they are.

In chapter 6, "The Great Ancestral Teacher," the circumstances that make things the way they are reified, even anthropomorphized, as *zaowuzhe*, 造物者, which literally means "that which makes things" (84). Western and especially religiously oriented translators reading this phrase tend to think of a Creator, a God responsible for the existence of the universe. But there is no good reason to believe that the phrase is being used literally to refer to a person or a conscious agent of any kind. Also, the term is indeterminate between singular and plural, and if the context allows it can be interpreted in the plural. It could thus simply refer to whatever processes are responsible for the production of things. Since the *Zhuangzi* text does not posit any kind of personal deity and the notion of such a deity seems inconsistent with the naturalistic tenor of the philosophical discussions, context requires that the phrase be read in a more neutral way. Indeed, there is no need to look beyond the concepts of *tian* or *ming* to find an appropriate candidate.

Transformation[17] *Hua* 化

> The Way is without beginning or end, but things have their life and death. . . . The years cannot be held off; time cannot be stopped. Vanishing, continuing, filling and emptying, end and then begin again. . . . The life of things is a gallop, a headlong dash—with every movement they alter, with every moment they shift. What should you do and what should you not do? Everything will change of itself, that is certain![18] (182)

Thus says Ruo of the North Sea, in chapter 17, describing the worldview of cyclical transformation shared by the early Daoist texts. The importance of transformation is also evident in the *Inner Chapters*, which opens with a metamorphosis of cosmic proportions: "In the Northern Darkness there is a fish whose name is Kun.[19] Kun is so vast I don't know how many thousands of miles it measures. It transforms and becomes a bird whose name is Peng" (29). The seasonal migration of this embryonic beast from the northern darkness through the light to the southern darkness represents the visible natural cyclical transformations at their most expansive.

In chapter 2, Zhuangzi describes life and existence as an array of phenomena that replace each other in endless cycles:

Joy, anger, grief, delight, worry, regret, fickleness, inflexibility, modesty, willfulness, candor, insolence—music from empty holes, mushrooms springing up in dampness, day and night replacing each other before us, and no one knows where they sprout from. . . . So I say, "that" (*bi* 彼) comes out of "this" (*shi* 是) and "this" accords with "that"— which is to say that "this" and "that" give birth to (*sheng* 生 produce) each other. But where there is life (*sheng* 生) there must be death; where there is death there must be life. . . . A state in which "this" and "that" no longer find their counterparts is called the axis of the Way (*daoshu* 道樞). . . . For this reason, whether you point to a little stalk or a great pillar, a leper or the beautiful Xishi, things ribald and shady or things grotesque and strange, the Way interpenetrates (*tong* 通) them continuously (*wei yi*, 為一). (37–41)

The indexical "this," *shi* 是, is here used to refer to a thing in the stage of its existence; the indexical "that," or "other," *bi* 彼, is used to refer to a counterpart phase, after transformation has taken place and something else exists in its place. A chrysalis will become a butterfly, a tadpole will become a frog, an egg will become a bird, Kun will become Peng, a living creature will die.

As we race through the busyness of our lives, we encounter things, people, and circumstances that cause us pleasure or suffering; their differences weigh significantly in our evaluations of them. Xi Shi was a courtesan known for her beauty, in comparison with which other faces appeared harsh. A stalk and a pillar appear to us as distinct entities with opposite qualities. We approve of Xi Shi's beauty or the strength of a pillar and shun the unsightly or the weakness of a mere stalk. Life and death, this and that, what is approved and what is rejected are portrayed as diametrically opposed counterparts, *ou* 偶, opposite points on a wheel that exchange places as it revolves. The circumstances of life incessantly alter before our eyes, and from one instant to the next our prospects may change radically. We respond to these changes emotionally, now joyful or hopeful, now worrying and anxious. In our youth we despise old age; as we mature, we watch with regret as we lose our suppleness and strength, and as the passage of time accelerates we dread the ultimate transformation that looms menacingly before us. We are flustered and perturbed, *bian* 變,[20] by the incessant alterations of circumstance and overwhelmed by the ever-increasing proximity of death.

In chapter 27, "*Yuyan*," "Imputed Words," the followers of Zhuangzi comment on the nature of cyclical change: "The myriad things are of all kinds, yield to each other with different forms, beginning and ending like a wheel, *huan* 環, where none maintains its position. This is called the potter's wheel of nature; the potter's wheel of nature is the grindstone of nature" (304–5). While a straight line has a beginning and an end, on a circle any point may be considered the beginning and any point may be considered the end. The process of circling is continuous and endless. The years, seasons, day and night, the growth and decay of all things exchange constantly without a beginning or end in sight. This is the potter's wheel of nature, *tianjun* 天均, which builds things up, and also the grindstone of nature, *tianni* 天倪, which wears things down. The image is that of a large, heavy disc revolving relentlessly about a central axis; the revolutions of the wheel represent the natural transformations that occur in cycles.

The image of circulation recurs in various forms throughout the *Zhuangzi* and encapsulates its understanding of the process of living and dying. That process can be understood in several ways, depending on how it is divided. Living and dying, presence and absence, or something and nothing may of course be seen as the two phases of a *yinyang* contrast. Or they may be thought of in a threefold way, as a limited phase of determinate existing, *you* 有, surrounded by two vast expanses of absence, *wu* 無 or *wuyou* 無有. There is the absence before we were born and the one that follows after we die. In comparison with these two expanses, even the longest life seems insignificantly fleeting. We emerge for an instant between two vast abysses,[21] unaware of anything but the ephemeral moment, identifying ourselves within its confines. To the extent that they intrude into our consciousness, we distinguish two distinct stages of absence before and after as antithetical to existence, and we fear death in particular as the enemy of life.

Now, we may of course think of ourselves as continuing to exist in some form or another after death, but this is not the concept of death as the end of existence, only physical death as the end of physical existence. Plato argues for the immortality of the soul on the grounds that since it is not a composite physical object, it cannot disintegrate, and therefore cannot cease to exist.[22] The materialist view of the self, in contrast, completely rejects the existence of anything nonphysical, and so affirms the absolute absence of personal existence after physical death. In both cases, life and death are still dichotomous and antithetical opposites, but for the Platonic dualist, since existence of the soul is eternal, death as the end of existence is impossible.

Zhuangzi's view, in contrast, does not start with a dualistic dichotomy of existence and nonexistence. Zhuangzi understands life as a process that is an integral part of nature. Living and dying are merely manifestations of cycles of processes that characterize the natural world in general and the integration, replication, and dissolution of organic entities in the biosphere in particular. Still, from the perspective of everyday life, the phase of existence fills the field of our attention so that the two stretches of absence on either side become invisible, or even unthinkable.[23] But *between* the light and the darknesses that surround this phase fall two shadows. Between the prior absence and our existence, there is a phase of gradual emergence, determination, and integration. And between our existence and its subsequent absence, there is a phase of disintegration and dissolution. There are intermediate stages between the absence of a thing and its existence as a thing, during which there is no clearly existing thing, and no clear existence of the thing.

Imagine the process of crystallization from a liquid, sugar from honey perhaps, or salt from ocean water. At first there is a relatively amorphous solution. Under certain conditions, cooling in the case of honey or evaporation in the case of salt water, a process of coagulation or crystallization begins. At the end of the process, crystals have formed with a relatively determinate and integrated structure. Between the two is the phase of integration and determination. It may be swift or slow, but it must take time. Even if the process accelerates rapidly toward its final steady state, the transition is never instantaneous.[24]

Zhuangzi uses the metaphor of emerging to refer to the transitional process of coming into existence. "The genuinely human (*zhenren*, see below) of ancient times knew nothing of loving life, knew nothing of hating death. They emerged (*chu* 出) without delight, and went back in (*ru* 入) without a fuss" (78). This is the gradual integration of a determinate entity or organism from a prior relatively indeterminate stage. Although not etymologically related, the images behind the words for life, *sheng* 生, and emergence, *chu* 出, are remarkably similar. A shoot is represented by a vertical line with offshoots rising up out of the base line, bursting forth from the ground into the light and air above. This image of springing to life, emerging from the darkness, functions throughout Daoist discussions of life and existence. From the vast and murky formlessness of the soil a process of integration begins, a coming together of a self-sustaining, self-propelling organism constructing and differentiating itself, yet inseparable, from its environment. The catalyst that begins the process is a seed, whose propensities shape the continued course of development; as it progresses, the root becomes the locus of continued production. The seed, the root, the inner tendencies of the developing organism are the conditions that enable the living processes to begin and to flourish. The botanical etymology can be applied metaphorically to the emergence into existence of all phenomena.[25] In this way, all "things/creatures" are said to be "born/produced"—there is no clear distinction being made between the living and the nonliving. But even when applied to the emergence of living things, that is, to their ontological emergence rather than their biological birth, it is no less metaphorical.

Likewise, things at the end of their term return to the vast expanse of indeterminacy from which they emerged. Zhuangzi calls this "*ru*" 入, entering, or reentering the source from which one originally came. The visible form of a plant shrivels as the organic substance gets reabsorbed into its root, once again becoming indistinguishable from the soil in which it is embedded. The organic functions of an animal begin to wind down and become less coordinated. After they have all eventually ceased, the organic matter itself begins to break down, and like decaying vegetation, reenters the soil from which it originally emerged. Determinate things thus return to their indeterminate ancestral condition. Of course, as with the phase of emergence, at one end of the process there is no *entity* to speak of. So of course, it cannot strictly be said that the same entity has returned to *its* own prior state.

Moreover, the living and the nonliving are mutually dependent. Living and nonliving matter turn into each other in cycles: living matter decomposes into and arises from nonliving material, yet the nonliving stuff is in some important sense simpler, and therefore more originary. Organic matter arises from the combination of inorganic substances, and inorganic substances arise from the decomposition of organic substances, but the inorganic substances are, in an important sense, simpler and more fundamental. Nonliving matter and inorganic substances are obviously not transcendent, yet they are in a significant sense the sources of their living and organic counterparts. The returning to the nonliving and to the inorganic is a process of decomposition necessary for the continued production of the living and the organic. The successful nurturing of life thus requires a correct understanding of its relationship to the nonliving.

In an extraordinary passage in chapter 2, the "*Qi Wu Lun*," Zhuangzi describes the incipient production of things through a close focus of attention on the manifestation of the intermediate phases, the gradual changes between something and nothing.

> There is a beginning. There is a not yet beginning to be a beginning. There is a not yet beginning to be a not yet beginning to be a beginning. There is something (*you* 有).
>
>   There is nothing (*wu* 無). There is a not yet beginning to be nothing. There is a not yet beginning to be a not yet beginning to be nothing. At some point, there is nothing. But I do not know, of something and nothing, which is really something and which is nothing. (43)

There is a stage of there being some particular thing and a stage of its not being there, and each of the stages gradually arises from a beginning, *shi* 始. But the beginning itself also gradually arises: there is a not yet begun to be a beginning, *weishi you shi* 未始有始, and again, a not yet begun to be a not yet begun to be a beginning. The same iteration applies to the arising of nothing, and both iterations can be continued indefinitely.[26] Between something and nothing there is no radical dividing line. Rather, the very transformation that makes them different also makes them one and continuous. Zhuangzi, in attempting to describe the indeterminacy of the boundary between something and nothing, thus raises the question how we are able to be sure we can tell the difference. The two counterparts are merely two phases of a single continuous process, so they cannot really be independent. But if this is so, is there any means by which to tell them apart? Are they of different kinds, or are they the same thing? The conclusion is unclear. Some draw a relativistic conclusion from the mutual dependence of something and nothing; others draw a skeptical conclusion from our supposed inability to tell the difference.[27] I suggest that we infer no more than that all things transform into their counterparts through a continuous process that preserves differences while lacking determinate boundaries.

The ontological significance of these intermediate phases escapes our attention so long as we are focused on the demands and burdens of our existential concerns. But from a cosmic perspective, the continuous emergence and disappearance of life, and indeed the blending of the two into a single process of becoming, is more evident. Of course, even the division into three separate stages and two intermediate phases is artificial: they can all be understood as one single process of transformation: living-dying. From the moment one emerges, one is already on the path that leads back.[28]

From the perspective of *tian* there is also no clear boundary between things that are beautiful and those that are ugly. "The myriad things are continuous (*yi* 一). We look on some as beautiful because they are rare or unearthly; we look on others as ugly because they are foul and rotten. But the foul and rotten reverts to the rare and unearthly, and the rare and unearthly reverts to the foul and rotten. Thus, it is called the continuous energy (*yi qi* 一氣) that penetrates (*tong* 通) the cosmos. Therefore, the sage values continuity ('oneness')" (chapter 22, p. 236). In the interconnected web of natural processes, the beautiful and the ugly constantly transform into each other; a stalk may grow large enough to be made into a pillar, which in turn may eventually decay, leaving behind only a stalk. "The way interpenetrates things and makes them one and continuous. Separating, they are brought to completion; brought to completion, they are destroyed" (41).

The beginning of chapter 27, "*Yuyan*," "Imputed Words," says that the potter's wheel of nature is also the grindstone of nature; the very same wheel that enables the creation of clay vessels insofar as it forms and develops things is also the grindstone that wears things down. In a world of natural transformations, the very process of formation and development of some things is dependent on and inseparable from the destruction and decay of other things that provide the raw materials from which they are made. Seen from the perspective of nature, the two processes are identical: two functions of the same wheel, or rather two aspects of one and the same process or function. Moreover, everything is equally beautiful or equally ugly from an ultimate perspective; any advantage a pillar may have over a stalk diminishes in significance as our perspective becomes more global.[29]

The sage who understands this, then, is not drawn into the endless exchange, does not identify with one phase of the cycle and oppose the other, is not emotionally moved by the success or failure of a favored side. Confucius said of Wang Tai, "This gentleman is a sage. . . . Life and death are great affairs, and yet are not able to perturb him (*bian* 變). Though heaven and earth were to overturn, it would be no loss to him. . . . He takes it as Circumstance that things should transform, and he holds fast to the ancestral" (68). Rather, the sage lets go of all the exchanging counterparts and draws in to the center, *daoshu* 道樞, the axis of the way, a point of emotional balance.

When one withdraws into the center, opposing sides draw closer together. At this ancestral core one sees not the differences of exchanging opposites but the identity of a single, continuous process. It is all one process of living and production, or it is all one process of decay and destruction. Neither need be affirmed at the expense of the other.[30]

Dreaming and Waking[31]   *Meng jue*   夢覺

Dreaming and waking are part of the cycles of transformation, but are also used as an existential metaphor. The second chapter of the *Zhuangzi* ends with the famous butterfly dream. Zhuangzi dreamt he was a butterfly, oblivious to the existence of Zhuangzi. When he awoke he was fully himself. Which experience was the dream, and which was waking? How can we know? Superficially, it is tempting to read this as a purely epistemological issue, the Chinese equivalent of Descartes' Dreaming Argument. How can we tell the difference between dreaming experience and waking experience? If there are no reliable criteria, must we be committed to skepticism and deny the possibility of genuine knowledge? In fact, the epistemological problem of how to distinguish dreaming from waking, or illusory experience from veridical perception, is not what is primarily at stake in this passage. Clearly there is some concern about how to make the distinction between what is real and what is not, but if this can be construed as an argument for skepticism, it cannot be of the Cartesian variety.

In fact, Zhuangzi makes his main point explicit at the end of the anecdote: "Between the two there must be a difference, a separation; this is what is called the transformation of things." The point appears to be ontological: the story of the butterfly dream demonstrates an aspect of the processive nature of things. The world consists of cycles of transformation, represented here by Zhuangzi and the butterfly, by waking and dreaming.[32] Knowledge does not necessarily continue between dramatically different stages of transformation. When awake we usually remain oblivious to the identities and experiences that manifest in our dreams, and vice versa. But the point is not simply about waking and dream experiences. Rather, these are metaphors applied to the process of transformation of production and dissolution of all things, and of the living and dying of all creatures.

A couple of paragraphs earlier, Zhuangzi has suggested that our ordinary attitude toward life and death is mistaken:

How do I know that loving life is not a delusion? How do I know that in hating death I am not like a man who, having left home in his youth, has forgotten the way back? . . . some day there will be a great awakening when we know that this is all a great dream. Yet the stupid believe they are awake, busily and brightly assuming they understand things, calling this man ruler, that one herdsman—how dense! Confucius and you are both dreaming! And when I say you are dreaming, I am dreaming too. (47–48)

We take our lives seriously and feel certain of our identity, taking it as the locus of all importance and our lives as measuring the span of existence. We love life and fear death as though it is a terrible end. What we think of as real, however, is in fact just the fleeting phase of coming to light, a mere moment of emergence in a vast expanse of indeterminacy; the life and identity that we take so seriously, just a petty role that we are thrust into unexpectedly. When this becomes the dreamlike experience, death might well turn out to be an awakening. All that which surrounds our life, as it were, before and after, all that which goes beyond our limited experience is seen to be of primordial existential significance. Our fear of death and dying is as foolish as fear of waking up after an engaging dream. This view is not articulated extensively in the text, though it is hinted at on occasion.[33] It has remarkable affinities with the idealist philosophy of Yogacara Buddhism, according to which all phenomena emerge like a fantasy from a backdrop of emptiness.

Vastness[34]   *Da*   大

Giant trees, an oversized gourd, a colossal bird, a gargantuan fish: vastness is a theme invoked allegorically throughout the first chapter, "Wandering Beyond" (*Xiao Yao You*). This image sets the stage for the *Inner Chapters*, and the idea is developed further in chapter 17, "Autumn Floods." The contrast between pettiness, *xiao* 小, and vastness, *da* 大, signifies the fundamental shift of perspective that Zhuangzi recommends: an ever-expanding frame of reference beyond the limitations of the human toward the all-encompassing range of the cosmos. This expansiveness has both cosmological and existential-phenomenological significance. In its cosmological aspect it signifies the unencompassable vastness of the cosmos itself; in its existential-phenomenological aspect it indicates a person's cultivation of breadth of perspective to approach that of the cosmos as a whole. One who cultivates such wisdom understands things not from the restricted viewpoint of a particular life, but from the broader perspectives within which that life is contained as a limited but integrated part.

According to Zhuangzi, the Ruists and Mohists are blinkered by their petty concerns and thereby prevented from understanding what lies beyond. The frog that peers up from the bottom of the well takes the patch of ground beneath its feet to be the whole of the earth and the circle of light above its head to be the heavens (175–76). The unending expansiveness of heaven and earth, of space and time, is utterly beyond its comprehension. Zhuangzi uses the term "petty" *xiao* to describe the parochial attitude of those who seem incapable of judging anything except from their familiar perspectives, and whose conception of the value of life is limited to success as defined by their community. This is how Zhuangzi sees the sociopolitical *daos* of the Ruists and the Mohists, both represented in the first of the *Inner Chapters* by the little creatures who can comprehend nothing that lies beyond the narrow confines of their imaginations.[35]

This is true, of course, not only of Ruists and Mohists but also of people in general. We see first and foremost what lies before our eyes, understand everything through the ubiquitous and semitransparent medium of our language, engage with things as they fit into our lifeworlds,[36] and are swayed by our emotional reactions to the vicissitudes of daily life. During the formative years of childhood, although our minds are open, ready to absorb, interpret, and internalize all experiences, we are nevertheless confined to a minuscule fraction of phenomena, aware first and foremost of our own pleasures and pains, our wants and needs, and what we like and dislike. I do not mean to suggest that humans are born egotistical. On the contrary, children are evidently both selfish and generous, but even their generosity and altruism lie within the context of a miniature world. We acquire a sense of identity as we distinguish ourselves from our surroundings, but as we grow older we learn to break down the boundaries through which we have thus confined and defined ourselves. We begin to develop the ability to see things from many sides and gradually take into greater account the emotional responses of others. This is the natural process of acquiring maturity, as we become educated, more ethical, and more integrated into our social environments.[37]

As Zhuangzi sees it, the *daos* of the Ruists and Mohists never expand beyond this arena, and remain inadequate so long as they do not take seriously the possibility of a vaster context of concern. To be fair, Confucius is not only aware of a *dao* that remains forever beyond our grasp but is also motivated by admiration for it. Still, he insists that we should always focus on what lies before our eyes. In the words of Zhuangzi's Confucius, he remains confined "within the four seas" (86–87), that is, within the social worldly realm. Zhuangzi takes the converse view. The deeper significance of social life itself can emerge only when we rise beyond it and understand the contexts within which it is contained. The further we open up those boundaries, the more integrated into the grand scheme of things we become. This requires cultivating an attitude of disinterested breadth of mind, or 'objectivity,' not as understood by empirical science, but more like the distancing of concern recommended by the Stoics or the sort of perspectivism advocated by Nietzsche. To do this we must open up our imaginations and venture beyond the confines of our everyday concerns. Only then are we able to refocus our attention, or rather relax the focus of our attention, so that the significance of our place in the grander scheme of things can emerge. As humans strive to approximate the all-inclusive impartiality of the cosmos, we cultivate distance from human concerns. "People like this ride the clouds and mist, straddle the sun and moon, and wander beyond the four seas. Even life and death cannot perturb them, much less the ends of benefit and harm" (46).

As with Ruist self-cultivation, the cultivation of expansiveness is unending: in the "*Xiao Yao You*" (31–32), Zhuangzi tells us that the sage Song Rong had transcended the petty concerns of social success and was unmoved by praise and blame, but he had much further to go. The level of ability that Liezi attained is described in superhuman terms, but he still did not reach the utmost possible. Zhuangzi then refers to an ultimate perspective from which anything is possible. This is the direction toward which the person of the highest achievement, the *zhiren* (see "Genuine Humanity" below), should set their aspirations, far above the realm of human concerns: "If he had only mounted on the alignment of the cosmos, steered the changes of the six energies, and thus wandered through the inexhaustible, then what would he have had to depend on?" (32). But if the cosmos is truly that which is inexhaustible, immeasurably vast, then no such ultimate perspective can ever be completely attained. Moreover, there can be no such thing as the point of view that encompasses everything. If it were possible to expand so far, one would no longer inhabit a point of view from within the cosmos; one could no longer be situated at a particular perspective.[38] The images of vastness then represent not an achievable endpoint but the *process* of expansion.

The discipline of cultivating expansiveness is not easy, at least for ordinary people. Daoist cultivation proceeds laboriously through the continuous accumulation of minuscule increments and requires dedication and diligence. The stories of acquisition of skill, for example, often involve years of training.[39] In this, the *Zhuangzi* agrees with the *Laozi* about the relationship between the vast and the petty, or the great and the small: "the journey of a thousand miles begins with a footfall; the construction of a tall tower begins by piling mud."[40] There is certainly room for the small in the grand scheme of things: we best attend to the cultivation of vastness by attending to the task at hand. Indeed, we can cultivate vastness only by tending to our current situation, through the resources we have at our disposal at any time, which will inevitably be limited. However, while we remain inextricably situated in our particular contexts, immersed in the details of our everyday lives and activities, we should be careful not to identify with the petty goals and parochial limitations through which they are ordinarily defined.

Our individuality is at most that of a focus within a field or context that cannot be encompassed all at once, but the focus has no identity apart from its function within the field as a whole.[41] Moreover, there is not just one field but many simultaneous fields, overlapping, interconnected, and nested within greater contexts. The food I am enjoying satisfies my hunger; this gives me energy to continue my work; my work provides a livelihood; the food itself was produced in a context of agriculture, shipped in a context of transportation systems; my work has its place within the functioning of an institution, which itself has a role in a larger social context. But this entire realm of embedded social significances is itself situated within the immense and inexhaustible context of the natural world. The recommendation of the *Inner Chapters* is that the details of our lives be properly given significance not through petty social constructs, but by casting them into relief against the humbling vastness of the cosmos: the sage lives immersed in every detail, but from the perspective of the whole.[42]

Traditional interpretations of the discussion of the great and the small, however, have tended to follow the commentary of Guo Xiang, who takes the great and the small to be equalized. The universe embraces multitudes: boundless varieties of things, qualities, experiences, and perspectives. Some may be larger than others and some may contain others, but none has greater importance than any other in the grand scheme of things, and all have their shortcomings. All things, all differences, must therefore be given equal value. This is a form of relativism: each thing has its own abilities and limitations, and it makes no sense to criticize any of them for not having the qualities of any of the others. In particular, it makes no sense to criticize the small for not being big. There is certainly some degree of truth to this claim. It makes no sense to criticize an ant for not being as large as an elephant, or to criticize an elephant for not being as large as a galaxy. Moreover, anything big is dependent on the smaller parts of which it is composed. "If wind is not piled up deep enough, it won't have the strength to bear up great wings. Therefore, when Peng rises ninety thousand miles, it must have the wind under it like that" (29–30). Even that which is immeasurably large is made up of the minute and cannot exist without it. An ocean may arise from the mindless and purposeless accumulation of insignificant quantities of water. The imperceptibly minute makes up the incomprehensibly vast. Each depends on the other for its place in the whole. If it were even possible to remove the petty, there would be nothing for the vast to be vaster than, and vice versa.[43]

Nevertheless, while it is true that each thing has its own appropriate size or degree, it does not follow that everything small is always equal in value to everything big. And although the vast and the petty may be mutually dependent, it does not follow that they are, or should be, equally valuable. Value is always value-*for*: for someone and for some purpose. Value arises from the perspective of a creature that has needs, wants, desires, or ends: light is valuable for a tree; social harmony is valuable for humans. And one judges the value of something by the degree to which it enables one to succeed. If one is a monkey, one must sleep in a tree, not under water. If one seeks knowledge, truth is more valuable than half-truth or falsehood. If one is trying to cultivate a flourishing life and emotional tranquility in harmony with the natural world, then expanding beyond one's limitations will be more valuable than remaining confined by them.

Moreover, while Zhuangzi certainly acknowledges the variety of natural things, the whole point of the discussion of the petty and vast is precisely to set up an *evaluative* distinction. Indeed, Zhuangzi draws this moral explicitly: "petty understanding cannot compare to vast understanding" and "small years cannot compare to vast years" (30). Again, this is the direction in which the person of the highest achievement, the *zhiren* (discussed in "Genuine Humanity" below), should set their aspirations, far above the realm of human concerns: "If one were to ride the true course of the cosmos (*tiandi*) and harness the transformations of the six energies (*qi*), what would one have to depend on?" (32). He unequivocally devalues the petty and quite clearly recommends abandoning the ways we ordinarily limit ourselves.[44] This distinction, far from being a form of radical relativism that equalizes all views, upholds Zhuangzi's own *dao* as the way of expansiveness, and criticizes rival ways that are still mired within human and social contexts. If Zhuangzi's views were truly relativistic regarding all *daos*, he would go out of his way to show us that his *dao* is no better than others. It would make no sense to ridicule them and recommend that we rise beyond them.

Wandering Beyond[45]　*Xiao Yao You*　逍遥遊

When applied existentially, the cultivation of vastness is interpreted as a sort of journey, *xiao yao you*. This is the title of the first of the *Inner Chapters*, and can be understood to mean something like "wandering freely beyond." In modern Chinese this phrase has a sense of living free and easy, enjoying life, and doing as you please. This sense of the term is captured by the translations "wandering at ease" and "free and easy wandering." Certainly, Daoist sages, including Zhuangzi, are often portrayed in this manner: they live on the outskirts of society, having relinquished all social obligations, and although they live in poverty, they also have the freedom to live in a joyful and tranquil appreciation of their lives. This sensibility infuses the stories of chapter 20, "The Mountain Tree." Those who feel trapped by the complex involvements of social life sometimes dream of escape. But social rules and regulations form an intricate, self-sustaining network in which we become increasingly enmeshed. The ties and obligations to family, friends, work, and society are so deep rooted that as we struggle to free ourselves responsibly in one area, we become more tightly entangled in another. It would appear that the only way to extricate ourselves is to break free altogether, paying no attention to any subsequent obligations.

Though we are not told how, the Daoist sages have somehow succeeded in extricating themselves from the system, which therefore no longer has authority over them. Since they wander outside of its bounds, the stresses and anxieties that come from having to conform to the demands of this external system of control simply cannot enter their lives. This idyllic scene, however, does only partial justice to the full significance of the term "wandering beyond." Obviously, not everyone who abandons their social obligations or lives freely and joyfully is a Daoist sage. Their motivation may be entirely selfish, or their lives entirely out of tune with the *dao* of the cosmos. The deeper significance of such wandering lies in the discipline by which one gets there. Wandering freely beyond is not the resulting state, since as we have noted, such a state is ultimately unattainable, but the means by which one cultivates it.

The clue to this deeper discipline lies in the character "*yao*" 遙, which has a sense of "remoteness" or "going beyond." That is, we do not just wander around aimlessly, but move outward, away from our locus of familiarity. We wander into the distance; the further we go, the stranger things get: we discover new climates, new customs, new creatures. But it is not just distance that shifts position from within the same perspective, not merely a horizontal meandering of a focal point to other positions on the same plane. Nor is it merely a horizontal wandering *between* other equal perspectives, that is, perspectives that share the same degree of limitation. The first is just a displacement in which I gain more experiences: I move to where you are and see the world from where you see it, but I still see it *as* I ordinarily would have done from my own perspective, as myself. I still bring my context, background, and presuppositions with me. This is tourism at its worst. The second is an attempt to transform my perspective qualitatively: I now not only see the world from where you are but also attempt to see it *as you do*. This is more challenging and requires the ability to empathize, to actively and imaginatively construct feelings and significances that would never otherwise have been available to me. This is an admirable form of ethical cultivation and is the kind of discipline required by the phenomenological anthropologist, but it is still not the perspectival wandering that is properly called *xiao yao you*.

Rather, as the allegory of Peng suggests, it is a wandering above into a higher-order perspective, with more comprehensive points of view, that contextualizes one's earlier standpoint. One does not merely shift position or exchange horizons, but expands them. From the new perspective one is able to see one's old point of habitation not only in a broader context but also in relation to rival positions. This movement to higher-order perspectives can, at least theoretically, be continued indefinitely. By learning to see, and so identify ourselves, from an increasingly "cosmic" perspective, we gradually are released from our former limitations.

Thus, *xiaoyao* wandering is explicitly associated with the modifier "*wu*." This is the form of negation we encountered in the *Laozi*, an optimal minimization that reverses priorities of significance.

Now you have this vast tree and you're bothered because it's useless. Why don't you plant it in the village of Have-no-thing, in the broad and empty wilds, stroll around the slopes of *Wuwei* (see below), and wander beyond (*xiaoyao*) as you rest beneath it. It will not come to an early end by the axe, and no thing will harm it. If there is nowhere one can be used, where can one come to grief or distress? (35)

Action Without Artifice[46]   *Wuwei*   無爲

When one engages from such a perspective, one's actions will not be so preoccupied, controlling, or manipulative; they will be *wuwei* 無爲. Unlike the *Laozi*, the *Inner Chapters* show little interest in sagely rulership and instead associate *wuwei* with life free of the confines of social structure. To live freely we must expand beyond ordinary human concerns and distance or disentangle ourselves from (*wu*) the social constructs through which we manipulate and control, and through which we are manipulated and controlled (*wei*).

In this section, I attempt to uncover the deeper conceptual connection between *wuwei* as living freely and *wuwei* as engaging with the world free from artificial constructs. As we saw in Chapter Two ("Activity and Artifice"), prior to reflection, we tend to take our socially constructed artifacts and ambitions to be independently real, and even of profound importance. This may be understood as a type of naïve realism.

Wuwei is the mode of activity of people who relate to the world distanced from such constructs or artifices. It is not that they do not categorize things or conceptualize the world at all, but their understanding is not determined by customary systems of significance. The concepts through which we deem (*wei*) things to be so are no longer thought of as simply what those things are (*wei*). According to chapter 2, "A road (*dao*) is made by people walking it; things are so because they are deemed so. What makes them so? Making them so (*wei*) makes them so. What makes them not so? Making them not so makes them not so" (40). When we are no longer misled into believing that there is only one way to understand the world, we are free to reinterpret things, not as we please, but in any of a plurality of ways that accord with their inner tendencies. We are able to apply other modes of understanding, multiple concepts and categories; to see the same thing in a new light or endow it with a different function (a pot may become a drum, a gourd may become a boat). We continue to live in a world in which we recognize pots, drums, trees, and so on, but we do not necessarily concede their independent objectivity *as (wei)* pots, drums, or trees.

This is not necessarily to be interpreted as skepticism (or radical relativism) regarding all objectivity. There is clearly something about the gourd that enables it to function as a pot or a drum, something about water that makes it an appropriate habitat for a fish. It means, rather, that the world as we ordinarily understand it does not have the kind or degree of ontological independence that we may ordinarily believe it does. Indeed, we are thrown into a world and must deal with it on its own terms, but what we make of it, *wei*, what we take it to be, may be construed in different ways. The stream before us manifests now as a freeway, now as an obstacle; as revenue, a dumping ground, or the lifeblood of the valley. Different contexts and purposes will reveal different possibilities of understanding. On a more radical level, we need understand it not as a unitary thing but as a multiplicity: different waters, rocks, plants, and aquatic life-forms. More radically still, we need not even recognize these entities, but see only molecules, atoms, subatomic particles, or energy and process. How far we can push the limits of reconceptualization is unclear, but the variations of our understanding must always be responsible to the natural tendencies of the phenomena.

Phenomenologically, we have the capacity to respond to the phenomena of experience with a level of subtlety that remains indeterminate with regard to specific concepts.[47] When we refrain from imposing fixed preconceptions, we become able to engage with them in a manner responsive to shades of difference that escape the crude boundaries of our ordinary linguistic concepts.

On an existential level, when we recognize the extent to which our lives are molded by social constructs, we become able to free ourselves from a type of emotional entanglement that disturbs our tranquility. The social ambitions that motivate us—money, wealth, power, privilege—lose their grip, become less influential. Other possibilities for a flourishing life may emerge, not determined by manipulative action and its attendant desires. With the diminishing of the hold of desires and conceptual constructs, one's mode of engagement with the world will be more accommodating, allowing events to happen without attachment to the outcome. Thus, the lessening of artifice goes hand in hand with the cultivation of a sort of indifference toward worldly success and failure.[48]

Paradoxically, natural behavior that is uncontrived (*wuwei*) is an achievement of Daoist cultivation. It cannot be accomplished simply by retiring from social engagement and doing as one pleases. Though our desires appear natural, they have been cultivated through socialization. To act more naturally, we must first reduce the influence of structures that have been internalized over decades. But deprogramming deeply ingrained impulses is no easy task, if it is even possible. Moreover, we can only ever optimally minimize artifice, never eradicate it altogether: both the nurturing and the mastery of naturalness themselves require a minimal degree of artifice.

Uselessness[49]   *Wuyong*   無用

When one is released from socially defined functions, one's life will appear useless, *wuyong* 無用, from a conventional perspective. Chapter 4 of the *Zhuangzi*, "*Ren Jian Shi*," ends with the moral "Everyone knows the use of the useful, but none know the use of the useless" (67). The use of the useful is its conventional utility, its socially constructed purpose. Objects of artifice are defined by their purposes, what they were made to be used for. As we deem practical things to be what they are, we thereby also determine their functions, *yong* 用. When a pen is broken and can no longer write, when the ink has faded so that a book can no longer be read, they become useless. But the objects are still interpreted in terms of their former functions: we do not usually say that a broken pen is not a pen, but neither do we see it as something that could be assigned a new function. We simply throw it away.

There is very little place in a socially constructed system for anything that has no conventional use at all. An expanse of grass will still be a "park," a "garden," or a "scenic spot" to be enjoyed from a specific vantage point, or to be hiked through for the exercise. Even when the uses are multiple, they are still culturally encoded and admit of little variation beyond the socially accepted functions. If something has no encoded social function, it is deemed useless: a large area of uninhabited land, a jagged piece of wood, a flash flood, an oversized pumpkin by a lake.

When we learn to disengage our prefabricated constructs, things no longer appear with predetermined functions. We may then begin to engage with things in increasingly unconventional ways. But for our imaginations to wander *beyond*, it is not enough merely to exchange existing functions. We might use a car as storage space, a tie as a belt, a wheelbarrow as a shopping cart, or a fork as a comb. This is still adapting things for preexisting social uses, and so still remains within the framework of our social and humanistic schemes.[50] We do not begin to wander beyond the bounds until we can reconstruct apparently useless things for what, from an ordinary point of view, appear to be useless purposes. The kinds of occupation valued from a cosmic perspective by a Daoist sage would not be recognized as worthwhile at all from the worldly perspective of a Ruist or a Mohist. What possible human relevance could there be in preparing oneself for a cosmic journey, seeing things from the limitlessly expanding perspectives of nature?

Huizi complains that Zhuangzi's ramblings about the vast and inexhaustible cosmos are so detached and distant that they have no relevance to the pragmatic concerns of human life whatsoever. "Your words, too, are big and useless, and so everyone alike spurns them!"[51] (35). Zhuangzi's diagnosis is that Huizi cannot see the use of what appears to be useless because he is blinded by social convention; the conditioning is so deep that he is unable to free himself from it. But as one cultivates expansiveness, concerns that once loomed large appear trivial; possessions and ambitions that once seemed desirable begin to lose their appeal. Conversely, issues that previously seemed remote and meaningless begin to take on a new significance, unfathomable from the earlier confined perspective. Zhuangzi several times points out, sometimes using the voice of Confucius himself, that Ruists, and by implication the Mohists also, will not be able to understand Daoist discourse: they confine themselves to the social arena, and this shortsightedness prevents them from seeing the value of more cosmic matters.

As with the *Laozi*, such cosmic "detachment" raises an ethical problem. There are occasions where the language of the *Zhuangzi* becomes almost unintelligible. It attempts to intimate the phenomenological attitude of the sage in paradoxical terms, and like the *Laozi* sometimes shows contempt for the cultivation of humanity and rightness. Indeed, the passages are often taken to express Zhuangzi's skepticism about ethical evaluations, either because ethical judgments are relative or because they are ultimately unknowable. A version of this sort of ethical problem can be found in chapter 23: Nanrong Zhu complains to Laozi, "If I am not humane, I harm others; but if I am humane, then on the contrary I make trouble for myself; if I do not do what is right, I do injury to others; but if I do what is right, then on the contrary I distress myself" (252). Nanrong Zhu is paralyzed in part because he sees the consequence of giving up humanity and rightness as harming others. Laozi does not deny this but responds, "You are confused and crestfallen. . . . You are a lost man—hesitant and unsure, you want to return to your inner conditions and natural tendencies (*qingxing* 情性) but you have no way to go about it—a pitiful sight indeed!" This, of course, is just an *ad hominem*; it does not even begin to address the objection. Insofar as it fails to do so, the objection remains unanswered.

For the most part, however, the concerns of the *Zhuangzi* remain invested in pragmatic values, though not defined by social and political interests. It is rather a naturalistic pragmatism, concerned with discovering and embodying the kinds of flourishing that flow from the more natural, less artificial aspects of our humanity. Zhuangzi's concern is that we be able to live out the full span of our natural years. Still, as in the *Laozi*, while Zhuangzi does not explicitly promote unethical virtues, the extent to which natural virtues are consistent or inconsistent with behavior that others would perceive to be harmful remains inadequately addressed by the text.

Completing One's Natural Years[52]   *Zhong Qi Tian Nian*   終其天年

As noted above, while the useful often come to an early end, the use of being useless is to enable us to live our full lifespans (35; 63–66). Only when we allow our natural tendencies to flourish are we able to fulfill our natural years, *tiannian* 天年. Like all natural creatures, we follow natural cycles of birth, growth, maturity, and death. But our lives are riddled with problems and accidents, plagued with anxieties and ill health, and haunted by the ever-present possibility of dying. Some of us will live well into our old age; others will be the victims of an untimely death (*yao* 夭). Zhuangzi attributes the prevalence of anxieties and early death to the degree to which we have become distanced from our natural lives, the degree to which our natural capacities have been strangulated by the artificial constraints in which they are embedded.

The concept of natural years is premised on the idea that each thing has its own natural fullest lifespan. This will, of course, not be the same for each of us, but will depend on our internal makeup and our environmental conditions, and how the two interact over the course of our lives. Developing a more cosmic scope of understanding, according to Zhuangzi, would enable one to appreciate the natural processes of living and dying, and thereby to better cultivate one's own vital capacities. If we foster our natural capacities, specifically those that allow us to live in the healthiest way possible, and avoid circumstances that impair our ability to thrive, then we will surely live as long as natural circumstances will allow. This does not completely eliminate the possibility of anxiety and early death, but it minimizes anxieties and any deleterious effect they may have on our health. Then, any apparently early death that may occur will not in fact be an untimely one. Thus, at least one use of the apparently useless cosmic concerns is their ability to enable us to live peacefully and in full acceptance of our circumstances and tendencies. Note that not all life and death are equal; only natural death and natural life are to be equally welcomed. A life cut short by political intrigue, revenge, suicide, or even high-minded self-sacrifice is not as good as a life that fulfills one's natural years.

The key to a flourishing human life lies in a discipline of cultivation of life tendencies, far from the harmful influences of social involvement. This includes diet, meditation, exercise, and breath control, the consequence of which is to enable us to live with greater physical and emotional health and to extend our natural lifespans to the fullest. The precise details of such psychophysical practices are not explained in the text, but appear to be presupposed in its recommendations. It is not unreasonable to believe that these practices have been preserved and developed through traditions influenced by Daoist philosophy: meditation, traditional medicine, martial arts, and perhaps most especially the traditional Chinese yogic discipline known as *qigong*. Harold Roth believes that the early text known as *Nei Ye* ("Inward Training") provides a clue to understanding these "mystical" practices.[53] Part of this method involves focused attention on and observation of internal processes as they appear to manifest in our experience: how it is that we emerge at each instant, how we are sustained through each moment, insofar as such processes appear to be available to phenomenological reflection. Daoist practice also involves psychophysical mimicry and embodiment of processes manifested in other natural phenomena. This ability depends on a nonverbal sensitivity to what lies beneath the surface of the observed phenomena and results in a nonverbal assimilation or internalization of those same tendencies. The assumption is that such fundamental biological or psychophysical tendencies are indeed available to first-person reflection and third-person observation, and that we naturally have the capacity to understand, embody, and cultivate them.[54] Just as it is possible to cultivate the seeds of a plant and tend to its natural conditions, so we should also nurture our own natural propensities. We must "hold fast" *shou* 守 to these ancestral conditions, protect *bao* 保 them, conserve them, and enable them to flourish to their maximum potential.

If this is possible, then it seems that by continued cultivation and renewal we might be able to keep these processes going indefinitely, though this indefiniteness is not necessarily understood to be infinite.[55] Hence, the later Daoist interest in longevity. This may appear to contradict the Daoist claim that dying is inseparable from living and that we must therefore learn to reevaluate our preference for living over dying. That is, to fully accept our naturalness we must surely also accept death as the necessary condition for the flourishing of life. But there is no contradiction here: the goal of cultivation of the life processes is not to defy death, but to extend the life processes to their fullest natural potential. Living and dying are one and the same process: a cyclical emerging and returning. To extend the process of living is also to extend the process of dying. Though it can be extended indefinitely, as with all natural things, it will eventually come to an end. When the natural time ultimately arrives, we welcome our inevitable return.

There is an intimate and paradoxical relationship between naturalness and cultivation. To live most naturally, we must engage in a rigorous discipline. This is not inconsistent, since there is a continuum between the complementary contrasts of nurture and cultivation. We nurture by ensuring the natural conditions that enable the development of the life potential of an organism. Cultivation involves more deliberate activity and control: we create artificial structures that will promote a specific kind of development in accordance with a plan of our devising. We nurture best not when we eliminate culture altogether, but when we optimally minimize it.

Attenuation of the Heart-Mind[56] *Xinzhai* 心齋

If the way to live out one's natural years is to live a life as free from artifice as possible, this means steering clear of complex social structures. But it does not necessarily mean avoiding social relations altogether. By critiquing sociopolitical structures and values, Zhuangzi is not rejecting social relations or asserting individualism. Indeed, the worldview that Zhuangzi promotes is inconsistent with individualism. Those who are in tune with the cosmos form a community of friends and live in mutuality, equal in their acceptance of the naturalness of death, identifying themselves with the transformations of the whole cosmos, and thereby are united in their recognition of the dissolution of the boundaries of selfhood (83–87).

Nevertheless, the world of politics is especially dangerous. It is unclear whether Zhuangzi believes that the political arena is essentially corrupt or this is just a contemporary problem.[57] Either way, in chapter 4, "In the Realm of Human Interactions,"[58] Zhuangzi attempts to advise those who through either personal calling or circumstance cannot give up social involvement and its attendant dangers. Even here, Zhuangzi's goal is to enable them to fulfill their natural lifespan, minimizing the possibility of an early and unnatural death. In Zhuangzi's narrative, Yanhui, the student most admired by Confucius for his devotion to virtue, feels compelled to approach the brutal Lord of Wei to admonish him and get him to change his ways. Yanhui has many strategies for trying to change the heart of the pitiless ruler, but Confucius is skeptical that any of them can work. Yanhui here is reminiscent of Mencius in his actual dealings with Xuan, the King of Qi, and Hui, the King of Liang. Using the character of Confucius, Zhuangzi's advice is that Yanhui should engage his own heart-mind, *xin* 心, on a fast, *zhai* 齋, empty it out, attenuate it, so that he may sense the *qi* of the ruler and guide it from within. Yanhui inquires:

> "May I ask what attenuation of the heart-mind is?" Confucius said, "Unify your concentration! Don't listen with your ears, but with your heart-mind. No, don't listen with your heart-mind, but with your energy (*qi* 氣). Listening stops at the ears, the heart-mind stops at the signs, but energy is tenuous (*xu* 虛) and waits on all things. Only the way accumulates the tenuous. This tenuousness is the attenuation of the mind." (57–58)

The metaphor is opaque, and even Yanhui at first fails to understand. But such language is unavoidable. After all, Zhuangzi is attempting to describe a phenomenological or meditative practice of altering one's attention: one must attempt to diminish the force of cognitive obstacles that prevent sensitivity to the implicit intentions of others. This is not the kind of activity that ordinary language evolved to describe.

This attenuation of the heart-mind involves emptying oneself of preconceptions, yielding cognitive power to a preexisting natural sensitivity to people's motives and intentions. We learn to sense what they are about to do, when they are amenable to suggestions, when they are likely to strike out. "Now I will tell you. You may go and wander in his bird cage, but never be moved by reputation. If you get in, then sing; if not, keep still" (58). In the same vein, Ju Boyu advises Yanhe, "If he wants to be a child, be a child with him. If he wants to act without guiding boundaries, do the same with him. . . . Fathom him through to the unblemished" (62).

We are born already attuned to the moods and gestures of others, though apparently not to equal degrees. To develop and hone this sensitivity, we must lessen the hold of our own intentions and diminish our own motivations. There are even people who can extend such an intuitive connection to other species. A tiger trainer can succeed in taming a tiger, not by changing its nature but by opening his or her own sensitivities to the animal's inclinations, understanding it on its own terms (63). In this way, one may be able to avoid an early death, though this is not as good as avoiding the predicament in the first place. But there is another danger (62). If one empties oneself of preconceptions and strives to flow along with the tendencies of the wild animal or brutal ruler, one surely runs the risk of the reverse influence. If one flows along with the amoral sensitivities of the ruler, developing a feel for them and refraining from activating one's own ethical values, might there not come a point at which one crosses over to their way of thinking and behaving? How does one attempt to understand and play along with brutal tendencies without giving up one's values? The two sensibilities are at odds with each other, and if a balance can be achieved, it is surely a precarious one.

Potency[59]　*De*　德

In chapter 5, "Signs of the Fullness of Potency," sages who live away from the center of social activity are said to have potency, *de*. It is a natural excellence that enables them to remain clear of entanglement in schemes for personal gain and from the corrupt games of power politics. In chapters 4 and 5, Zhuangzi warns against political involvement, and his sages idealize a life on the outskirts of social acceptability. They tend to be the human counterparts of the "useless": social misfits, outcasts who are often physically deformed, live in poverty, and sometimes depend on charity to survive.

Physical deformity can occur in two ways, either naturally or through human mutilation. In ancient China, physical mutilation was a typical form of punishment, and therefore was taken as a mark of a criminal. Some people are born with bodies that might appear to have been deliberately mutilated in this way. Their bodies form in a way that is not the norm for humans. An ordinary physical body is thought of as complete in its parts and abilities, and it comes with an ordinary kind of potency. The potency valued by Ruists is full-bodied and useful to society. It manifests as a charismatic influence through which one spreads the socially inculcated virtues. But, in Zhuangzi's estimation, the potency of social usefulness is a tool of artifice. Instead, he reverses the perceived value of so-called deformity and regards deviations in body and ability as signs of the fullness of potency.

Those whose potency is out of the ordinary, whether physically or psychologically, often lack a socially defined role. Their remarkable physical appearance and intensity of character are considered by those who represent the norm to be unattractive; their humanity is often even perceived as in some way incomplete. Indeed, ordinary language supplies us first and foremost with negative terms that reinforce exclusion: "lame," "crippled," "deformed," and so on; the same is true of the classical Chinese terms. But Zhuangzi senses a deeper magnetism and an overflowing potency in such people. One might say that their humanity is exceptional. In chapter 4, the giant twisted tree that seems useless has extraordinary natural powers: it produces bitter and pungent phytochemicals, so powerful that the merest touch produces blisters and hallucinations.

> Ziqi said, "What tree is this? It must certainly be of extraordinary caliber!" But, looking up, he saw that the smaller limbs were gnarled and twisted, unfit for beams or rafters, and looking down, he saw that the trunk was pitted and rotten and could not be used for coffins. Lick a leaf and it would blister your mouth and make it sore; inhale, and it would make you delirious for three days. "It is really a tree of no caliber," said Ziqi, "and so it has been able to grow this big." (65)

From the perspective of an ordinary human *dao*, it is warped, gnarled, unattractive, and useless. Ziqi fails to see that what the tree lacks in socially acceptable beauty and usefulness, it makes up for in terms of extraordinary natural powers. In a similar way, people born blind often have sharper hearing and sensitivity to subtle changes of light and shade; people without hands develop exceptional flexibility and dexterity with their legs and feet. People with autism sometimes have extraordinarily powerful personalities and intellectual capacities. Intellectual geniuses are often socially inept. Why this should be is unclear, but that it happens to a significant extent seems undeniable.

It is to such people that Zhuangzi looks to find his exemplary characters. His "misfits" are social outcasts: they live out their natural years content with a simple life, while others come to an early end or suffer from the side effects of the rat race, political intrigue, or existential anxieties. In an extraordinary turnabout, however, Zhuangzi suggests that such outcasts also have the genuine potency of a sagely Daoist ruler. Among them he finds not only sages who understand life from the perspective of nature but also those who have the capacity to govern others from such a perspective. Shushan Choptoes, for example, had a wordless teaching that succeeded in harmonizing his followers (71); Ai Taituo had a charisma that drew people in droves and enabled them to live contented. The character of Confucius says, "Now Ai Taituo is believed before he speaks, accomplishes nothing and is loved, so that people want to turn over their states to him and are only afraid he won't accept" (68). Shushan and Ai Taituo had no theories or doctrines and refused involvement in worldly affairs, yet their influence spread so that the whole community could function harmoniously.

However, though they exuded excellence and even inspired worldly minded rulers with confidence in their ability to govern, they chose not to sully themselves with such a lowly occupation (32–33). From a cosmic perspective, such social success and utility are utterly meaningless. The natural world provides the only real riches; the rest are traps and snares that endanger one's life and health. This ideal of sages who succeed in ruling only by cultivating the fullness of their own potency provides a seed that will eventually bear fruit in the Syncretistic metapolitics of the *Outer* and *Miscellaneous Chapters*.

Genuine Humanity[60]   *Zhenren*   真人

Zhuangzian sages are sometimes described as "*zhenren*." The word "*zhen*" 真 may be translated as "genuine," "real," or "true," and the term "*zhenren*" is sometimes translated "True Man." But there is potential for misunderstanding if we naïvely equate "*zhen*" with a semantic concept of truth or a metaphysical concept of reality. As already noted in Chapter One above, early Chinese philosophy is primarily pragmatic in spirit, motivated to a large extent by the political and ethical situation during the Warring States period. So its concern is likely to be pragmatic rather than semantic or meta-physical. Indeed, the term "*zhen*" and its opposite, "*wei*" 僞, are simply not applied to sentences, thoughts, and the like in Daoist texts and so are not used as semantic terms. This means that translating them as "true" and "false" is highly misleading at best. They are also not used in a metaphysical sense to distinguish the way the world really is from the way it merely appears to us. So, "real" and "apparent" would also be inappropriate translations.

The most common usage of these terms, especially in classical philosophi-cal texts, is a hybrid of the normative and the ontological. That is, it applies to people, our behavior, and the things we do and make. The closest Eng-lish terms might be "genuine" and "artificial." The concept of genuineness in classical Chinese has a cluster of associations: what is innermost, what is sincere, the stuff of which one is made. The most genuine core of something is its natural makeup; the natural behavior that follows from it is spontane-ous, exhibiting the minimum of artifice. Genuineness is authenticity, being "true to" oneself. The term "*zhen*" also has the sense of what arises naturally from the way things are in their innermost nature, without any interfer-ence, redirection, or artifice. It thus also implies sincerity insofar as it is what flows from one's nature without contrivance. Indeed, we have already seen in Chapter Two above that the meaning of "*wei*" has a sense of being contrived and artificial. It has a sense of being 'false' insofar as this implies what is not true to nature or what lacks sincerity. The significance of "*zhen*" and "*wei*" can thus be seen to arise from the most fundamental Daoist concern: draw-ing us away from artifice and back to the realm of the natural. It is related to the contrast between *tian* and *ren*: what naturally and spontaneously occurs and what occurs as the result of human contrivance.

Chapter 6, "The Vast Ancestral Teacher," opens with the problem of understanding what is genuinely natural, *zhen tian*, and what is genuinely human, *zhenren*.

Those who understand what nature (*tian*) does, and what humans do, have reached the peak. Understanding what nature does, they live from nature, and understanding what humans do, they use what their wits understand to nurture what they do not understand, and live out their natural years without being cut off midway. This is the frui-tion of understanding. However, there is a difficulty. Understanding is dependent on something for it to be correct, but what it depends on is exceptionally unsettled. How, then, can I know that what I call "natural" is not human, and what I call "human" is not natural? There must first be genuine humanity (*zhenren*) before there can be genuine understanding. (77)

Given, as noted in Chapter Two above, that the artificial can only be defined in terms of what is human, the question arises, "What, if anything, is natural about being human?" According to Zhuangzi, there *is* something salvageable about our humanity: it is not pure artifice. There is a central core of genuineness that is natural. When we nurture this genuine humanity, we reconnect with the natural world, become more distanced from the everyday hopes, fears, and anxieties that plague us, and are more tranquil and accepting of all our circumstances. In chapter 6, the person who has genuine humanity is described in almost impenetrably paradoxical terms, reminiscent of the language of the *Laozi*, but also with characteristics of stoic fortitude and serenity.

Prior to chapter 6, the ideal person is referred to as the *zhiren*, 至人, the utmost person.[61] This is someone who has reached the pinnacle of human achievement. The term is paradoxical, insofar as the Daoist ideal is a person who has cultivated naturalness to its apex and diminished humanistic concerns to their natural optimal minimum. Although the utmost person and the genuinely human person are not explicitly identified, the characteristics of utmost humanity and genuine humanity are not dissimilar, so I shall take them to be effectively the same thing. Ordinarily, we evaluate what happens to us according to our personal goals. We distinguish success from failure, good fortune from bad, and allow these judgments to rule our hopes, fears, and anxieties. From a cosmic perspective, however, these evaluative judgments lose their grip: things and situations have different values from different standpoints, but the differences dissolve as the perspectives increase in breadth and inclusiveness. Those who cultivate their genuine humanity, the *zhenren*, are not perturbed by things. Circumstance has no control over them and even death has no power to make them flinch.

The genuinely human (*zhenren*) of ancient times knew nothing of loving life, knew nothing of hating death. They emerged without delight, and went back in without a fuss. . . . They were happy to receive it, and forgetfully returned it. This is what I call not giving up the way on account of the heart-mind, not using the human to come to the aid of nature. This is what I call the genuinely human. (78)

The transformations that all things undergo are simply the way they are, and the person who lives from the perspective of nature knows how to understand and accept what cannot be changed.[62] He or she identifies with this ancestral source, trusts the inner potency that derives from it, and is thereby able to remain tranquil amid the turmoil and insecurity of life.

A common objection to this sort of stoic ideal is that a life of emotional indifference is a diminished life. Is it not important to feel everything vividly, to live through every detail of our lives with passionate intensity? This objection rests on a misunderstanding. The person who cultivates a stoic attitude is not cold and impassive, apathetic and emotionally dead. On the contrary, the ideal is precisely to live in fullest appreciation and joyful acceptance of every moment of one's life. "Therefore, sages wander in the realm where things cannot escape, and all are preserved. They delight in early death; they delight in old age; they delight in the beginning; they delight in the end" (81).

A stoic would insist that being thrown around and controlled by the passions prevents one from being able to live fully. It is the power of the negative emotions, in particular, that stoicism seeks to undo: hatred, disgust, fear, anger, anxiety. These passions do not increase the value and beauty of a human life, but diminish it. If we are controlled by hatred for our companions, fear for the future, and disgust with our environment, we cannot be free at the same time to accept and appreciate them.

Huizi, however, with his humanistic goals, remains suspicious of such ideals. Is the pinnacle of humanity really indifferent to benefit and harm, to life and death? How is such a philosophy relevant to ordinary humans? If we are to accept and appreciate all that the world has to offer, are we also to accept and appreciate cruelty and injustice? Doesn't social progress depend on the actions of those who are moved to oppose cruelty and injustice? Yanhui, for example, is moved by the plight of the people; he finds that he has no choice but to come to the aid of those who are oppressed by their tyrant ruler. If Yanhui were to accept everything with equanimity, he would not be moved to help improve their conditions. Indeed, if the people were to accept their own situations with equanimity, they would not be moved to help themselves. Again, the stoic position is more subtle.

It is not that everything must be accepted just as it is, that all situations are to be accepted equally. Rather, it is only the circumstances beyond our control that we must learn to accept with equanimity. Moreover, we are not supposed to accept them as "just," only as "unavoidable," and to suffer injustices that are unavoidable with equanimity does not mean that we cannot work to alleviate other injustices. Of course, all this depends on having the capacity to recognize cruelty and injustice as such and values by which to judge human behavior and social structures. If Zhuangzi's brand of Daoist stoicism requires that we give up all evaluations of right and wrong, *shifei*, as inapplicable from the standpoint of the cosmos as a whole, then Huizi's objection remains valid.

Dichotomous Evaluation   *Shifei*   是非

> When the Way relies on little accomplishments and words rely on vain show, then we have the dichotomous evaluations of the Ruists and Mohists, by which we affirm what we deny and deny what we affirm. If you want to affirm what you deny and deny what you affirm, there is nothing better than *ming* 明 clarity. [Watson has: What one calls right the other calls wrong; what one calls wrong the other calls right. But if we want to right their wrongs and wrong their rights, then the best thing to use is clarity.] (39)

We come, finally, to what many contemporary, especially Western, scholars consider to be the philosophical heart of the *Zhuangzi*, or at least of the *Inner Chapters*: Zhuangzi's discussion of *shifei* judgment, or dichotomous evaluation, and the way of life or overall attitude that he proposes in its place. This is concentrated in chapter 2, hereafter referred to as the "*Qi Wu Lun*" ("Discussion on Smoothing Things Out"[63]), the most difficult chapter of the entire collection. It is dense, convoluted, and abstract, with very little context to help with interpretation. Many passages are so obscure as to be almost impenetrable. This has not deterred scholars from telling us what every passage means, nor has it weakened the resolve of modern translators determined to find an intelligible rendering for every sentence in their own language. Still, despite the obstacles, when it is read carefully and contextually, several competing philosophical possibilities emerge with varying degrees of clarity and plausibility.

From the perspective of everyday engagement, we not only understand the world through systems of distinctions,[64] we also respond to these things with likes and dislikes, *haowu* 好惡, judge things to be beneficial and harmful, *lihai* 利害, and thereby make judgments about what is to be approved, *shi* 是, and what is not, *fei* 非. The word "*shi*" 是 means "this"; as a sentence modifier it means "it is the case that," and as a verb it means "to affirm." It is paired with "*fei*" 非, which means "it is not" or "it is not the case that," and as a verb means "to deny," "to reject." These terms can be used to judge whether something is or is not the case, but also contain an implicit evaluation. To *shi* something is also to approve of it; to *fei* something is to disapprove of it. This is all encapsulated in the Mohist technical term *shifei* 是非, translatable as "approval and rejection," "affirmation and denial," "right and wrong," or "evaluative judgment."[65]

Zhuangzi thinks of our tendency to respond to circumstances and events through such distinctions, emotions, and judgments as an integral part of what makes us human, our *renqing* 人情—the makeup of our humanity.[66] The word *qing* is a notoriously difficult term when used philosophically. Even its ordinary meaning contains a puzzling ambiguity: it can refer to the circumstances that surround us and to our responses to those circumstances. It has a dual sense of both "circumstances" and "emotions." Complicating the term still further, when used to refer to external circumstances, it can mean either general circumstances or particular conditions, and when used to refer to a particular kind of thing, can have the sense of the specific conditions that go to make up that kind of thing. This last sense is close to, but not necessarily identical with, the concept of an essence: the characteristics or qualities without which something cannot be the kind of thing it is.[67]

In chapter 5, "*De Chong Fu*" ("Signs of the Fullness of Potency"), Zhuangzi explicitly characterizes human *qing* in terms of *shifei* judgments, and says that we must abandon these. "Lacking the *qing* of a person,[68] approval and rejection (*shifei*) do not take hold of him" (75). This might mean that a person who does not respond emotionally to circumstances is not moved to make judgments of approval and rejection. Or it could mean that if one lacks the particular conditions, the makeup of a person, then one will not be moved to make such judgments. Either way, Huizi is disturbed by this claim: "How can you call a person who is without *qing* a person?" Zhuangzi replies, "That is not what I mean by *qing*. Being without *qing* means not allowing approval and rejection (*shifei*) to harm yourself."[69]

In the "*Qi Wu Lun*," Zhuangzi directs his most trenchant attacks against the Ruists and Mohists, Ru-Mo, or *renyi shifei*. In this pairing, it seems that "*renyi*" refers to the virtues of humanity and rightness emphasized by the Ruists and Mohists, while "*shifei*" refers to the dichotomous ethical evaluations of the Mohists.[70] There are in fact *two* discernible aspects to Zhuangzi's critique of *shifei* judgment. The first concerns the variety of stances from which differing judgments are made: judgments of value will vary depending on the creature, the culture, or the individual making the judgment. The second bears on the significance of the paradoxes or contradictions that arise insofar as we are led to simultaneous affirmation and denial of the same thing: it is and is not a horse; it is both acceptable and not acceptable. Interpretations of Zhuangzi's critique of *shifei* judgment must account for both of these.

According to the traditional account, Zhuangzi is criticizing the Ruists and Mohists for arguing with each other at all, for failing to see the relativity of all ethical judgments and philosophical positions, and for not recognizing the validity of each other's standpoint. This derives from Guo Xiang's relativism equalizing the vast and the petty. Graham's interpretation continues in a similar vein.[71] He sees this relativism as deriving from a recognition that all language is conventional. If words can be given any arbitrary meaning, then the world can be categorized any way we please. In particular, virtues can be defined any way we wish, and different *daos* can be articulated in relation to those virtues. Since all definitions are internal to each system, disputes between systems must be meaningless. Every *dao* is right from its own point of view: there is no ultimate viewpoint from which to make a final judgment.

Graham has two approaches to the paradoxes and contradictions that Zhuangzi raises.[72] In some places, he dissolves the contradictions by relativizing each opposing element to a different point of view: you affirm that something is a horse or approve it from your point of view; I deny or reject it from mine. In others, he sees the contradictions as arising from the very nature of rational analysis. When opposites are defined, they are separated by a boundary, but where does the boundary itself lie? According to Graham, Huizi has shown that the spatiotemporal boundaries belong to both sides, and thus the point of transition falls on opposite sides simultaneously.[73] Midnight belongs to both yesterday and today. Zhuangzi follows this logic, according to Graham, and concludes that not only spatiotemporal distinctions but also all other distinctions require a boundary that defies bivalent logic in this way, and so all distinction making entails contradiction. Zhuangzi is thus led to reject all rational analysis, and instead recommends a direct intuition of the world as an undifferentiated whole that, in itself, escapes all linguistic distinctions. The sage nevertheless recognizes both the usefulness and the limitations of all distinctions, and is thereby able to apply them flexibly. The wise person's mode of judgment is thus *yinshi* 因是, "adaptable judgment," or, as Graham translates it, "the 'That's it' that goes by circumstance."[74] This is contrasted with "deeming judgment," *weishi* 為是 (in Graham's translation, "the 'That's it' which deems"), a form of naïve realism that takes things inflexibly to be what they are deemed to be.

Chad Hansen's interpretation[75] begins by attributing to Zhuangzi a recognition of the relativity of all judgments, but he rejects Graham's portrayal of Zhuangzi as a "mystical" monist who eschews rational discourse. Hansen sees all *daos* as linguistic: they are guiding *discourses*. They are composed of systems of discrimination, which he characterizes as conceptual schemes or discrimination patterns. In Hansen's reading, there are countless such guiding discourses, all equally justified by nature, and each judging itself to be right from its own point of view. Unlike Graham, however, Hansen does not draw the antirealist conclusion that there can be no single correct discourse; rather, he draws the skeptical conclusion that if there is a right one, we cannot know which it is. But if one cannot know which is correct, then it does not really matter. One is then free to accept *all* possible points of view and adopt *any* of them temporarily but wholeheartedly, at any time. Thus, he sees the "*Qi Wu Lun*" as articulating a hybrid epistemology: a form of skeptical relativism. This epistemological metastance is *ming* 明, an attitude of insight from the perspective of the axis of the way, *daoshu* 道樞, a central position from which all contrasting perspectives may be surveyed. From there, all things can be affirmed and denied simultaneously: hence the possibility of paradox and contradiction.

Recently, Lisa Raphals[76] and Paul Kjellberg[77] have interpreted Zhuangzi's position not as a form of relativism or epistemological skepticism, but as a way of life comparable to that recommended by the ancient Greek Skeptics. Now, "skepticism" in modern and contemporary epistemology (and as used by Hansen) refers to a view that denies the possibility of knowledge. This, at least ostensibly, was not the position of the ancient Skeptics. Their Skepticism was a way of life based on a method of always withholding judgment about disputed issues that go beyond experience. What appears in experience should be accepted at face value, but whether what appears to be real, good, or true is ultimately real, good, or true is not something that we should worry about. We should withhold judgment about those ultimate issues (hold them in suspension, *epoché*).[78] To do so, we should actively find reasons in favor of all the possible alternatives, until they all seem equally plausible. At that point we will realize the futility of trying to find certainty regarding ultimate things. Withholding judgment in this way will give us peace of mind (*ataraxia*) and enable us to cope with a world in which we can be certain of nothing.

Raphals and Kjellberg argue that Zhuangzi should be interpreted as offering a similar way of life. We should recognize that arguments about *dao* and about right and wrong are futile. Zhuangzi attempts to undo our dogmatism by shaking our confidence not only in our own belief systems but also in our capacity to evaluate them. In the "*Qi Wu Lun*," he raises a version of the problem of the criterion. All disputants take themselves to be right—so who can we get to judge between them? There can be no judge who does not adopt a prior viewpoint, so there can be no unbiased judgment. It would be better, then, to avoid the arguments altogether. One can only resolve disputes where the parties share criteria of evaluation; but when these very criteria are at stake, no resolution seems possible. When all viewpoints are made immune to criticism in this way, we are able to let go of the apparent persuasiveness of our own. We are also thereby freed from any emotional anxiety that comes from needing to know who, after all, is right.[79]

Radical relativism[80] and skepticism are ancient and familiar doctrines, and the problems with them have been amply documented over the centuries. The relativist claims that one can never pass judgment on the values of other perspectives, and yet in doing so, passes judgment on those who do so. Radical relativism is therefore inherently self-contradictory: there is no way to put it into practice without at the very same time contravening its own principles. When applied to ethics, it also results in horrifying consequences: the radical relativist typically refuses to judge those who practice genocide, or slavery, on the grounds that those who practice mass slaughter or own slaves believe they are doing a good thing. To those who claim not to know what is wrong with this consequence, I have nothing to say. This skeptical posture may seem invincible, but one cannot have a fruitful discussion about ethics with someone who appears to lack even the most minimal ethical intuitions.

Radical skepticism is also not easy to save from inconsistency. The episte-mological skeptic who asserts that one cannot claim to know anything seems to be making a strong knowledge claim in that very assertion. And the thera-peutic skepticism of the ancient Greeks is also committed to inconsistency, even if it never explicitly asserts the skeptical doctrines on which the practice depends. After all, why would one recommend refraining from ever making judgments, if one did not believe that such judgments could never be justi-fied? One may try to save skepticism from inconsistency by claiming that skepticism itself is not known or is itself to be kept under *epoché*, but the upshot of either of these solutions is that we can neither approve nor recom-mend skepticism as more effective than other ways of life.[81]

Of course, the fact that skepticism and relativism are hard to free from inconsistency does not mean that they are not correct interpretations of the "*Qi Wu Lun*." It might well be that the *Inner Chapters* espouse an inconsistent philosophy with serious ethical problems. But, as mentioned in the first chap-ter, philosophers do not simply rehearse ancient philosophies for their own sake or for the sake of historical knowledge, but study them in order to learn from them, to move beyond them, and via a deliberate "fusion of horizons," to construct new philosophies that address the problems of the old ones. It seems that Hansen attempts to do precisely that. He tries to circumvent any inconsistency by appealing to the notion of a special, meta-level perspective or discourse, a *dao* of *dao*s. That is, he claims that Zhuangzi's *dao* should be construed as a meta-level *dao*: it can be thought of as a perspective on all other perspectives or a discourse about all other discourses. This perspective is centered in the *daoshu*, the axis of the way from which all other ways can be surveyed. In effect, it is not itself a perspective at all. If a perspective is a view of the world from a situated point, then the *daoshu* cannot itself be a perspective. It is the somehow unsituated recognition of the multiplicity of perspectives and the acceptance of their internal positive self-evaluation. This recognition or insight, *ming* 明, also enables one to adopt temporarily any perspective wholeheartedly, without being committed to it. As a meta-discourse, it is not itself about the world, but is the verbal expression of the acknowledgment of the equality of all discourses about the world. It is a discourse that somehow escapes perspective but enables one to choose the perspective from which to temporarily make discriminations without committing to it.

Although this is a valiant attempt at resolving, or rather precluding, the inconsistency, I am not sure that it succeeds. Once a discourse has been defined as a set of discrimination patterns on the world, the notion of a discourse about discourses makes no sense. Something similar follows for a perspective on perspectives. The very notion of a meta-discourse that has no discrimination patterns and makes no judgments seems incoherent. More importantly, the meta-attitude itself is supposed to be unsituated and value free: it ranges freely over all other sets of values, which are applicable only from within the discourse in which they themselves are embedded, not from the meta-discourse. But the notion of an unsituated, value-free *dao* is surely incoherent. Here we reach a logical inconsistency that lies at the heart of radical relativism. Radical relativism, by definition, aims to be value-neutral regarding *all* values. Now, we can certainly accept the context dependence, or culture dependence, of some values: kinship and partnership relations, conceptions of modesty, and ways of showing respect vary significantly from culture to culture, and few people think it appropriate to impose their own way of life on others. And here we see the liberal pluralism that seems to motivate some forms of relativism. But one cannot be value-neutral about value-neutrality itself. Value-neutrality is itself a value, one that cannot be relinquished even temporarily without giving up radical relativism. To reject dogmatism is to value broadmindedness and flexibility. So, no dogmatic view can ever be adopted, since to adopt it is to abandon the value-neutral position, and therefore the radical relativism, from which one entered it in the first place. And yet radical relativism can make no exceptions regarding which views are acceptable.

All these interpretations begin with arguments in favor of relativism. And while there undeniably are passages that appear somewhat skeptical and passages that appeal to a multiplicity of views, they are, I believe, not necessarily indicative of radically skeptical practices or relativistic doctrines, and are only peripheral to the Zhuangzian *dao*. Zhuangzi certainly advocates *fallibilism*: the pragmatic recognition that no matter how obvious or clear things may be, we should certainly be open to being proved wrong. He also adopts an attitude of epistemic humility, never claiming to know more than he does, but does not shy away from making knowledge claims (that humans should not sleep under water), and from advocating certain forms of knowledge (the kinds of embodied knowledge manifested in physical skill).

The relativistic arguments (45–46) never really establish more than the contextual dependence of all evaluations.[82] Different types of creatures will inevitably value different aspects of the world, depending on their particular needs. Radical relativism of the sort that accepts *all* perspectives equally does not follow from this: if the passages in question imply that it does, they are mistaken. Moreover, Zhuangzi does *not* accept all points of view as equally valid, especially not those of the Ruists and Mohists. His rejection of both ethical systems is clear. Mohism is subject to his criticism that belief in clear judgments of right and wrong, *shifei*, is overly simplistic and out of touch with the complexity of phenomena that we encounter in our lives. Both are vulnerable to his criticism that emphasis on *renyi*, humanity and rightness, is too shortsighted; it fails to see human concerns from a broader perspective. Thus, while Zhuangzi acknowledges that they each believe themselves to be right from their own point of view, he does not recognize the validity of either standpoint, and indeed finds both to be petty, inadequate to cope with the vastness of the cosmos. He proposes his own *dao* as superior and criticizes those who are unable even to understand it. His view is *pluralistic* insofar as it recognizes and celebrates the varieties of things, but it does not accept all proposed *daos* as equally good.

This should not be taken to mean that Zhuangzi's position is a form of "absolutism." It is sometimes thought that to reject radical relativism is to adopt absolutism. However, if absolutism is the imposition of one's own actual values as universally applicable, then the dichotomy between relativism and absolutism is a false one. There are many intermediate positions: forms of naturalism and pragmatism that create a productive but provisional middle ground while avoiding the imperialist dogmatism of absolutism. Their recommendations are pluralistic and tentative, while avoiding the nihilistic extremes of relativism and skepticism.[83]

Zhuangzi certainly has an ideal, a holism, in comparison with which all lesser views are partial and inadequate. It might be thought that such a holism requires that one include all former perspectives as one develops. But this is not correct. The broader perspective *supersedes* lesser perspectives, just as a more inclusive scientific theory is broader in scope than narrower theories but does not have to include the falsified ones. This is why Zhuangzi is able to criticize the Ruists and Mohists. Nor does the broader theory include the former theories as "approximations," insofar as their predictions are close to those of the correct theory. Newtonian mechanics may work as well as relativity theory for getting rockets to the moon, but the latter rejects the concepts of absolute space and absolute mass. Moreover, it is not always the case that superseded theories provide practically workable approximations.

The theory of phlogiston, for example, is completely falsified by the theory of oxygen; and the theory of *élan vitale* is completely contradicted by contemporary biological theories of biological processes. In a similar way, while the Daoist perspective may contextualize the judgment of some lower perspectives (for monkeys, sleeping in trees is good, but not for fish) and thus is able to be pluralistic, it clearly rejects others (the Ruist and Mohist ways that assert that cultivating humanity and distinguishing clearly the boundary between what must be affirmed and what must be denied are the best ways for humans to flourish).

Another philosophical significance is allowed to emerge when we displace the discussions of skepticism and relativism from the center to the periphery of the philosophy of the "*Qi Wu Lun.*" Certainly, Zhuangzian philosophy manifests fallibilist and pluralist tendencies, but these are subordinate to a more general sense of respect for the wholeness, continuity, and expansiveness of the cosmos. The natural world as a whole is given greatest value; our task is to cultivate an attitude of expansiveness that brings us into greater attunement with it. As our perspective broadens, we notice the continuities between what seemed previously to be disparate things. We see instead a holistic, organic world in which things arise and decompose, mutually constituting each other as they do so, through interdiffusing sets of continuous processes. But also, as we rise above the clamor of human discourse and human desires, the distinctions and values on which they are based lose their cogency, and they begin to seem petty when set against the stark beauty of the cosmos. Zhuangzi's attitude toward the multitude of competing humanistic *daos* is to rise above them: he does not accept them all equally, but criticizes them all equally.

One may indeed move flexibly between lesser perspectives for pragmatic purposes, but one never loses sight of the fact that all lesser *daos* remain unequal to the *dao* of the cosmos. As soon as a *shifei* judgment made from within a particular perspective loses its grip, one abandons it for a *dao* that is more adequate to the task at hand. It is emphatically not that alternative *daos* are equally right, only that they may be of limited and variable practical value in different contexts. They may be adopted, but only for as long as they prove adequate to the purpose at hand. This is *yinshi*, adaptive judgment, given a purely pragmatic significance, rather than a radically (or skeptically) relativistic one.

But when relativism is no longer presupposed, we have the problem of understanding why Zhuangzi promotes paradoxes and contradictions:

"Affirm what you deny and deny what you affirm" (39), "To use a horse to show that a horse is not a horse is not as good as using a non-horse to show that a horse is not a horse" (40). Graham and Hansen attempt to dissolve the contradictions by relativizing the affirmations and denials: the Ruists affirm what the Mohists deny, and vice versa. This helps us escape the contradictions, but the problem is that the passages in question contain no explicit reference to points of view; on the contrary, they literally encourage us to contradict ourselves.[84] The question is: Why? Graham acknowledges that the *shifei* terminology is taken from the Mohists, but he interprets the discussion as criticizing their naïve realism: there is one set of distinctions between right and wrong that accurately maps the way the world actually is. Graham has Zhuangzi respond by replacing what appears to be their naïve dogmatic absolutism with an all-inclusive relativism that delights in a multiplicity of mutually inconsistent *daos*.

However, when one examines in detail the discussion of *shi* and *fei* in the later Mohist *Canon*, another possibility comes into play. The Mohists argue that distinctions can, and must, be expressed clearly and mutually exclusively. Only when opposites are precisely distinguished from each other can we be clear about what is the case and what is not, what is right and what is wrong, and only then can we live in a unified and harmonious way.[85] When the "*Qi Wu Lun*" is read against these presuppositions, we see another significance emerge: *shifei* judgment that sharply separates opposites for human convenience is not genuine but artificial. It is a product of human emotions and linguistic constructs: we classify things, like or dislike them, and then make judgments. The natural world, however, does not conform to these crude structures: natural processes slip through the frameworks in which we attempt to contain and control them, as water leaks across irrigation channels. The same is true of the significances through which we understand the world. The boundaries that we articulate to define and distinguish entities and processes are always indeterminate and porous, and inevitably disintegrate.[86] Thus, what is at stake is not primarily physical boundaries, though the claim holds true of these, but boundaries of meaning, through which we are able to distinguish what is (*shi*) from what is not (*fei*).[87]

The standard example the Mohists use is a horse: we must be clear about what is and is not a horse. We must always affirm the term "horse" only of horses and deny it only of things that are not horses.[88] In Zhuangzi's process worldview, all opposites are in constant transformation, displacing one another, yielding to and becoming one another. The transformations are continuous, with no clear and determinate boundaries isolating one thing from another or preventing things from disintegrating into their contradictories. The natural phenomena of birth and death are precisely the processes by which a horse gradually arises from and returns to a state in which there is no horse. We find that the apparently sharp artificial boundaries through which we understand things are in fact necessarily blurred, and that in the shadows between opposites the bivalent logic ("Yes, *shi*" or "No, *fei*," but not both) favored by the Mohists breaks down. If we look only at clear cases of horses, we tend to be blind to the intermediate cases. But if we start from the outside of the transformative process (with a non-horse) and work our way in, we bypass this cognitive obstacle. Is a horse skeleton a horse? At which exact point did the horse stop being a horse? In the penumbra, there is no clear answer, and we see more clearly that a contradictory answer ("Yes, *shi*, and no, *fei*") is not obviously wrong.

From a cosmic perspective, all things and processes form a continuum. But the cosmos is not thereby reduced to a monotonous and indifferent blob; it still retains its distinctiveness and variegation. It is just that the multiplicity and variety are not fixed—either sharply or uniquely—by the artificial boundaries of linguistic distinctions. The natural world is not carved into distinct entities, nor are processes sliced into discrete events. Rather, it is permeated with channels of porosity,[89] regions of vagueness through which one distinctive area or process bleeds as it becomes another. In the penumbrae, where things become their opposites, whether we should say that something or its opposite is or is not remains exceptionally undecided, *te weiding* 特未定; we may say neither or even say both simultaneously. However, this does not entail that we can make the world into anything we please: vagueness and indeterminacy remain confined *within the penumbrae*. Moreover, the channels move in some directions and not in others; the tendencies of development retain their distinctiveness, however one chooses to carve them up. There is a continuity of transformations in which things exchange in cycles, become each other through gradated changes, whether swift or slow.

The cosmos is ultimately, inexhaustibly vast, while internally it is continuous and indeterminate. Cultivating an expansive attitude leads to a life of tranquility, distant from human concerns, but hopefully not inhuman. The wise, though above the din and disturbances of the world, nevertheless remain alive in it. They live immersed in every detail of life, but from the perspective of the cosmos. From such a vantage point, the distinctions that seemed so real, the fears and anxieties that once overwhelmed us, lose their significance. The vicissitudes of life are accepted in all their magnificent variety: gains and losses, health and illness, life and death are all phases in the inevitable transformations of things, and are to be welcomed with equal openness. Recognizing the fluidity of the transformations of a continuous whole, the sage also recognizes realms of indeterminacy and paradox for all judgments. Linguistic distinctions can help us understand, but remain too crude to match the fluency of natural change. To deal successfully with the subtleties of such change requires abandoning the crude and unwieldy tools of language. They can be adequately mapped and dealt with only by a non-verbal, embodied understanding of the subtleties of natural tendencies and natural processes. This issue will be taken up in Chapter Seven below, where I provide an analysis of the Daoist philosophy of skill.

CHAPTER FIVE

The *Outer* and *Miscellaneous* Chapters of the *Zhuangzi*

From Anarchist Utopianism to Mystical Imperialism

The *Zhuangzi* anthology as a whole does not represent the philosophical ideas of a single school, let alone a single person, but rather the development of different lines of thought over several centuries. Still, ideas that resonate with those found in the *Laozi* and in the *Inner Chapters* remain clearly recognizable throughout the *Outer* and *Miscellaneous Chapters*, with the single notable exception of chapter 30, which does not contain any distinctively Daoist ideas. From a careful examination of the complete anthology, we can see that over the course of time, these ideas began to develop their own momentum, and interpretations began to diverge significantly. Moreover, influences from non-Daoist schools can also be found: ideas from Confucianism, Mohism, and Legalism, for example, appear in later passages written by more eclectically inclined thinkers. Despite the hankering for unity and simplicity of the *dao*, the streams of thought develop branches that grow and diminish, subdivide and reconnect, creating the variety of permutations represented in the *Outer* and *Miscellaneous Chapters*. From a distance, in addition to the Zhuangzian mainstream, two distinctive courses can be discerned leading to opposite ends of the political compass: a quasi-anarchistic type of utopianism and a composite theory of rulership based on a form of mystical cultivation. Both rightly claim their heritage in the pre-Qin Daoist texts, but while the utopian branch stays close to the source, the syncretist branch, through a shift in emphasis, follows the momentum in a surprising direction.

The division between the *Outer* and *Miscellaneous Chapters* does not appear to be based on considerations of style or content. It is true that many of the *Miscellaneous Chapters* (23 to 27 and 32) are more heterogeneous than others in the anthology—Graham refers to them as "ragbag" chapters—but overall the dividing line after chapter 22 appears to be somewhat arbitrary. While a few of the *Outer* and *Miscellaneous Chapters* are composed of extended essays, the majority are collections of assorted stories, parables, and philosophical musings of varying length: some just a few sentences long, others developed more extensively. Some chapters of the anthology fall together in neat groupings—they are written in similar styles, use similar terminology, and express similar points of view—but most contain a selection of themes and viewpoints, and a few appear to be almost random collections of passages. Apart from the Utopian essays, I prefer to refer to the strands of thought that can be discerned in scattered passages throughout the text, rather than to chapters as a whole.

Modern scholarship from China, Japan, and the West over the last hundred years or so has enabled us to disentangle several of these strands.[1] Some passages advocate a clearly identifiable philosophical position, while others suggest intermediate positions consistent with the thought of more than one branch. Consequently, grouping and classifying each chapter, and even individual passages within each chapter, under separate strands has proved to be no easy task.

A few overall distinctive tendencies can be discerned. Several chapters show signs of direct influence of the quasi-anarchistic views espoused by significant portions of the *Laozi*. Six chapters, 8 to 10 and 29 to 31, are written in relatively lengthy prose and with consistent literary style. With the exception of chapter 30,[2] they, and passages consistent with them, can be attributed to a utopian strain of Daoism that is largely social libertarian or anarchist in spirit. At the other end of the spectrum, a minority of passages exhibit the syncretistic, or eclectic, approach typical of Han dynasty thinkers and advocate a holistic political philosophy in which a single ruler is able to take control of a vast state system through esoteric forms of inner cultivation and delegation of practical duties. These are scattered through chapters 11 to 16, which are otherwise miscellaneous in character; chapter 33, however, appears to be a single Syncretist essay. The remainder of the anthology explores ideas that resonate closely with those of the *Inner Chapters*. These are classified by Graham as the "school" of Zhuangzi and were included in Chapter Four above. This Zhuangzian philosophy and passages consistent with the utopian strand of Daoist thought form the bulk of the *Outer* and *Miscellaneous Chapters*.

Even when the various philosophical positions represented in the anthology as a whole differ dramatically—the Utopian chapters and the Syncretist passages have political views that are almost diametrically opposed—their ancestral commonalities are not altogether lost. Indeed, insofar as similar views can be found in either the *Laozi* or Zhuangzian passages, the early "Daoist" part of their heritage remains impeccable.

In the following, I shall explore some philosophical issues raised by the utopian Daoists and briefly discuss the characteristics of syncretistic Daoism. I end with a rough guide to the strands of Daoism in the chapters of the *Zhuangzi* anthology.

DAOIST UTOPIANISM

There are several chapters, and a large proportion of passages throughout the *Zhuangzi* anthology, that appear to owe as much to the *Laozi* as to the *Inner Chapters*; they explicitly develop a critique of Ruism and call for a return to simplicity, to nurturing life, and to cultivating one's natural tendencies. Chapters 8, 9, 10, 28, 29, and 31 and many of the passages in chapters 11, 16, and 22 express versions of this philosophical attitude.[3] They extol the virtues of a simple life, reject the cultivation of humanity and rightness, and rail against the oppressive nature of social arrangements. They call for abandoning concern with political power and describe a utopian era when social groups were small and life was simple. Liu Xiaogan classifies this as a form of anarchism.

Chapters 8, 9, and 10 are so strikingly similar in style and philosophical content that they could have been written by a single person. A. C. Graham believes that these chapters, which are long essays, were indeed written by one author, whom he refers to as "the Primitivist." However, although the chapters contain very similar critiques of social artifice and claims that we need to nurture our natural tendencies, *xing* 性, they have enough differences, particularly in terminology, to suggest the possibility of different writers, or of the same writer formulating thoughts and objections at different times. The first part of chapter 11 expresses a similar view, but it is written in a markedly different style and is composed of several medium-length essays. Graham believes that although chapters 28, 29, 30, and 31 present similar ideas about political activity, they are significantly different in style and content from those he attributes to the Primitivist. The chapters are also different enough from each other in style and terminology that they do not appear to be from the hand of a single author. Graham notices that the view expressed in chapter 28 is precisely that attributed to Yang Zhu (Yangzi) in the *Lüshi Chunqiu*, and so he refers to the authors of these chapters as Yangists.[4]

Philosophical Overview

The Confucian philosopher, Xunzi, sees social cultivation as absolutely necessary for our development as humans. He argues that without culture and artifice, without regulation and control, our natural tendencies will flow unrestrained and run amok. "The natural tendency of humans is ugly; as for their being good, it is because of artifice (*wei* 偽)."[5] According to the utopian ideas of chapter 8, "Webbed Toes," and chapter 9, "Horses' Hooves," however, it is the very process of enculturation itself that damages our *xing*. This is reminiscent of Mencius' argument that our natures should not be damaged by the imposition of external structures. But Mencius and the Utopians have radically opposed understandings of the relationship between nature and the virtues. Mencius argues that virtues such as humanity and rightness derive from our natural tendencies, while wickedness results from neglecting or harming them. The Utopians assert that such harm results not only in wickedness but also in striving for virtuous behavior. In chapter 8, "Webbed Toes," we read:

> Nowadays the humane people of the age lift up weary eyes, worrying over the ills of the world, while the inhumane rupture the conditions (*qing* 情) of their natural tendencies (*xing* 性) and lifespan (*ming* 命) in their greed for eminence and wealth. Thus, I think that humanity

and rightness are not the natural condition of humans (*renqing*). . . .
Depending on curve and plumb line, compass and square to "rectify"
things, this is to hack away at their *xing*. (100)

The direct attack on all ethical concepts in favor of ethically neutral natural
tendencies gives rise to the recurring problem for Daoist ethics. But, as we
shall see in the section on reluctant rulership below, unlike the *Laozi* and
Zhuangzian philosophy, the Utopians may have a solution to this problem.

It is not only the inculcation of ethical ideals that disrupts our natures
and causes confusion but also the purposive acquisition of knowledge. The
recommendation of the Utopians is that we should reject the dysfunctional
excesses of culture and civilization—the systems of measurements and laws
through which we attempt to control what ultimately cannot be controlled,
and technological innovations by which we try to improve on nature—and
instead return to natural simplicity, *pu* 樸. We will thereby be able to nourish
our natural tendencies and keep our lives whole.

Why might the very tools designed to bring about social harmony cause
social turmoil? The simple answer is that culture diverts us from what is most
genuine. Civilization and regulation are additions to nature that arise from
human hubris: dissatisfied with our natural condition, we desire to improve
it; we set up goals and intentions, and construct plans of action and social
structures that will enable us to achieve those goals. Natural processes are
fluid, free, and flexible, and have their own appropriateness, but we cut them
down to our preferred specifications and stretch them to fit our rigid constructions. "What is long by nature needs no cutting off; what is short by
nature needs no stretching. . . . I think, then, that humanity and rightness are
not the human condition" (100).

Chapter 10, "Rifling Trunks," warns against using intellectual artifice to
control nature in order to benefit people:

With increased knowledge of bows, crossbows, nets, stringed arrows,
and triggered contraptions, birds flee in confusion to the sky. With
increased knowledge of fishhooks, lures, seines, dragnets, trawls, and
weirs, fish flee in confusion to the depths of the water. . . . This is how
the great confusion comes about, blotting out the brightness of sun
and moon above, searing the vigor of hills and streams below, overturn-
ing the round of the four seasons in between. (112–13)

Interfere with nature and you will only throw it out of joint: the natural seasons will fall out of order, the birds and beasts will be in disarray! The more we seek knowledge, the more we use it to interfere with natural processes, and the more we inevitably throw them out of balance. At one time, such anxiety might have been dismissed as excessive and unrealistic alarmism, but from our present vantage point we can see that the authors of the Utopian chapters displayed a surprising and eerie prescience.

Chapter 10 seems to draw its primitivist inspiration directly from the *Laozi*. "Cut off sageliness, cast away wisdom, and then the great thieves will cease. Break the jades, crush the pearls, and petty thieves will no longer rise up" (110). It might be considered an early Chinese exercise in deconstruction, asserting that the cultivation of humanity results in inhumane behavior and therefore is inhumane, and that sagacity, *sheng* 聖, produces thieves, and therefore is itself a form of brigandry. This is developed further in chapter 29, "Robber Zhi" (see "Hypocrisy as a Philosophical Criticism" below). The critique of sagacity here echoes the attack on cleverness in the *Laozi*: those who are crafty can use their wits to outsmart and exploit the gullible.[6]

Moreover, the existence of artificial measures and values arouses people's desires: they strive to acquire the objects valued and cheat to conform to the measures and regulations, and thereby harm their own natures.[7] Xunzi also argued that following desires leads to excess, but recommended that desires be regulated through artifice. As with the *Laozi*, however, the analysis and recommendation of the Utopian chapters is just the reverse: the very structures through which we attempt to control behavior are excessive and result in harm. By defining what is valuable—profit, fame, humanity—they lead us away from a natural state of contentment and down a spiraling path of increasing artifice, acquisition, and control. If, however, we are in tune with our natures and potency, if we can settle into and find peace in *an* 安, our natural tendencies, then the senses cannot be thrown off balance.

Natural Tendencies[8] *Xing* 性

The Utopian writers are particularly concerned that humans should preserve their natural life tendencies, and not sacrifice or exchange them for anything else. They are referred to as *xing*, sometimes as *xingming* 性命, or *xingming zhi qing* 性命之情, the circumstances (*qing*) of natural tendencies (*xing*) and lifespan (*ming*). Here, "*ming*" appears to have the sense of "lifespan" rather than Circumstance. "*Xing*" is etymologically related to, and indeed sometimes interchangeable with, the word "*sheng*" 生, meaning "life." The heart radical, 忄, suggests the heart of life, the inner region from which the life processes originate, as it were: our life capacities, perhaps, or life impulses. These tendencies not only enable us to live but also make us what we are, and provide the conditions for the development of each individual natural lifespan. Our life tendencies are produced by nature and provide our distinctive predispositions, not only as the individual things we are but also as the kinds of things we are. They are naturally born in us, but they must nevertheless be nurtured if we are to complete our natural lifespans. However, since our ability to live to our fullest natural potential is as much the product of environmental circumstances as it is of our inner tendencies, the concept of *xing* tends to include some of those nurturing conditions.[9]

The Daoist conception of *tian* is not of a hegemonic ruler, a lawgiver that controls and governs the myriad things. It is rather a way of referring to the background conditions that enable or allow things to flourish in accordance with their own inner dispositions. Seeds do not grow into plants because they are commanded; they do so because that is their natural tendency. The natural disposition of horses includes, among other things, eating grass and galloping; the natural tendencies of water include falling and adopting the shape of its container. To be sure, modern science posits "laws" that "govern" all natural phenomena. However, the metaphor of "obeying" scientific laws is misplaced. The so-called "laws" of nature are rather principles that simply describe the most general repeating patterns in accordance with which natural phenomena occur. Since they describe the patterns that things actually follow, there is no sense in talking about obeying or disobeying them. To the extent that what happens does not correspond to our stated laws, it is not the events that are at fault, but our understanding of the natural patterns that actually took place. We need not to punish the event, but to come up with a better theory as to what patterns it actually followed.[10] In every case, what happens naturally is simply what happens, not just as a matter of fact, but as a matter of the outward unfolding of inner processes. It is inevitable, given the way things are: it can neither be forced nor avoided.

Still, seeds do not always grow. If they do not get sufficient water they will not sprout; if they are overwatered they will drown. It seems that in unsuitable circumstances they cannot follow their natural tendencies. But is this right? Surely it is the natural tendency of a seed to decompose when soaked in water for an excessive amount of time. The rotting of organic matter is just as natural as the growth of an organism. Nevertheless, there is still an important distinction here that we should not be eager to lose too quickly: these natural tendencies are of two quite distinctively different kinds. The ability of a seed to follow its inner tendencies to grow into a plant of a particular species is something quite specific, quite different from its tendency to decompose. There is a sense in which decomposition is a *general* tendency that occurs when the species-specific processes are *prevented* from developing. This notion of the proper development of an organism of a specific species is comparable to Aristotle's notion of the proper function of an organ. At any rate, even if it could be argued that there is no objective distinction between the two kinds of processes, it remains the case that the Daoists are looking to learn from the aspects of nature that enable life to flourish. Even if all processes follow their natural tendencies, some of those processes are more conducive to the flourishing of life than others, and it is these that are emphasized in the concept of *xing*. We may choose to follow and develop our cognitive, manipulative, and evaluative tendencies, but according to the Utopians, we harm our natural life tendencies when we do so.

There are also nonbiological tendencies that may result in flourishing or conflict. A stream will follow a channel down a hill, but a rock in the channel will block the path of the stream. The rock may break if the current is powerful, or slowly and imperceptibly be worn down and polished by the flow. Such physical processes are very different from biological phenomena and organic processes, where some sense can be given to the proper function of an organ or organism. Nevertheless, even in nonliving physical processes, where there is no sense of proper function, we may discover principles of natural flourishing that can be applied to the process of living. Living things, after all, are also physical; the events that occur and the processes they undergo also have general physical properties, not specific to the proper function and development of the living thing. They are also subject to mechanical laws and the law of gravity; they can move quickly or slowly, clash softly or roughly— and by observing nonbiological phenomena, we can learn which other kinds of interactions will promote flourishing and which kinds will hamper it. If there is a general Daoist claim, though not necessarily a universal principle, about such interactions, it is that a more natural and lasting success lies in understanding the *yin*, yielding, qualities while the *yang*, forceful, qualities will have a tendency to be more destructive. The natural world flourishes best when it is a dance of yielding processes, because mutual yielding allows mutual flourishing, but it is the recuperative *yin* qualities that embody the secret of successful engagement.

When this is applied to human life, the moral is that we should minimize action that hampers our natural tendencies. Popularizations of Daoism in the West have for decades interpreted this as "going with the flow," dropping out from the rat race and following your desires. Although some of the depictions of Zhuangzi's happy-go-lucky sages on the outskirts of society might seem to corroborate this interpretation, in fact, it is quite mistaken. On the contrary, the path of cultivation of natural tendencies is a difficult discipline. Humans are the product of thousands upon thousands of years of cultural development: we are thoroughly civilized creatures, and all our actions are shaped by artifice. We are born into a social world in which everything is evaluated, approved or rejected. It is a world of cultural habit and significance: we are rarely, if ever, confronted with purely natural objects, but are surrounded by artifacts that have social functions. From the moment of our birth we are shaped as cultural beings. The actions we perform are almost never merely physical movements or purely biological functions, but have meanings, motivations, and purposes that are thoroughly imbued with social and cultural significance. But in choosing the path of artifice, we neglect our natural capacities and leave them to atrophy. What they would have become if allowed to develop with minimal manipulation is either lost or buried deep beneath layers of socialization. Thus, the undoing of artifice, the recovery of spontaneity, and the cultivation of natural tendencies, if they are even possible, cannot be achieved by merely "going with the flow."

Hypocrisy as a Philosophical Criticism

Chapters 29, "Robber Zhi," and 31, "The Old Fisherman," are literary masterpieces that engage in a savage critique of Confucius. The plot of chapter 29 echoes chapter 4 of the *Inner Chapters*, where Yanhui goes to visit the brutal lord of Wei.[11] Here, it is Confucius who goes to visit the crime lord Zhi to convince him to change his ways. In reply, the ferocious and volatile Zhi launches a furious attack on Confucius, accusing him and all moralists of hypocrisy. Note that he refers to Confucius disrespectfully using his personal name, "Qiu":

"In your flowing robes and loose-tied sash, you speak your deceits and act out your hypocrisies, confusing and leading astray the rulers of the world, hoping thereby to lay your hands on wealth and eminence. There is no worse robber than you! I don't know why, if the world calls me Robber Zhi, it doesn't call you Robber Qiu!" (328)

He gives several instances of people whose way is praised and commended by Confucius. But all of these either were unvirtuous or acted in ways that caused harm or even death, either for themselves or for others:

"Yao was a merciless father, Shun was an unfilial son, Yu was half para-lyzed, Tang banished his sovereign Jie. . . . All these . . . men are held in high esteem by the world, and yet a close look shows that all of them for the sake of profit confused their genuineness, that they forcibly turned against their *qing* and *xing*." (328–29)

In practice, the Confucian way, in promoting unvirtuous people, would appear to be either hypocritical or self-undermining.

There is not much explicit argument, but the story is narrated in a beauti-ful and compelling way.[12] Zhi and his band have their own code of criminal conduct and ideals of excellence. Comparing it with the *dao* that Confucius teaches, he finds that the latter does not even result in a more harmonious society: in pursuit of Confucian virtue, people still suffer and lose their lives. The accusation of hypocrisy is essentially that there are no significant differ-ences between the brigandry of Zhi and the way of Confucius, and that Con-fucius therefore has no right to preach. It is important, however, to note the rhetorical function of this chapter. Zhi's *dao* of brigandry is not being pro-moted as an equally good ideal, but rather is being used as a device to show how the results of Confucian practice are inconsistent with its own ideals. That is, the deeper agenda behind Zhi's tirade is to show that Confucianism and brigandry are *both* unacceptable, two sides of the same coin: a meddling interference with natural tendencies that causes contention.

The writer or writers of these stories seem at times to presuppose that there can never be any motivation other than profit of some kind, whether wealth or reputation. "Never-Enough said to Sense-of-Harmony, 'After all, there are no people who do not strive for reputation and seek gain'" (335). Even Confucian striving for virtue is really just vying for some sort of personal advancement. As with those who believe that humans always act out of selfish motivations, the narrator does not say why Confucius is just striving for profit, but merely makes the accusation. The claim, however, is unjustified: it assumes dogmatically what it sets out to prove. *Prima facie*, we act sometimes selfishly and at other times altruistically. While it is true that one can always assume an egoistic story behind any stated altruistic motivation,[13] that is not the same as *proving* that the ostensibly altruistic motivation was really selfish, and even if that is true in some cases, it certainly does not follow that *all* altruistic behavior is disguised self-interest. In the absence of such proof, there is no noncircular reason not to accept the altruism at face value.

Now, even if turns out to be true that Yao was a bad father or Shun a bad son, this would not invalidate the virtues of being a good father or son, even for someone who reveres Yao and Shun. One can revere virtues and respect a person as virtuous while also recognizing the extent to which they fail to be virtuous. There is neither inconsistency nor hypocrisy in that. And the claim that Confucianism is self-undermining is compelling only if the practice of Confucian cultivation necessarily results in an unvirtuous society; that is, if it can be shown that Confucianism is *necessarily* self-undermining.

A similar type of criticism can be found in postmodern critiques of enlightenment ideals. The ideals of objectivity, truth, and progress are deconstructed[14] by showing how those who professed them systematically used them to justify all sorts of injustices: slavery, racism, hostile colonial occupations of other people's countries, religious conversion forced under threat of torture, and so on. But the fact that some people use ideals to justify unethical behavior does not by itself invalidate those ideals. The *ad hominem* attack is not sufficient to refute the values behind the ideals. Nor would it be even if every proponent of the ideals also engaged in unjust, unethical practices. What is needed is to show that something in the very nature of the ideals themselves results inevitably in injustice. The accusation of logocentrism is an attempt to provide precisely such a contaminating factor.

Derrida points out that the very structure of definitive judgment necessarily seeks to exclude what is deemed incomprehensible and therefore either rejected as evil or dangerous, or not acknowledged as even having any existence. The ideals of objectivity blind us to the value of what cannot be encompassed from the perspective of those ideals.[15] All moralism that seeks logical universality excludes, and thereby does "violence" to, an "other" that does not conform. If this type of criticism is correct, the hypocrisy is not deliberate, but is something that the proponents are incapable of seeing. It is thus hypocritical not in intention, but in deed: one does not mean to be causing harm, but one's commitment to a certain set of ideals necessarily results in a harm that one is rendered incapable of recognizing. One is ideologically bound to refuse to classify it as a harm. The missionary who tortured those who refused to convert was ideologically bound to insist that the torture is beyond criticism. In a similar way, the Ruist insistence that virtue is more important than life results in devoted scholars inflicting damage on themselves, living in dire straits, ending their lives early, and encouraging others to do the same.

The presence of such *aporias* in the very nature of evaluative judgment is taken by some to entail the radical relativist conclusion that we must therefore refrain from making all such judgments: nothing can be criticized; everything must be accepted as it is. This sort of reasoning leads to the following kind of absurdity: the moralist who condemns murder or racial hatred is oppressing those who murder or hate people of other races. The unintended consequence of such a desire to avoid all violence thus becomes a paradoxical defense of those who are most violent, while criticizing those who judge that violence to be bad. The absurdity would be funny if such bizarre views weren't becoming increasingly prevalent in popular culture. There is a second problem with this view: it falls prey to its own criticism. The radical relativist who claims that we ought not make evaluative judgments and criticizes those who do is thereby making an evaluative judgment! The relativist criticism of "absolutism" is itself a rejection of absolutism, and as such does "violence" to absolutists. Thus, the refusal to make any evaluative judgment must be accompanied by the refusal to reject absolutism: the radical relativist must thus both reject absolutism and accept it at the same time.

If this is correct, how do we respond to Zhi's deconstruction of virtue? How do we acknowledge the force of the *aporia* and not fall into the absurdity of radical relativism? Conversely, how might we make ethical judgments and not become oppressive absolutists? I think the answer lies in the fact that we do, *ipso facto*, appear to share a deep level of basic intuitions about harm and suffering independently of our ideological commitments. Even those who insist on their right to inflict what are ostensibly harms (pain, deprival of freedom, inequitable treatment) do not simply assert the infliction of harm as a good; rather, they always seek to justify the necessity of the harm in accordance with an ideology. To act in accordance with values at all *requires* inflicting harm to some degree. Deep disagreements lie in the ideologies in terms of which such harms are justified. Perhaps the best we can hope for is to minimize the infliction of such harms, and in the dispute over the justification of necessary harm, remain genuinely open-minded and willing to change our stance.

Reluctant Rulership

Chapter 28, "Yielding the Throne," expresses a view broadly consistent with chapters 8, 9, and 10, but is written as a collection of short narrative passages. The stories echo the theme of the last of the *Inner Chapters*, "Responding to Emperors and Kings," and begin to set up the possibility of a new type of Daoism. A ruler or emperor wishes to yield the throne, usually to a Daoist or recluse of some sort. The recluse refuses and explains that nurturing life is more important than gaining control of a state.

> Shun tried to cede the empire to Shan Juan, but Shan Juan said, "I stand in the midst of space and time. . . . When the sun comes up, I work; when the sun goes down, I rest. I wander through the cosmos, and my mind has found all that it could wish for. What use would I have for the empire?" (309–10)

However, if there has to be a state and a ruler, then surely the best ruler would be precisely a person who does not care for ownership of the state and is devoted only to the nurturing and preservation of life and the cultivation of *xing*. Prince Sou of the state of Yue fled his state for fear of assassination, but the people pursued him. They wanted him to be their ruler precisely because he had no personal stake in ruling them (311). People who have any kind of motivation to rule, who are tempted by power, are not to be trusted. For them, life is simply one factor in the calculation of gains and losses: life may have to be lost for territory to be gained. In contrast, a person who sees life as more important than power will not yield to such machinations. "The empire is a thing of supreme importance, yet [Zizhou Zhifu] would not allow it to harm his life. . . . Only one who has no use for the empire is fit to be entrusted with it" (309).

This concern with cultivation of life, moreover, is not selfish. When the state of Bin was attacked by the Di tribes, King Danfu refused to go to war, saying, "To live among the older brothers and send the younger brothers to their death; to live among the fathers and send the sons to their death—this I cannot bear! My people, be diligent and remain where you are. What difference does it make whether you are subjects of mine or of the people of Di?" (310). His concern for the lives of all his people outweighed his concern for rule. If Graham is right that this chapter represents the view of Yang Zhu, then the contrast is not between selfishness and concern for others, as Mencius sees it, but between concern for personal profit and caring about the lives of the people. It is therefore not a form of egoism. This might provide the beginnings of a solution to the recurring ethical problem for Daoist thought. Unlike Zhuangzian philosophy, the Utopians, while rejecting artificial distinctions, still presuppose a naturalistic distinction between benefit and harm, and by extending this concern to others raise the possibility of articulating naturalistic concepts that are genuinely ethical.

HAN SYNCRETISM: MYSTICAL RULERSHIP

Chapter 28 thus forms a pivot that, with a single aikido move, as it were, transforms utopian anarchism into a form of effortless imperialism.

> Hence it is said, the genuineness of *dao* lies in regulating one's person . . . its offal and weeds are for governing the empire. Looking at it this way, the accomplishments of emperors and kings are superfluous affairs for the sage, not the means by which to keep the person whole and nurture life. (312–13)

Cultivation of one's natural tendencies now becomes the very means of bringing about a peaceful and harmonious life, not only for an individual or a small group but also throughout the entire empire. The sageliness of self-cultivation spills over by itself into a peacefully functioning social structure. This quasi-anarchistic attitude can be discerned even in chapter 7 of the *Inner Chapters*, where the "nameless person" says, "Let your mind wander in the neutral, blend your energy with the vacant, follow along with things as they are of themselves, and do not accommodate impartiality toward oneself—then the empire will be governed" (94).

There are a number of passages that start with this idea and, drawing on a comprehensive awareness of the various schools of thought, use it as the foundation for a more explicitly political form of Daoism. This is a kind of mystical rulership, also hinted at in the *Laozi*,[16] rooted in Daoist cultivation, but now combined with a concern for the details of rule. Thus, the practice of cultivation of life tendencies is now combined with a distinctive interpretation of *"wuwei"* and promoted as a quasi-anarchistic method of ruling a vast empire. In this eclectic system, values and policies of Confucianism and Mohism can be identified, as well as a Legalist-type interpretation of the *Laozi*, according to which the ruler is devoted to what is most essential, while the activity of government must be entrusted to the subordinates.

The first to think in an eclectic way was the Confucian philosopher Xunzi, who criticized the proponents of various rival doctrines as unable to see the limitations of their own views and unwilling to evaluate others with objectivity. They happen upon an insight and become obsessed with it, taking it to be the whole of the way: Mozi promoted utility; Songzi argued for the lessening of desires; Shenzi championed the law; Shen Buhai believed in circumstance; Huizi was obsessed with language; and Zhuangzi was mesmerized by the cosmos. According to Xunzi, only Confucius had enough presence of mind to be free from obsession: his *dao* was able to balance utility with form, the lessening of desires with their need to be satisfied, and the value of the natural with the importance of the human, for example. In this way, the Confucian *dao* was promoted as an all-encompassing one.

This spirit of eclecticism and search for an overarching *dao* became the hallmark of Han dynasty philosophy. Rather than choosing and championing one particular *dao*, philosophers recognized each to have some value, though none could be thought complete. Hence the desire to construct a comprehensive *dao* by synthesizing philosophical positions, extracting what was of value in each, and eliminating what was problematic. Doctrines of competing schools were thus integrated into a larger system in which each was able to contribute its particular virtues to the smooth functioning of the whole.

Chapter 33 of the *Zhuangzi*, *"Tian Xia"* ("All Beneath the Heavens")[17] echoes Xunzi quite closely:[18]

> How thorough were the people of ancient times! . . . They had a clear understanding of root policies and connected it even to petty offshoot regulations. . . . Many in the empire seize upon one aspect, examine it, and pronounce it good. But like the ear, the eye, the nose, and the

mouth, each has its own understanding, and their functions are not interchangeable. In the same way, the various skills of the hundred schools all have their strong points, and at times each may be of use. But none is wholly sufficient, none is universal. (363–64)

Mozi, Songzi, Shenzi, and Zhuangzi are both praised for some of the doctrines and critiqued for their partiality and lack of comprehensiveness. Huizi receives criticism but no praise, and the philosophy of the *Laozi* is described without any apparent criticism. Rather than Ruism, the "way of the ancients" is identified as all-encompassing: the way of "sageliness within and kingliness without" (364). Most notable are the various ways in which Ruism and Daoism are merged in the Syncretist passages. Ruist values such as *ren* and *yi* are not lost, but are subordinated, at least theoretically, to those of Daoism. Even Legalist and Mohist policies are relegated to the outermost branches of this system. Sagely government is rooted in the cosmic (*tian*), ancestral (*zong*), potency (*de*), and *dao*; the chapter goes on to the cultivation of ethical virtues, the judicious application of law, and administrative concern for the welfare of the people. Beginning with Daoist principles and ending with Mohist goals, it incorporates Confucian ideals and Legalist procedures.

Chapter 13, "*Tian Dao*" ("The Way of *Tian*") distinguishes between the way of the sage ruler and everyone else. The way of the sage is rooted in stillness, emptiness, and *wuwei*. This allows the way of the ministers to manifest in movement and activity, *youwei*, the counterpart of *wuwei*. The kingly way is merely to oversee from the perspective of *tiandi* (the cosmos), *dao*, and *de*, while the ministers busy themselves with details of the tasks of administration:

> Emptiness, stillness, limpidity, vacancy, silence, *wuwei*—these are the level of the cosmos, the pinnacle of the *dao* and its potency. Therefore the emperor, the king, the sage rest in them. . . . Still, they may be without active interference (*wuwei*); as they are without active interference, it is those employed in service who take on the responsibilities. (142–43)

The potency of emperors and kings takes the cosmos as the ancestral, the way and its potency as principal (*zhu* 主), and *wuwei* as constant.... Superiors must adopt *wuwei* and make the world work for them;

inferiors must adopt action and work for the world. . . . The heavens do not actively give birth, yet the many things are transformed; the earth does not rear, yet the many things are nourished. The emperor and the king do not actively administer, yet the world is benefited. (144–45)

It is worth recalling at this point that in the *Records of the Historian*, Sima Tan follows a similar pattern to Xunzi and the Syncretists. As we have seen in Chapter One above, he analyzes the faults and virtues of six families of philosophical thought—*Yinyang*, Ruism, Mohism, Legalism, the Linguistic school, and *Dao(de)jia*. In his account, *Daojia* emerges as the most perceptive and inclusive, adopting and absorbing what excels from the other schools. Emptiness and *wuwei* are also central to the practice of Sima Tan's Daoist ruler. Whether this eclectic *Daojia* is the same as the Syncretistic way of the ancients of the "*Tian Xia*" chapter, or of chapter 13, is far from clear. Furthermore, whether either or both of these are to be identified with the eclectic Han dynasty school known as "Huang-Lao" is also unclear. They may well be three alternative formulations of syncretist philosophy. If the Mawangdui silk manuscripts have been correctly identified as belonging to the Huang-Lao school, then Randy Peerenboom has given quite a persuasive argument that its philosophy is distinctively different from the Syncretism of the *Zhuangzi*.[19]

Below is a list of the chapters of the *Zhuangzi*, grouped according to the philosophical tendencies discussed above that are dominant in each. Given the complexity of most chapters, this should only be taken as a rough classification.

"*INNER CHAPTERS*," *ATTRIBUTED TO ZHUANGZI*

1. Wandering Beyond   *Xiao Yao You*   逍遙游
2. Discussion on Smoothing Things Out   *Qi Wu Lun*   齊勿論
3. Nurturing the "Principal" of Life   *Yang Sheng Zhu*   養生主
4. The Realm of Human Interactions   *Ren Jian Shi*   人間世
5. Signs of the Flourishing of Potency   *De Chong Fu*   德充付
6. The Vast Ancestral Teacher   *Da Zong Shi*   大宗師
7. Responding to Emperors and Kings   *Ying Di Wang*   應帝王

UTOPIAN DAOISM (GRAHAM'S "PRIMITIVISM")

8. Webbed Toes   *Pian Mu*   駢拇
9. Horses' Hooves   *Ma Ti*   馬蹄
10. Rifling Trunks   *Qu Qie*   胠篋
11a. Let It Be, Leave It Alone   *Zai You*   在宥
16. Healing Natural Tendencies   *Shan Xing*   繕性

UTOPIAN DAOISM (GRAHAM'S "YANGISM")

28. Yielding the Throne   *Rang Wang*   讓王
29. Robber Zhi   *Dao Zhi*   盜跖
31. The Old Fisherman   *Yu Fu*   漁父
(Graham includes chapter 30 in this category.)

DEVELOPMENTS OF THE PHILOSOPHY OF THE INNER CHAPTERS, WITH UTOPIAN AND OTHER PASSAGES

16. Healing Natural Tendencies   *Shan Xing*   繕性
17. Autumn Floods   *Qiu Shui*   秋水
18. The Height of Happiness   *Zhi Le*   至樂
19. Penetrating Life   *Da Sheng*   達生
20. The Mountain Tree   *Shan Mu*   山木
21. Tian Zi Fang   *Tian Zi Fang*   田子方
22. Knowledge Wandered North   *Zhi Bei You*   知北遊
23. Geng Sang Chu   *Geng Sang Chu*   庚桑楚
24. Ghostless Xu   *Xu Wugui*   徐無鬼
25. Ze Yang   *Ze Yang*   則楊
26. External Things   *Wai Wu*   外物
27. Imputed Words   *Yu Yan*   寓言
32. Lie Yukou   *Lie Yukou*   列御寇

HAN SYNCRETISM

33. The Empire   *Tianxia*   天下

MIXED COLLECTIONS, CONTAINING
SYNCRETIST PASSAGES

11b. Let It Be, Leave It Alone   *Zai You*   在有
12. Heaven and Earth   *Tiandi*   天地
13. The Way of *Tian*   *Tian Dao*   天道
14. The Turning of the Heavens   *Tian Yun*   天運
15. Constrained in Will   *Ke Yi*   刻意
16. Healing Natural Tendencies   *Shan Xing*   繕性

NOT DAOIST?

30. Discoursing on Swords   *Shuo Jian*   說劍

CHAPTER SIX

The *Liezi*

AUTHORSHIP

Liezi,[1] like Laozi, is probably a legendary character rather than an actual War-ring States thinker. According to the *Liezi* itself, he is supposed to have lived in the Butian game preserve in the principality of Zheng, but was eventually driven by famine to live in Wei. The first chapter of the *Zhuangzi* refers to Liezi, so if this name refers to an actual person, he would have lived prior to the writing of that chapter. This means that he would have flourished some-time before the end of the fourth century B.C.E.[2] He was said to have been a student of Huzi (Huqiu Zilin) and a fellow student of Bohun Wuren (whose name, "Wuren," notably means "no person"), and teacher of Baifeng. Though there are references to his philosophy in the *Huainanzi* and the *Lüshi Chun-qiu*, Liezi is not explicitly mentioned in any of the early classifications of philosophical thought and thinkers, in Xunzi, Zhuangzi's *Tianxia* chapter, and Sima Qian.[3]

TEXT

The extant text has eight chapters, each of which contains a series of stories, developing themes whose antecedents can often be discerned from the *Zhuangzi* and sometimes from the *Laozi*. In style, it is modeled to a large extent after the *Zhuangzi*: mythical, poetic, literary, humorous, indirect, and polysemic. Several themes are developed in each chapter, and some chapters overlap in themes, but overall it is a little less miscellaneous in character than the *Zhuangzi*. About one quarter of the text consists of passages that can be found in other early works, such as the *Zhuangzi*, the *Huainanzi*, and the *Lüshi Chunqiu*.[4] The remaining majority of the text, however, is distinctive in style, and with the exception of the *"Yang Zhu"* chapter, quite consistent in the worldview and way of life that it advocates. Most of the text contains material of philosophical interest. However, myths and folktales based on similar themes, but with no apparent philosophical value, can be found side by side with stories that have profound philosophical significance.[5]

Chapter 7, *"Yang Zhu,"* is problematic. It appears to start from the Daoist premise that one must tend to one's life, and infers from it a hedonistic philosophy of pleasure seeking that is inconsistent with the cultivation of indifference toward worldly things that is characteristic of much of the rest of the book, especially chapter 6, "Effort and Circumstance,"[6] and of early Daoist philosophy in general. Whether this really is the philosophy espoused by Yang Zhu, as the tradition has maintained, or Graham is right that the philosophy of the real Yang Zhu can be discerned in the *Miscellaneous Chapters* of the *Zhuangzi* is unclear. Graham hypothesizes that this chapter probably belongs to an early hedonistic phase in the philosophy of the author.[7]

The received eight-chapter text with Zhang Zhan's commentary dates from the Western Jin. Zhang Zhan narrates a story about its provenance, ostensibly trying to establish the authenticity of a newly rediscovered ancient text. The Zhang Zhan edition includes a preface by Liu Xiang, the Western Han scholar, who says that he edited and collated material from other collections to create an eight-chapter edition. However, Chinese scholars have long been suspicious of the authenticity of Zhang Zhan's text and have classified it as a forgery. They claim that the textual material was compiled, edited, and written by a single author who intended to deceive readers into believing that this was the ancient text to which Liu Xiang refers.[8] Linguistically, the style of the original parts of the text appears to be typical of the Warring States period, but Chinese scholars insist that the style does not ring true.

Unlike most Western scholars at the time, Graham concurred that the evidence suggests that the text is rightly understood to be a forgery, dating to around the end of the third century C.E. To convince non-Chinese scholars, Graham undertook a thorough analysis of linguistic differences that are inconsistent with the earlier dating.[9] He also argued that the evidence strongly suggests that the parts of the *Liezi* that are shared by pre-Qin texts, such as the *Zhuangzi*, were in fact directly copied from those earlier sources and not vice versa. Philosophically, many passages show signs of reconciliation of Daoist and Confucian ideas, and possible Buddhist influence, all of which suggests a dating later than the Warring States.

However, even if the text is a forgery, it is not clear why this should be considered sufficient reason to neglect it as a work of philosophical interest. Whoever wrote it, and whenever it was written, it contains much material that expresses distinctively recognizable strands of Zhuangzian thought, with sufficient complexity and sophistication to warrant serious study as a development of early Daoist philosophy.[10]

PHILOSOPHY OF THE *LIEZI*

A large proportion of the ideas has clear affinities with the philosophies of the *Laozi* and the *Zhuangzi*. The *Laozi* is sometimes quoted with approval, although the quotations are attributed either to the *Book of the Yellow Emperor* or to Lao Dan. Although the *Liezi* does not refer to the *Zhuangzi*, it shows many signs of influence from the latter. It thus clearly stands in the same tradition, deals with many of the same issues, and on occasion has almost identical passages. It continues the line of philosophical thinking of the *Xiao Yao You* and the *Qiu Shui*, developing the themes of transcending boundaries, spirit journeying, cultivation of equanimity, and acceptance of the vicissitudes of life. It also continues the line of thought of the *Yang Sheng Zhu* and the *Da Sheng*, about cultivating extreme subtlety of perception and extraordinary levels of skill.[11]

Unlike the *Laozi*, the *Liezi* displays little interest in critiquing the Ruists, and unlike the *Zhuangzi*, it contains no criticism of the "Ru-Mo"—the Ruists and Mohists. On the contrary, it shows signs of reconciliation of Ruist and Daoist ideas, and many Ruist principles are given Daoist interpretation.[12]

Like the *Zhuangzi*, it relies to a large extent on the methods of narrative and phenomenological exploration.[13] The text begins with themes from the *Zhuangzi* but develops them in interesting new directions. In particular, it takes the imaginative tendencies of the *Zhuangzi* to a new level, comparable with the Indian and central Asian imagination, referring to other realms of existence. There are also places where the philosophical logic draws closer to the explicitly metaphysical. This is very unusual for early Chinese thinking, which, as we have seen, remains thoroughly holistic and naturalistic, even when dealing with the most fundamental cosmological issues. As we shall see, the *Liezi* explicitly articulates concepts in a way that, more strongly than other Daoist texts, suggests metaphysical transcendence. The logic of complementary contrasts is also imbued with a new significance: the necessity of transcending the apparently opposing alternatives, which again suggests the possible influence of Indian philosophy, specifically through Buddhism.[14] This conjecture, however, is based on philosophical evidence alone. It is, of course, possible that this new direction of thought developed from entirely within the philosophical resources of the Chinese tradition.[15]

As I have argued earlier in this book, the early Chinese worldview ought for the most part to be thought of as naturalistic, holistic, processive, and pragmatist in spirit. That is to say, the world is understood as no more and no less than nature itself, a continuous whole consisting of natural processes that are interconnected through paths and cycles of mutual productiveness. We as humans are an integral part of this world, not set apart from our natural environment but produced by it, created and sustained by it as we ingest, transform, and interact with it according to our needs and purposes. All things in nature, especially in what a modern scientist would call the biosphere, are created, sustained, ingested, and transformed in similar ways: they arise from and create other things in complex cycles of interaction. Such a world is not seen as in need of any external explanation: it is understood in terms of the many things, which in turn are understood in terms of their relations to each other. Some aspects of worldly existence are understood to have a primal status—the *yin*, the ancestral, and *dao*—but, as we have seen, they are not posited as altogether outside the natural world, but are manifested as and within natural phenomena. Their primordial role is not that of external origins but innermost sources, located at the heart of things. The early Daoist texts are certainly concerned in some sense with the origins of things in the cosmos, but this concern presupposes the productive potency of the cosmos itself and does not require that it be explained. Such naturalistic descriptions of the structures and processes of the origination and completion of things are better described as cosmological than as metaphysical.[16] This is also true of other early texts concerned with originary phenomena. The *Yijing* (the *Book of Changes*) and the *Zhongyong*[17] are cosmological in the same way: the primal phenomena to which they appeal—the images 象 *xiang*, energy 氣 *qi*, the Genuine 誠 *cheng*[18]—remain deeply embedded, as it were, within the world.

Our ordinary concepts are pragmatic: that is, they play a role in making sense of our ordinary experiences. We seek explanations, to discover the truth about what is real, but always within a context of concern. Our practical knowledge claims, precisely because they are limited by our everyday contexts, are not intended to be absolute. They are not perfect or infallible. When we ask for explanations, there is always something we take for granted: the context within which the explanation can make sense. We seek to fit what we do not understand into a framework that we do not call into question: familiar knowledge and beliefs that we presuppose and that help us to make sense of the world around us. When we ask about an unusual-looking flower, for example, we might well accept as an explanation that it is a species of ginger from Micronesia. We don't usually need to follow up with "But what is ginger?" "What does it mean to be related to ginger?" "How do you know it is related to ginger?" "How do you know it really is native to Micronesia?" If we did continue to ask those other questions, that would lie within the context of new pragmatic concerns. Perhaps I have now become a botanist, and I wish to deepen my knowledge of plant species. If so, there will still be a context of familiar knowledge and beliefs in terms of which I understand the answers to my more detailed questions. This new context of knowledge must be accepted if I am to understand any answers at all.

But it is also possible to call this broader context into question. Perhaps I am a philosopher of science, wondering about the best method to encourage the growth of scientific knowledge. Now I can call into question presuppositions about the nature of scientific experiment and its relation to the objectivity of knowledge claims. This procedure of emerging out of a context to raise new questions in a broader context can be iterated indefinitely. But this also raises a new possibility: Is it possible to extricate oneself from all contexts, to find the ultimate of all explanations? That which explains absolutely everything, and does not presuppose anything itself? It is clear that if there could be such a thing, it cannot be contained within the world that we experience. If it were, it wouldn't be an ultimate explanation of absolutely everything but a foundational stratum within the natural world, precisely the sort of ancestral origin appealed to in the *Laozi* and the *Zhuangzi*. It would have a special status among natural phenomena that appears paradoxical in our attempts to understand it, but it would not be metaphysically transcendent in the strict sense.

As with the *Laozi* and *Zhuangzi*, the *Liezi* ponders the origins of things, but unlike the earlier texts, it begins to move from the cosmological to the metaphysical.[19] It takes up the search for the ancestral and seeks for ultimate origins, asks about the conditions of existence, production, and transformation. The earlier texts posit an ancestral wellspring that is not separate from the natural world. "*Tian Rui*" ("Cosmic Signs"), the first chapter of the *Liezi*, however, makes further inquiries about the world itself: does it have an origin that is distinct from the source of the many things? Does it have an end? Or is it the kind of thing to which such questions do not apply? By following these questions through, it attempts to explore the boundaries of our understanding of the possibilities of origination. It also pays closer attention to the resulting paradoxes and antinomies, not just noticing them and asserting them as mysteries, as in the *Laozi* and the *Zhuangzi*, but raising them as philosophical puzzles and pondering different possible theoretical responses.

CONCEPTS

The Unproduced[20]   *Busheng*   不生

There is the produced (*sheng* 生, the living, or existing), and the unproduced; there is transformation, and nontransformation (the unchanging). The unproduced is able to produced the produced (can generate the living); the nontransforming is able to transform the transformations. (17)

In the *Zhuangzi*, living is juxtaposed with dying, and their mutual blending into a single process is explored. They are two sides of a single function of organic transformation, *hua* 化, not only of the biosphere but of the whole natural world: the realm of things that are produced, develop, come to completion, and then disintegrate. In the first chapter of the *Liezi*,

"Cosmic Signs," a different contrast is developed, between *sheng* 生 and *busheng* 不生. These terms appear at first sight to be straightforward, but cause great problems for translation and philosophical interpretation. The term "*sheng*" refers not only to life and birth but also to the existing or enduring of all things, living and nonliving; to the processes of producing such things; and to the processes of their continuing to exist. The term "*busheng*" has several senses: "nonliving," "unborn," and "unproduced." When applied to nonbiological phenomena, it might be translated as "not existing." It cannot have the sense of "not producing" in this chapter, since it is defined not only as that which has the ability to produce but also as that which produces whatever exists.

In the *Liezi*, *hua* (化 transformation), although not actually separable from *sheng*, is referred to separately. While "*sheng*" refers to the enduring and production of things, "*hua*" refers to their transformation and the process of transforming them. Produced things have embodied form, *xing* 形, and observable qualities. "Whatever has features, likeness, sound, color, is a thing" (37). For a thing to be produced, to exist, is for it to be shaped, made tangible, colorful, and productive of sound.

Further, what life produces dies, and what has form must come to an end (*zhong* 終). However, living and dying, being formed and ending, constitute a constant and unceasing process of transformation. "The produced cannot be unproduced; the transforming cannot be untransformed: thus, they constantly (*chang* 常) produce and transform. What is constantly produced and transforms is never not produced, never does not transform" (17–18). Here, constancy is explicitly explained as having the meaning not just of regularity, as it does in the *Laozi* and *Zhuangzi*, but of presence at all times: "There is no time where there is no living or transforming."

But a distinction is made between these phenomena and what brings them about: "There is the produced, and what produces the produced; there is form, and that which forms form; there is sound, and that which sounds the sounds; there is color, and that which colors the color; there is flavor, and that which flavors the flavor" (20). This productive role is assigned to *busheng* and *buhua*, the unproduced and the untransforming. Each is singled out as that which produces its complement, *sheng* and *hua* respectively. "That which is unborn, *bushengzhe* 不生者, is able to produce the living; that which does not transform is able to transform the transforming"[21] (17).

In a move of profound logical significance, the text states that the unproduced does not itself have observable qualities: it sounds the sounds, but does not make a sound itself; it makes visible the visible, but is not visible itself:

> What the produced produces will die, but what produces the produced has not yet experienced ending. Whatever form forms becomes realized, but that which forms the forms has not yet experienced being there. Whatever sound sounds will be heard, but that which sounds the sounds has not yet been emitted. Whatever color colors will be patterned, but that which colors the colors has not yet experienced appearing. That which flavor flavors will be tasted, but that which flavors the flavors has not yet savored taking form. (20)

Incidentally, there is, of course, a logical problem with quantifying and identifying (and even referring to) what neither exists nor has qualities, so the text cannot explicitly identify the unproduced with the unformed, etc.; but for the same reason, it is even more problematic to take them to be different "things." The logical significance of this type of discourse is that it seems to be attempting to articulate a condition of the possibility of observable qualities which, as the very condition of their possibility, must itself lack those qualities. With this emphasis, one step is taken toward giving the unborn a transcendent status, but the move toward genuinely metaphysical transcendence remains incomplete so long as it is left unstated whether the living is able to produce the nonliving. If the productive power is mutual, then neither side is transcendent. Though the crucial step of explicitly denying the reverse is never articulated, it appears to be strongly implied. It seems that the *Liezi* text goes as far as possible in the attempt to develop the concept of the transcendent without taking the final step of explicitly asserting absolute asymmetry between producer and produced.

Note that it is not enough merely to deny symmetry between the two sides. As we have seen, the cosmologies of the *Laozi* and *Zhuangzi* both presuppose a mutual but asymmetric relation between *yin* and *yang*, and between *wu* and *you*. This sort of asymmetry merely establishes one side as of greater importance, as more central within the system; it does not establish one aspect of a duality as transcendent to an ontologically dependent system. What is required is an absolute asymmetry: one side must be absolutely dependent for its existence on the other side, and not vice versa. The *Liezi* seems insistently to imply this, but if the text stops short of asserting it explicitly, so should we.

However, an intriguing passage briefly refers to a concept that hints at the possibility of a deep asymmetry: *ben busheng* 本不生, the radically unproduced. The passage asserts that what has *sheng* must return to *busheng*, and what has form, *xing*, must return to the unformed, *buxing*. But the text then goes on to state, "The unproduced is not the *radically* unproduced (*ben busheng* 本不生); the unformed is not the *radically* unformed (*ben wuxing* 本無形)" (23). Unfortunately, however, this concept is not developed further, and may turn out to be inconsistent with the ontology as explicitly stated in the rest of the text. In the absence of further contextual explanation, it is hard to know the exact significance of this radical form of negation. But the text appears to be stating that in addition to the state of indeterminacy to which determinate things revert, there is something radically unproduced. Perhaps the point is that the *busheng* that has productive power is not the same as the empirical phenomenon of the indeterminately productive ground. Again, we have a gesture toward the possibility of transcendence, but insufficient confirming or disconfirming evidence to be sure.

Finally, in typical Daoist fashion, the text overturns our conception of what it means to exist. "When a form stirs, it produces not a form but a shadow. When a sound stirs, it produces not a sound, but an echo. When nothing stirs, it produces not nothing, but something!" (22). That is, what is produced by the movement of shape and sound is something less real, a shadow or an echo. In this way, the *Liezi* demotes the existence of the cosmos, likening its status to that of a shadow or echo. Between something and nothing, it is nothing that is given the more primordial and more real status. This ontological reversal can be seen again in the discussion of dreams and illusions.

Dreaming[22] *Meng* 梦

The concept of dreaming first appears with philosophical significance in chapter 2 of the *Zhuangzi*, the "*Qi Wu Lun*." The contrast between dreaming and waking is juxtaposed with the relationship between living and dying. The suggestion is made that the world of experience in which we play out our lives is not as real as we ordinarily believe, that it is comparable to a dream, and that our ceasing to exist might in fact be an awakening to a greater reality. But this "riddle" is not taken up again in the text. It is, however, taken up in chapter 3 of the *Liezi*, "King Mu of Zhou," where ontological and phenomenological issues are explored in greater depth, although always within the existential context of understanding the significance of living and dying.

How do we distinguish between dreaming and waking experience? According to philosophical realism, waking experience corresponds to an enduring external reality that is independent of our experience and is also experienced by others. Dream experience, on the other hand, is fleeting and private, a fabrication constructed from remembered and imagined experiences. Even the most vivid dream experience is not really of an independently existing world, though it may be based on experiences of an external world.

According to antirealism and idealism,[23] however, the world does not simply exist independently of us but is actively constructed by us, either through the mind or language or some other cognitively significant faculty. Any world we can understand must have significance, which must come from something capable of imbuing it with significance. Buddhist philosophy, with its empiricist roots, has a tendency toward idealism. This is developed extensively in Mahayana Buddhism, most notably in Yogacara philosophy. The philosopher Vasubandhu, for example, explicitly articulates arguments against the existence of an independent external world.[24] He tries to show how the world cannot be anything other than a mental construct: only in ignorance do we take the entities that we "project" to be independently real. According to such idealist philosophies, any world that can be made manifest to us must be understood in accordance with the structures of our understanding; indeed, the very notion of a world that is somehow independent of those structures would thereby have to be incomprehensible. That is, the very meaning of "independent existence" is itself a mode of understanding, so even the independent existence of objects is something we attribute to them. Insofar as we take this sort of independence to be objective, we are actually mistaken.

This is not to say that the world is not *real*. Neither antirealism nor idealism asserts that. Rather, the only reality we can know has to conform to the structures through which we are able to know it. Everything that we know as real must thereby be, at least in part, a construct. From this standpoint, the difference between waking and dreaming cannot be accounted for by appealing to an independent world, but only by distinguishing the ways in which the mind constructs objects from experience. Idealist philosophies thus blur the distinction between dreaming and waking experience, placing them along a spectrum of experiential possibilities. If all experience is a product of the constructive activity of the mind, the difference between waking and other types of experience—dreams and illusions, for example—might turn out to be a matter of degree rather than a radical difference in kind. The criteria for reality, for example, could not include independent existence, but would have to include degrees of consistency and continuity of experience.

The narratives in chapter 3, "King Mu of Zhou," play with other ways of structuring the relationship between waking and dream experience, but while deconstructing the distinction, they retain the terminology of "waking" and "dreaming." "The spirit encounters it and we dream; the body connects with it and it happens. Thus by day we imagine (*xiang* 想) and at night we dream" (67). Earlier, our waking experiences (*jue* 覺) were defined as what happens when the body connects with something (66). Here, we are informed that our waking experiences are imaginings; our sleep experiences are still called "dreams." But which we would interpret as *real* may largely be a matter of which we spend time in. If the dream world we experience in sleep outlasted our waking experience, then might we not take our dream experiences to be real and our waking experiences to be illusory? "At the South corner of the far West there is a country.... Its people sleep most of the time, without food or clothing; they awaken once in fifty days. They think that what they do in dreams is real, and what they see waking is absurd" (67). Waking up sporadically from a coma filled with consistent dream experience, for example, wouldn't we judge our waking experience to be less substantial? If antirealism is correct, the question must be an epistemological one: how do we tell the difference between waking and dreaming? Given certain types of experiences, some more consistent than others, or some shared with other people, we can only ask about the criteria through which we classify these; we cannot simply refer to a reality that is independent of our experiences to settle the question, since that involves making an epistemologically unjustified presupposition.[25]

The *Liezi* goes further, and considers other, still more baffling possibilities. What if dream experiences could be shared with people we know from waking experience?[26] Might we not conclude that the dream experience constituted a parallel reality? Furthermore, what if shared dream experiences could bleed over into the world of waking experience? The hypothesis seems barely coherent, yet it is not obvious why two such constructs could not overlap at some point.

It is notable that, unlike the Buddhist philosophical texts, the *Liezi* gives no arguments attempting to prove idealism or refute realism. It tries to persuade us to reconceive our worlds purely through narrative. As a rhetorical strategy, it is not very convincing: the narratives are too counterintuitive to be persuasive. Or perhaps it aims to do no more than engage our imaginations, in order to open us to the possibility of seeing the world as a construct and to encourage us to conceive of ways in which we might be able to reconstruct our experiences and thus re-create our world. One does not need a watertight argument to achieve this result.[27]

Phenomenal Construct[28]   *Huan*   幻

The term "*huan*" 幻 literally means "unreal" or "imaginary," and is used in Buddhist texts to translate the term "*maya*." It can be understood as expressing the idealist concept of an object as a construction (or "projection") of the mind. Dream objects may be thought of in this way as phenomenal constructs. In chapter 3, "King Mu of Zhou," it is stated that not only our dream experiences but everything that has form, exists, and changes is a construction of fantasy:

> "The energy of all that is produced, the appearance of all that has form, is *huan*.[29] What is begun by the creative transformations, and what is changed by *yinyang*, is called living and dying; the countless extensive changes, shifting and exchanging according to the form, are called transformations, or *huan*. . . . It is when you realize that the *huan* and transformations are no different from birth and death that we can begin to study *huan*. You and I are also *huan*; what need is there to study?" (65)

But if our ordinary experiences are also constructions, perhaps it ought to be possible to *re*construct our experiences; from an antirealist perspective, this would be tantamount to reconstructing our lives and our worlds. Such an ability to control the constructions is referred to as "*hua*" 化, the ability to "transform" things by transforming how people perceive things. "In the time of King Mu of Zhou, there came from a country in the far west a person with the power of transformation . . . the thousands and myriads of ways in which he altered and transformed things could not be exhausted. He not only altered the observable forms of things, he also changed the mental activity of people" (61). If we can understand how things are phenomenally constructed, it is possible that we might be able to gain control of the process of construction. If things are what we make of them, then what something is is a matter of the significance we bestow upon it. In the last story of the chapter, a man is tricked into seeing the wrong city as his homeland and the wrong grave as his father's grave. He imbues these places with deep significance and is filled with a sense of reverence and nostalgia for his homeland. In an important sense, the foreign land has become his hometown and the stranger's grave has become that of his father. This place and this grave now have this significance because he has bestowed it upon them. After all, what makes things significant is not the mere physical facts and objects, but the meaning with which we invest them. When he finally sees his actual homeland and his father's actual grave, they no longer have the power to overwhelm him. He has distanced himself emotionally from the constructs and thereby gained the ability to re-create them anywhere. Any city can be his homeland; any grave can be his father's grave. And they can hold as much or as little power over his emotions as he allows.

If the world is in part a phenomenal construct, and it is possible to reconstruct it, then it might, at least theoretically, be possible to *de*construct it. Like Buddhist idealism, the *Liezi* does not take the structures through which we ordinarily understand things to be fixed necessary conditions; on the contrary, it emphasizes their contingency and dispensability. The journeying upward and outward explored in the *Zhuangzi* is taken up with an additional significance. In the *Liezi*, spirit journeying, *shenyou* 神游, seems to function in part as a metaphor for "phenomenological explorations" in which we progressively undo the structures through which we understand things. We deconstruct our understandings of spatial relations, temporal relations, and the functions of things, and thereby rise beyond the definition and confines of the ordinary. This is comparable to Zhuangzi's highest understanding of the ancients.[30]

One clue to understanding how such deconstruction of the phenomena of experience might be possible is to recognize the role of memory in their construction. At the most fundamental level, awareness of any thing, process, or event must be sustained from the past through to the present.[31]

Without a minimal sustained awareness, we have only a fleeting series of impressions. On an existential level too, our lives can only form a narrative in relation to a history of events: who we are is built on our past; our lives are given meaning through past events. If the past is forgotten, we lose our understanding of events, and our lives lose what gives them significance. Indeed, in the absence of memory altogether, there is no "one" to whom the life belongs. The tale of the amnesiac, Huazi of Yangli, shows how these constructed significances also affect our emotions. If we continuously forget what has happened, no event can hold any power over our emotional states. "'Formerly, when I forgot,' said Huazi, 'I was boundless; I was oblivious to what was present or absent in the whole cosmos. Now suddenly I remember; and all the disasters and recoveries, gains and losses, joys and sorrows, loves and hates of the past several decades have risen up in a thousand tangled threads'" (71). So long as we remember possessing nothing and being attached to no one, we cannot experience loss; if we remember no grievances, we cannot hate anyone. The state of the thoroughgoing amnesiac appears to be a state of uninterrupted tranquility.[32] Without memory things can have no value, and can have no claim on our emotions. The possibility of such a condition strikes us with dread, but according to the *Liezi*, the sage understands its deeper value.

Whether more radical deconstruction than this is possible, we can imagine, at least theoretically, that the less we synthesize our experiences, the less familiar and stranger constructs would become. Phenomena would become increasingly vague, with unclear boundaries and less than full stability. Perhaps the insubstantial flux of experience would become more prominent as objectification decreases, though in the absence of contrasting stability it would not be recognizable as "flux." The process is gestured at in the story of King Mu of Zhou:

> Not long afterward [the man with the power of transformation, *huaren* 化人] called on the king to join him on an excursion. . . . They soared upward and did not stop until they were in the middle sky. They came to the palace of the *huaren*. . . . It emerged above the clouds and rain, and one could not tell what supported it below. To gaze upon, it was like a cumulus cloud. All that the eye observed and the ear listened to, the nose inhaled and the tongue tasted, were things not to be found in the human world. (62)

The phenomenological dwelling place (the palace) is described as floating, in the process of integrating, but not yet fully integrated: it lacks solid foundations, yet is able somehow to cohere. In comparison, the things of ordinary experience seem crude, heavy, and ugly, while the phenomena that manifest in a more primordial manner seem more refined. Sights, sounds, colors seem more ephemeral, more beautiful than in ordinary human experience, and at the same time become increasingly hard to comprehend. Phenomenologically, the passage of time does not feel different; but as in waking from a dream, one knows that it has passed differently only when one returns to one's former state and measures the time elapsed. But to complete the process of deconstruction would take us into the realm of complete disorder, noise, and incomprehension. Such a point of view, if practically possible, would be neither bearable nor sustainable for a human being.

> When it seemed to the king that he had lived there for several decades . . . the *huaren* again called upon him to join him on an excursion. They came to a place where they could not see the sun and moon above them, nor the rivers and seas below them. Lights and shadows glared, till the king's eyes were dazzled and he was not able to maintain his sight; noises echoed toward them, till the king's ears were disoriented and he was not able to maintain his hearing. (62–63)

King Mu begs to return to the ordinary realm. When he does, he realizes that what appeared to be decades in the other realm passed in a mere instant— "the wine had not yet cooled, the meats had not yet gone dry"—and he is informed that, since he traveled not physically but phenomenologically, he inhabited two worlds simultaneously. The *huaren* explains, "Your majesty has been with me on an exploration of the spirit. Why should your body have moved?" (63).

One might think that in such a view all possible constructions are given equal value, as with dreaming and waking experience. However, the *Liezi* does not seem to equalize them. Deconstruction and forgetting appear to be given the highest value; the simpler the world we inhabit, the more harmonious our responsiveness to it, the more we are able to live in tranquil affinity with the cosmos. Reconstruction is valued insofar as it brings us closer to an appreciation of the role of construction in our experience of ourselves and our worlds, and thereby closer to an ability to deconstruct it.

Infinite and Infinitesimal[33]   *Wuji, Wujin*   無極,無盡

The first chapter of the *Zhuangzi* raises the question of the relation between the vast, *da* 大, and the petty, *xiao* 小, and appeals to a text called "The Questions of Tang." Chapter 5 of the *Liezi*, which has precisely that name, also questions the relation between *da* and *xiao*. Here the questions are phrased in terms of the limits of space and time, and like chapter 1, "Cosmic Signs," attempt to reorient us toward the possibility of something altogether beyond. The issue of space is raised in terms of containment, *han* 含: spaces contain smaller spaces, like nested boxes.

> Thus, there are inexhaustible and endless relations of containment between the greater (*da*) and the lesser (*xiao*). Just as it contains the myriad things, so (something) contains the cosmos. Containing the myriad things is indeed limitless; containing the cosmos is also indeed endless. How do I know that enclosing [each] cosmos is not another cosmos? (96)

The question of time is raised in terms of temporal priority, or what came before, *xian* 先, and again echoing chapter 1, in terms of beginnings, *shi* 始, and ends, *zhong* 終. The Shang emperor Tang asks whether in the process of expansion one reaches the outer extremes, *ji* 極, and whether the process of contraction is exhaustible, *jin* 盡 (94). The concept of limitless (*wuji*) expansion appears to be a formulation of the concept of the infinite; conversely, the process of inexhaustible (*wujin*) contraction appears to be a formulation of the infinitesimal.

Emperor Tang asks Xia Ji whether at the ancient beginning there were things. Xia Ji replies, "If at the ancient beginning there were no things, how could there be things now?" Tang continues: "In that case, do things have no before and after?" Xia Ji replies, "The ending and starting of things have no limit from which they began. The start of one is the end of another, the end of one is the start of another" (94).

Rather than a fixed "before and after," beginnings and ends continuously give way to each other. There is only a natural temporal whole, a continuous, unbounded, organic process with no initial beginning and no final end. So far, this is the familiar cosmological view we have encountered in the *Laozi* and the *Zhuangzi*. "But," Xia Ji continues, "what lies beyond (*wai* 外)

things, and before events, I do not know." It appears that the whole world of things and events is now reified, and the question of what lies outside and before is asked about the whole itself. Is there something that is outside all things? Perhaps the reference is to some ultimate transcendent that is utterly beyond, *wai* 外, the natural world, containing it absolutely as though it were a thing. Comparing this with chapter 1, where the concept of a radically productive Unproduced is hinted at, one might expect Xia Ji to posit something atemporal as the condition of the production of the temporal cycles of transformation. However, the answer he gives is the epistemically modest, "I don't know." Still, the two answers are not incompatible. That is, a primordial beginning before all beginnings is something absolutely outside of the realm of the knowable. The limits of containment of the world are the limits beyond which we cannot understand. The statement of ignorance regarding what lies outside the temporal cycle *might* thus be construed more strongly as implying the unknowability of such things.

The discussion is also applied to space. Can the process of expanding outward be continued indefinitely? Is there no limit to expansion? At first, Xia Ji gives the familiar answer that he does not know, but when pressed, responds more cryptically: "Nothing, *wu* 無, is limitless; something is exhaustible."[34] It seems that a contrast is being made between what is limited and the unlimited "nothing" from which it arises. Even though the cycles of arising and falling, living and dying, exchange endlessly, what exists, *you*, is finite. But what cannot be used up is the limitless source from which all things continuously flow. *Wu*, nothing, is the condition of the possibility of the arising of the many things. If things have boundaries and limitations, the absence of boundaries and limitations would have to be no thing.

But this passage also seems to hint at a notion of the transfinite: higher orders of infinity. "Beyond (*wai* 外) the limitless is another limitless nothing; within the inexhaustible is another inexhaustible nothing." In chapter 17 of the *Zhuangzi*, "Qiu Shui," "Autumn Floods," the notion of the infinite is first mentioned, and is characterized as that which is neither increased when added to nor decreased when subtracted from (176). However, the possibility raised here in the *Liezi* suggests that there might be an unlimited that is in some sense greater than the infinite: a higher-order infinity. If the many things are contained in the vastness of the cosmos, then perhaps the cosmos itself is contained in a higher-order vastness. Beyond the unlimited nothing, *wu*, that contains the world, there may well be a higher order of unlimited nothing in which it is contained, and so on. This is reminiscent of nineteenth-century German mathematician Georg Cantor's concept of 'transfinite' numbers. Cantor discovered that if infinite sets are compared with one another, some are actually larger than others: the set of integers is infinite, but it is only a subset of the rational numbers, which in turn is only a subset of the real numbers. The size of the infinity is called its "cardinality," and if thought of as a number, is said to be transfinite. One cannot, of course, simply equate the two since the mathematical tools for the precise articulation of the full concept were not to be become available for at least another fifteen hundred years. Xia Ji raises the possibility of this intriguing notion, but appears to maintain a stalwart agnosticism.

Sameness and Difference[35]   *Tongyi*   同異

The process of expanding beyond the realms of familiarity brings with it both theoretical and pragmatic questions regarding the same, *tong* 同, and the different, *yi* 異. Emperor Tang wonders what there is outside the four seas (96). Do things become increasingly different, or are they all the same? The first answer Xia Ji gives is that things are similar (*you* 猶)[36] to the central regions. Tang then asks how he would verify that. After all, Xia Ji did not experience all things everywhere. His response is reminiscent of Mozi's epistemology: "I have traveled East as far as Ying; the people were like here. When I asked what lay East of Ying, it was again like Ying. . . . This is how I know that the four . . . limits are no different from here." That is, knowledge through observation, testimony, and inductive inference justifies the claim that things everywhere are similar. He observes similarities in contiguous regions, and relies on the testimony of others to learn of similarities beyond his experience. He then infers the similarity of the places he has experienced with the places he has not. If the places in the far east are the same as in the east, and the places in the east are the same as here, it follows from the transitivity of sameness that the places in the far east are the same as here. Iterating the procedure, he draws the tempting inductive inference that no matter how many times the process is repeated, the places at the furthest extremes will be the same as here.

However, this response is problematic for three reasons. First, assuming that iterating the procedure will yield the same results everywhere simply begs the question. Second, while exact sameness is a transitive relation, similarity is not. Consider the color spectrum: any small segment is similar to its immediately neighboring segments, but the similarity decreases the farther away the segments lie. Yellow and leaf green are similar; leaf green and deep green are similar; deep green and turquoise are similar. But the farther along the spectrum we travel, the less like our starting point the color becomes. By the time we reach turquoise, the similarity to yellow has vanished. It is true that they are both colors on a spectrum, but the similarity shared between yellow and leaf green is not shared with turquoise: similarity is not transitive. Third, all things may be seen as similar or different in some respect. From the perspective of a city lover, the hills and valleys are equally rustic; to a nature lover, they are entirely different kinds of terrain. To a layperson, liver and gall are equally physiological organs; from the perspective of a hepatologist, they perform dramatically different functions.

If Xia Ji and his interlocutors report similarities, perhaps it is because the cognitive capacities of creatures are primed to seek out similarities when encountering differences. To understand something is, in part, to recognize what it is like, to have identified some similarities with something else that one knows. Understanding presupposes classification of similar things, events, or qualities. What we understand, what we recognize, lies within the boundaries of familiarity that are set, at least in part, by such classifications. When we know how to classify something new, we have some basis on which to deal with it. When we encounter new kinds of phenomena, creatures, people, or cultures, we may at first be struck by their strangeness. To increase understanding, we must emphasize what we recognize: they all smile, they are born, they have mothers, they eat, they cry, they have purposes, they are creative. We feel most comfortable when we find universal characteristics. We also quickly interpret their cultural phenomena in terms familiar to us: their food, their families, their art, their social institutions, must surely all correspond to our own; to understand theirs, we need only find the equivalent in ours; and to the extent that there are differences, they can be nothing more than superficial variations. But this tendency to assume universality, though a necessary first step, is a little too easy, and if combined with the assumption that all difference must be shallow, is faulty. Cultural phenomena that seem alike on the surface might in fact have hidden structures, purposes, and significances that are vastly different. Moreover, such differences might combine and accumulate. To the extent that we fail to recognize their significance, we fail to understand the other phenomena.

And yet, understanding is at its heart the identification of similarities: to the extent that differences can be understood, they too must be recognized and classified according to what we understand. That is, even differences must be approached in terms of similarities: similar differences enable us to classify similar subspecies of phenomena. It follows that differences that have no ready equivalent create problems for understanding, and the accumulation of such deep differences creates *aporias*, phenomena that seem to evade our efforts to understand and classify them. When confronted in such a way with radically deep difference, there are two basic types of response, depending on our ability to process difference. We may see only what we are capable of recognizing and deny the very possibility of any deep difference; or we may acknowledge on some level the presence of an obstacle to understanding, an *aporia*, and continue to struggle to interpret and reinterpret the phenomena that never quite match our presuppositions.

Even when acknowledging the existence of deep differences, there are three types of response. First, we may exclude them as unacceptable insofar as they fail to conform to our expectations of normality. Second, we may other them and exoticize them, treating them as weird and wonderful forms of entertainment. The third response is found throughout the rest of the chapter: diversity is neither to be marveled at nor rejected, but to be accepted without judgment. We realize that what we ourselves take to be normal is just one among many possible variations equally embraced by the cosmos. Broadmindedness and tolerance of difference arise with increased experience of the world, and are antidotes to the imperialist tendency to absolutize our own personal preferences. However, there are again two possibilities: a moderate pluralism, in which many alternatives are accepted, and an extreme relativism, in which no negative judgment is ever allowed and absolutely everything is accepted. This radical relativism insists that no alternative system, no alternative culture, can ever be judged to be bad. Since cultures provide their own standards of judgment, it makes no sense to say of another culture that the standards it uses are themselves bad. We see the beginnings of this possibility in two of the examples that Liezi provides: the people who eat their firstborn and those who abandon their grandmothers. We are told, "These are what their superiors call governing, and what those below take to be custom. There is no need to consider them strange" (104). Initially, this might seem necessary to enable diversity to flourish, but on further reflection it will only end up undermining the very possibility of such flourishing, because of internal inconsistency. It will be powerless, for example, to oppose the most violent forms of intolerance, since it is ideologically committed to accepting and defending them.[37]

Circumstance[38]   *Ming*   命

The problem of difference within sameness, when applied existentially, leads to meditations on the vicissitudes of life and differences in fortune. Two people can apparently be the same in all relevant respects, and yet one of them live long and the other die young, or one be successful while the other lives in dire straits. Beigongzi and Ximenzi were from the same clan, alike in age, appearance, ideas, and actions. Yet, where Ximenzi succeeded, Beigongzi invariably failed. Master Dongguo attributes this difference to cosmic circumstance, outside of human control. He says to Ximenzi, "Beigongzi is rich in potency, but not favored by Circumstance; you are favored by Circumstance, but lacking in potency. But your success is not due to wisdom, nor is his failure due to foolishness. It is all *tian*, not *ren*" (122–23).

The last three chapters provide different approaches to this problem: chapter 6 has a stoic approach like that of the *Inner Chapters*; chapter 7 advocates a form of hedonism, in stark contrast to other Daoist writings; chapter 8 renounces the anti-intellectualism of the Utopian and mystical Daoists and promotes furthering knowledge through reflection and observation in order to understand and deal successfully with such variable circumstances.

Chapter 6, "*Li Ming*" ("Effort and Circumstance"), and chapter 8, "*Shuo Fu*" ("Explaining Conjunctions"), inquire into what, if anything, determines this difference. They provide answers that are dramatically different, in places diametrically opposed. According to chapter 6, experience shows that the difference cannot be determined by effort, *li* 力, since there are those who are diligent and yet die young or never succeed, while others who are contemptuous of effort become rich and powerful and live long, healthy lives. Even if those who put in greater effort have greater virtue, *de* 德, it is still not sufficient to guarantee success. Circumstance said to Effort:

> "If all this were within the reach of your effort, why would you make one live long and the others die young, why would you make the sage destitute and the unscrupulous eminent . . . ?" [Effort replied,] "If it is as you say, then I certainly have no effect on things. But that things

are so, is it you who controls them?" Circumstance answered, "Since we call it 'Circumstance,' how can there be anything that controls it? I push it straight, but let go and it twists and turns. Long life and short, destitution and eminence, high rank and low, wealth and poverty, bring themselves about." (121–22)

It seems that a thorough examination of cases of success and failure, health and illness, long life and short can never find any determining factor. The difference is simply that of circumstance, *ming* 命.

Two possibilities exist: either there are reasons or there are none. If there are none, then the difference is random and therefore unpredictable. That is, the difference in outcome is just the way things happen to be. It is just so of itself, without any further reason for its being so.[39] In this case, it is not that circumstance controls, *zhi* 制, or determines the outcomes of things; rather, *ming* is simply a way of referring to any and all circumstances that lie beyond our control. Alternatively, it may be that there are reasons why things turn out the way they do but that they are beyond our capacity either to discover or to understand. That is, the difference may lie in external circumstances about which we have no knowledge,[40] or in the firmly entrenched patterns that make things what they are: *guran zhi li* 固然之理, or perhaps, the reasons why things are the way they are (123). In several passages, the text suggests that this applies universally to all circumstances, even those that we think we have the ability to bring about. In fact, these passages suggest a radical form of determinism, according to which things are never the result of human ability, *neng* 能, or human effort; we are always simply unable not to do, *bude bu* 不得不, what nature or the cosmos, *tian*, inevitably brings about.[41]

It is only when we are able to accept this, to trust circumstance, *xinming* 信命, and the natural tendencies, *xinxing* 信性 (130), and to understand and accept the times, *zhishi* 知時, *anshi* 安時 (132), that we can live in tranquility. Only when we realize that things have their limits beyond which no action can affect them are we able to accept them for what they are. We are then able to appreciate all events of our lives as successes, a simple life as noble, and whatever lifespan turns out to be ours as a full life. Chapter 7, "*Yang Zhu*," draws the simplistic conclusion that if virtuous effort cannot ensure social success, we should live with abandon, maximizing our pleasure before we die. "What are humans to live for, to delight in? In beauty, riches, and sensual pleasures" (139). "The people of old understood the transience of life and death. So they acted following their hearts, and did not resist whatever fancies happened to arise" (140). In advocating hedonism, however, the chapter presupposes that maximizing pleasure lies within reach of our abilities. This is because the satisfaction of desires is immediate: we do not have to wait to see whether we have been successful. However, although specific desires can be immediately satisfied, we cannot be sure whether refraining from satisfying them immediately will not bring about greater pleasure in the long run. This is Xunzi's argument in favor of regulating desires. The "*Yang Zhu*" chapter remains philosophically weak so long as this argument is unanswered.

Whether there are no reasons, external reasons, or internal tendencies that account for the variability of comparable lives, the assumption in chapter 6 is that the outcome lies beyond our capacity to predict and control. Chapter 8, however, contradicts this directly, and in doing so moves Daoist thought in a dramatically new direction from the mystical or anti-intellectual tendencies of much of the *Zhuangzi*, and of chapter 6 of the *Liezi*. Success is attainable by the wise: those who understand how things happen. "Therefore, the sages watch the emerging to understand how it goes back in; observe what has passed to understand what will come. This is the pattern by which they know in advance" (159). Only those who observe carefully how things arise are able to understand how they will end up. Moreover, success and failure are only judged well after all processes have worked themselves out: an early success may result in a later tragedy, and vice versa. The correct judgment is the final one in which all earlier events are given their long-term significance (168–69). Again, such knowledge may be beyond ordinary people, but it is not beyond the capacities of the wise. This does not mean that there are universally applicable rules.[42] "In the world there are no patterns that are always right, no affairs that are always wrong. What worked before we now set aside, and what now works we will later abandon. There is no fixed judgment regarding whether it can be applied" (163). In these cases, judgments can only be made contextually: any rule regarding behavior that will lead to success will have exceptions depending on the details of the circumstances, and no one can predict all possible differences in the details. At best, the wisest people will have extensive personal experience, innate intelligence, and access to a vast array of past cases and their outcomes.

CHAPTER SEVEN

Philosophy of Skill in the *Zhuangzi* and *Liezi*

Those who understand what nature does, and who understand what humans do, have reached the pinnacle. Understanding what nature does, they live with nature. Understanding what humans do, they use what understanding understands to nurture what it does not understand, and fulfill their natural years without being cut off midway—this is the flourishing of understanding. (77)

We flourish best when we are able to foster our health and well-being, so that our lifespans may reach their fullest natural completion. We live wisely when we are able to cope skillfully with circumstances. From the perspective of ordinary people, the most accomplished sage might seem to have superhuman or even inhuman abilities. According to the Daoists, in following the path of artifice we have neglected a significant range of natural abilities and allowed them to atrophy; only by cultivating the potential with which we are endowed by nature can we overcome such limitations. Moreover, to deal successfully with the circumstances of life, we need also to understand the propensities of things. We must at the very least pay attention to how natural processes, both environmental and internal, develop. Thus, Daoists often retired from the cities and retreated either to the periphery of social life or into the mountains, where they could learn from nature, the "great ancestral teacher," reflect inwardly, and cultivate their natural potential.

A contemporary reader brought up on the pseudo-philosophy of popular wildlife documentaries might well interpret the claim that a good life is a natural life as entailing a form of predatory survivalism. Lions and wolves hunt in packs: creatures sustain their own lives at the expense of others. Those lower on the food chain live in fear, and those above maintain their status through violence. People who have such a view may find it hard to shake, but this idea of nature as wild, predatory, and brutal is certainly not universal. Chinese conceptions of nature, and Daoist conceptions in particular, have not generally been so bloody.[1] It is not that the philosophers were naïvely unaware of the aggression of much of the animal kingdom, but that they focused on those aspects that had the capacity to promote harmonious flourishing. If our goal is to learn how to flourish in harmony with our natural environment, then we must be highly selective about what we choose to model ourselves on.

Now, what is life promoting and health promoting is creature and context specific: fish live underwater, birds nest in trees. Neither of these would be taken by a Daoist as a model for human life. The guiding question, "What promotes the healthiest and most harmonious mode of flourishing?" comes from a human point of view, and even though the sage rises beyond this perspective, the question never completely loses its human orientation and significance. We reflect on processes that may provide a positive model for human flourishing while minimally interfering with the natural environment—those that promote life and health and that are maximally symbiotic. Death and illness also have an essential role to play in nature, and even disharmony cannot be completely eliminated, despite the claims of the Utopian idealists. Thus, while we should not seek to promote them, flourishing in harmony with nature requires that we also make our peace with these aspects of the natural world.

In this way, the Daoists advocated learning from natural phenomena, not as static objects, but through their movements, their tendencies, their interactions and transformations.[2] We observe the properties and behavior of the soil and the terrain, and also the effects of time, the seasons and cycles of change; we pay close attention to the fluidity of water, the power of the wind, the air and breath. The Daoist emphasis on *yin* also draws our attention to the value of what is ordinarily devalued: the rigidity of a branch might be a weakness, for example, or the insubstantiality of the wind and the softness of water may be their strengths.

To study nature is also to observe vegetative processes, and to the extent we learn from animals, it is their movement, balance, and dexterity, their ability to withstand hardship and interact harmoniously, that we are to reflect on. Having recognized those structures that are available to observation and reflection, we attempt to internalize and embody them through our natural imitative abilities. We especially pay attention to the biological processes of production, living, decaying, and dying, to the extent that these may be accessible to observation and reflection unaided by technological devices. Natural flourishing is manifested physically in health, emotional well-being, and longevity, so we should observe the interactions with our environment, the efficacy of the manner in which we move and breathe, and the effects of the ingestion of foods, water, herbs, and medicines on our physical and mental well-being. Most importantly, we should not just describe, but directly imitate and embody those processes and modes of behavior and interaction that lead to health, tranquility, and longevity.[3]

KNOWING: NATURAL ABILITY
AND LINGUISTIC ARTIFICE

While humans inhabit a cultural world of language, artifice, and explicitly articulated knowledge, the rest of the natural world does not do so to the same degree. Nature does not control the seasons or command the weather: the rain does not know how to fall, and a seed does not know how to grow. Humans, of course, also have natural abilities and natural modes of activity: besides talking, writing, ordering, and constructing devices, we also breathe, walk, observe, move, and express our emotions. Indeed, the first group of abilities depends on the second: we could not talk, write, or construct things if we were unable to observe and move. From a Western philosophical perspective, these two modes of activity may be understood in terms of different modes of knowledge: verbal and embodied.

In the mid-twentieth century, Gilbert Ryle distinguished between "knowing that" and "knowing how."[4] The first is explicit, cognitive knowledge, the content of which may be expressed verbally as the "that" clause of a sentence attributing knowledge to a knower. I know that the Sun is approximately ninety-three million miles from the Earth. I know that my neighbor can ride a unicycle. The sentences, "The Sun is ninety-three million miles from the Earth," and "My neighbor can ride a unicycle," constitute the content of my knowledge. Knowing how, on the other hand, is essentially nonlinguistic. "Know-how" refers to what we are able to do without being able to explain it verbally. While we can pass on cognitive knowledge simply by communicating the content of the "that" clause, no amount of verbal description can ever pass on know-how. I can tell you that my neighbor can ride a unicycle, and you thereby immediate acquire the same piece of information. But while my neighbor can attempt to describe in great detail how to balance and control a unicycle, no amount of description will by itself result in your being able to balance and control one. Whatever is communicated in the verbal description, it is not the know-how itself.

There are strains of Daoism in the *Zhuangzi* and the *Liezi* that are dismissive of the capacity for and the necessity of verbally expressible knowledge. While humans dwell in language, speaking, cogitating, writing, commanding, advising, and strategizing, nature does not. Natural phenomena do not follow verbal instructions in order to flourish. Nature functions nonverbally, *buyan* 不言, and in the most subtle and complex ways that often cannot straightforwardly be captured by ordinary language.[5] Natural forces are also *wuwei*: they simply come into play without taking deliberate control, and natural phenomena do not always know what they do. Moreover, even when natural creatures know what they do, they do not necessarily know how or why they do what they do. Although we may seek to increase our understanding of how phenomena occur, observe the manner in which they arise, develop, and fall, at the most fundamental level we eventually must resort to accepting that that is simply how they are, *ming* 命. We place our trust in the fact that they have the natural capacity to flourish without our understanding why.

In chapter 13 of the *Zhuangzi*, "The Way of Nature," Wheelwright Bian chides Lord Huan for wasting his time reading the words of the ancient sages (152). The words are the mere dregs of a once living skill and simply cannot contain the abilities they attempt to describe. In the preceding passage,

Zhuangzi says, "Writing does not go beyond speech: speech has value, and what is of value in speech is the idea; the idea has what it follows, but what it follows cannot be transmitted with words" (152). Applying Ryle's distinction, it appears that Bian is thinking of the knowledge or wisdom that Lord Huan seeks as a kind of know-how, comparable to his own excellence in making wheels: just as Bian cannot capture it in a theory of woodworking and pass it down to his son, so wisdom cannot be passed on with words.

What is at stake here is the extent to which the skill can be verbalized. The most Bian can say is, "Not too slow or loose, or the chisel won't catch; not too fast or tight, or it will slip" (152–53). Certainly these words communicate something, but it is so vague that the actual knack, the artistry that they are attempting to convey, remains elusive. The actual meaning of this utterance—exactly how much is just right—can only be gained from extensive experience. The words "tight" and "loose" can only be useful in a context in which specific embodied examples have already been used to delimit the meanings of the terms. The instruction presupposes this prior training: it cannot convey the knowledge by itself.

To be fair, there are other kinds of instruction that can capture basic practical knowledge. The kind of "procedural" knowledge contained in instruction manuals, for example, can indeed be put into words: "Hold the handle and push." True, the sentences require some experience, if only to understand what the terms refer to, but since even the crudest application of such instructions will succeed, they do not require extensive experience with the skill itself. A skill that requires artistry, however, can only be taught by demonstration and learned by imitation. A gifted few may seem to have a natural aptitude, but most people can acquire and perfect it only through years of direct experience. The expert can surely guide the apprentice, but whether the apprentice achieves artistry cannot be assured through instruction alone.

Some Daoist writers express a suspicion of all planning and conscious activity: successful activity is always spontaneous; knowledge and cogitation are always irrelevant to success. This extreme dogmatic view, typical of chapter 22, "Knowledge Wandered North," and the fatalist voice in chapter 6 of the *Liezi*, has no real justification. Sometimes verbal instruction and conscious deliberation and control are necessary for the most skillful activity. We cannot always accomplish our goals simply by responding: though improvising and extemporizing sometimes work, they are not always successful. Understanding a situation theoretically in advance often enables us to anticipate possible problems and to narrow down the best courses of action. In fact, there are times when regulated behavior (that can be described verbally) is essential to success.[6]

Indeed, even in the teaching of the highest levels of physical skill, words can express more than Bian will allow. A great music teacher or sports coach does not only teach by example. They can often find the right similes, images, and metaphors to convey a subtle sense for which literal description proves insufficient: "Drop like a hammer," "The sound should trickle," "Imagine stepping on a sheet of thin ice." A deftly chosen image can sometimes obviate weeks of frustrating practice.

There is a sense in which the Daoists were also demonstrably wrong about the capacity of verbally expressible knowledge to describe the inner workings of natural phenomena. It is true that at some point we must resort to an acknowledgment of the contingency of things—"That is just how they are"—but over the last few centuries that point has retreated and continues to retreat as we peer deeper into the inner workings of things. Modern science has constructed complex mathematical theories describing their behavior, enabling us to explain, predict, and thereby control their development. We even have theories describing the behavior of subatomic particles, and we have created apparatuses capable of manipulating and recording events at a subatomic level. We have theories describing the objects and events at the farthest reaches of space and perhaps the earliest moments of time, and have constructed telescopic devices that enable us to witness them. Genetics, the theory of evolution, neuroscience, and biochemistry have enabled us to understand and even modify the intricate physical mechanisms associated with life and consciousness. The list of sciences goes on and the increase of knowledge and technological proficiency proceeds exponentially.[7] This is not to say that these theories are perfect as they stand, or that there are no problems with their practical and ethical application. But if the Daoist claim was ever that such forms of knowledge and practice are impossible, then it has been proven empirically to be mistaken. Indeed, the success of science and technology is based on the very techniques criticized by the Daoists— explicit verbal description, and technological manipulation in accordance with human desires.

This, of course, is certainly not an inexcusable mistake. After all, the scientific method that would eventually enable us to do precisely what was previously considered impossible, or relegated to the realm of magic, was not formulated until two thousand years later. The Daoists, however, were right that this kind of knowledge could not be achieved through the methods of observation and the language that were available at the time. More importantly, they were also right insofar as precise knowledge or verbal descriptions are neither relevant nor efficacious for excelling at certain kinds of physical practices. A skilled archer does not need to know how the eyes or muscles work, or the formulae for computing the flight of the arrow in fluctuating environmental conditions, in order to excel at archery: there is no necessary connection between the possession of such knowledge and the achievement of consummate skill. Moreover, our natural physical dexterity *cannot* follow from an intellectual understanding of precise mathematical formulae. We simply lack the means to apply such formulae in our actions: we would need to be able to accurately distinguish measurements and rates of change that lie far beneath our thresholds of conscious discernibility. Our embodied knowledge is honed through trial and error, the tacit processing and coordination of sensory and proprioceptive input. Bian's basic claim that the content of a verbal proposition cannot transmit expertise remains correct. The skill can be conveyed only by experiment with actual movements, which the teacher then attempts to correct and adjust (by manipulation, further exemplary practice, or more insightfully chosen analogies and metaphors). Without the embodied practice, no amount of words can impart the skill to the student—except by lucky accident.

Furthermore, the suspicions and fears of the utopian Daoists regarding the consequences of a way of life based on measuring and controlling are currently being corroborated. While the efficacy of modern technology cannot be denied, the problems inherent in attempting to control nature are becoming increasingly evident. One can only unconditionally celebrate the course of progress while remaining stubbornly blind to the problems it is causing. Waste piles so large they must be shipped to other countries, acid rain, nuclear contamination, depletion of the ozone layer, oceans filled with mercury, artificially accelerated climate change: the resulting damage to the life and health of humans, animals, and the environment is escalating faster than our attempts to gain control of it.

TERMINOLOGY

While both the *Zhuangzi* and the *Liezi* contain stories praising people who have consummate levels of expertise, adeptness, or artistry, neither resorts to consistent terminology to name what they admire and what they criticize. Some skillful characters claim to have an art, *shu* 術, or a way, *dao* 道, while others deny it. Butcher Ding denies having a mere technique, *ji* 技, and to make matters worse, the term *qiao* 巧, which approximates the English word "skill," has negative connotations of contrivance, trickery, and craftiness. The Daoist authors are careful to distinguish the sort of skill that manifests an embodiment of *dao* from a more superficial technical dexterity. Thus, some types or aspects of skill are admired, while others are belittled. The skill that the Daoists praise is intuitive, natural, fluid, and of the sort that is essentially nonverbal. It involves the ability to sense, interpret, and respond to the subtle tendencies of the phenomena one is engaged with, subtle differences that lie beneath the threshold of ordinary perception and description.

The modes of skillful action that are most highly valued are *shu* (an art) and *dao* (a way). The heights of achievement in skillful action may be called "mastery," "expertise," and "craftsmanship," while the qualities of such action may be called "virtuosity," "adeptness," "artfulness," and "artistry"; other qualities would include responsiveness, fluency, and *shen*, a spiritlike quality (discussed below). A skill may involve control of one's own body (as in singing or walking), or it may involve media: the materials one transforms (which may be mineral, vegetable, animal, human, and even conceptual). It may also involve the use of tools: the means by which one modifies the media. Ordinary, everyday activities may be perfected as skills: walking, breathing, observing, cooking; specialized activities for complex social purposes: teaching, governing, designing; activities for pleasure, such as games and sports; and, of course, arts such as carpentry and poetry. There are also the meta-level skills of skill acquisition and skill development. And finally, there is the overall skill of living a flourishing life.

Again, we see that we should not assume a *radical* dichotomy between the human and the cultural, or between the spontaneous and the artificial. It is rather the degree of artifice that has divorced us from a fuller and more intuitive understanding of the natures of things, and of ourselves, that the Daoists object to. Whatever cultural arts we perform, whatever cultural products we make, we should allow the natural tendencies of the medium to flourish to their greatest potential, with the least interference and manipulation from us.

The types of skill that Daoists devalue include techniques, methods, and procedures. Methods and procedures are externally imposed, following fixed steps, expressible as a series of rules or instructions. Techniques are not necessarily expressible verbally, but they can be improved (made more fluent, for example) by repetition alone, and do not require the kind of sensitivity that is necessary for artistry. Although one may achieve artistry in following a procedure, it is not the procedure itself that accounts for this. The additional layer of artistry is what the Daoists praise as the skill, or way, of the sage. Other types of action that are rejected include manipulation, scheming, control, trickery, and sleight of hand. Thus, the difference between the arts of which the Daoist texts approve and mere technique, is not the difference between "high" and "low" art. There is artistry in the cutting of meat and the making of wheels. Indeed, most of the examples in the *Zhuangzi* and *Liezi* are crafts, sports, and working-class professions.

The importance of skill in these two texts lies in acquiring not simply a specific skill, but the meta-level skill of being able to develop skills and acquire new ones. This skill of skillfulness can then be applied to the art of living itself. A flourishing life, a life lived well, for a Daoist, is one performed with consummate artistry. Hence, the title of the third of the *Inner Chapters*, "*Yang Sheng Zhu*," means "what is central in cultivating life," and in the *Outer Chapters* the title of the corresponding chapter is "Penetrating Life." Lord Wenhui, after observing Ding, says, "I have heard the words of Butcher Ding, and learned how to nurture life!" (51).

In the following I extract a Daoist philosophy of skill development and acquisition from the several stories in these two chapters of the *Zhuangzi* and from chapters 2 and 5 of the *Liezi*.[8]

NATURAL ABILITIES

The path to phenomenal skill must begin somewhere. It is rooted in the natural abilities we are born with: we can perceive what lies around us, we can move our bodies, and we can respond to what we perceive. But we are not born with these abilities fully developed; they must be nurtured and refined as we grow. We learn to better interpret what is going on in our environments, gain greater control over our movements, and respond to what happens with greater accuracy. The way we develop these abilities will depend on the kinds of environment in which we grow up. The more opportunity we have to develop those abilities, the more comfortable we will be in those environments. The swimmer at Lüliang Falls[9] could swim comfortably in the most dangerous waters. He tells Confucius:

"I have no way. I began with inner conditions (*gu* 故), grew up with my natural tendencies, and become complete with Circumstance. I go under in tandem with the swirls and come out together with the eddies, following the way of the water without imposing myself on it.... I was born on land and was comfortable on land—these are the inner conditions. I grew up in the water and became comfortable in the water—these are my natural tendencies. What is so without my understanding why it is so—this is Circumstance." (205)

His effortless ability to survive in the dangerous water arose because the skills he was born with were developed in the water. It is notable that he refers to the growth and development of his inborn natural abilities as *xing* 性. This reflects the fact that what is inborn is incomplete and must be developed in response to environmental circumstances, and therefore that the distinction between what is natural and what is learned does not have sharp boundaries.

He also says that he came to completion through circumstance, *ming* 命. This is, however, not a third stage in the process, but rather the underlying condition of all natural processes. In uncovering how things happen, we may identify the conditions, *gu*, and natural tendencies, *xing*; but we may keep inquiring further about what makes these conditions and tendencies so. At some point we must acknowledge the brute fact of the circumstances, which are simply not susceptible to further scrutiny or analysis: what is so without our knowing why. This is what the swimmer calls "*ming*." One can, or course, analyze it to some extent: he has already explained, for example, that he cooperates with the water and does not impose his own personal predilections. We can also observe closely and reflect on variations in technique—how to practice most efficiently—and evaluate the efficacy of the results. We can conduct experiments and even use modern technology to discover things about the nature of efficacious movement that are not available to first-person reflection. Nevertheless, one may either continue asking questions indefinitely, stop for pragmatic reasons, or hit rock bottom. At some point, we must acknowledge either that we have no ultimate answer or that things just are the way they are.

DISCIPLINE

Though different people have different aptitudes, the development of natural ability to extraordinary heights usually requires many years of training. In the *Liezi*, the unlikely superstar Shang Qiukai is a scruffy old man who discovers in old age an extraordinary athletic prowess: when goaded to jump off a tall building, he lands with unselfconscious ease and grace; he dives into a river and fishes out a pearl from its depths; and he runs into a burning building and emerges unscathed (*Liezi*, 39–42). But innate talent of this sort is extremely unusual. People with special aptitudes are usually discovered at an early age, if social circumstances provide the opportunity for their talents to be manifested. Often, years of dedicated training are required. The discipline required to recover and cultivate the sort of spontaneity promoted by the Daoists can be seen in skillful activities such as *qigong*, *taiji*, and martial arts. The naturalness that the Daoist admires is that of the athlete or skillful individual who has gained expertise after many years of concentrated effort. In chapter 3 of the *Zhuangzi*, Butcher Ding outlines three stages in the development of his skill: "What I cherish is the way, which goes beyond mere technique. When I first began cutting up oxen, I saw nothing but oxen. After three years I did not see the whole ox. Right now, I encounter it with spirit and don't look with my eyes" (50–51). At first, with an untrained eye and limited ability to discriminate, he sees nothing but an ox carcass. After three years of extensive and detailed observation and practice, he no longer sees the whole. After nineteen more years of extensive practice, Ding says that he no longer sees with his eyes but encounters, *yu* 遇, the material with his spirit, *shen* 神.

These three stages can be compared to the stages of learning a language: first, the stage of foreignness; second, the stage of apprenticeship; and third, the stage of fluency or mastery. This could also apply to riding a bicycle or driving a car, or even learning to walk. At the stage of foreignness, we might know how to name the object or medium we are working with, and maybe even some of its parts, but we really have no deep understanding of its natural makeup. During the stage of apprenticeship, the more we immerse ourselves in the practice, the closer and more intensely we concentrate as we learn the nature of the material and develop familiarity with it. We become so aware of increasingly minute levels of difference that for a while, we might even lose the capacity to see holistic interconnections. Only with increasing practice and familiarity do we gain greater ease in engaging with the medium. The more familiar we become, the less explicitly we need to focus our perceptual awareness. At the stage of expertise, we no longer pay focused attention to the myriad details; our gaze relaxes, and we simply encounter the material, the medium, and the circumstances in all their complexity with immediate familiarity, and respond swiftly and intuitively.

SKILL ACQUISITION

In addition to our natural skills, we may cultivate new skills, but we do so through the development, adaptation, and appropriate transference of related skills that we already have.

> Good swimmers quickly develop the ability because they forget the water. As for divers, they may never have seen a boat before but will know how to handle it, because they look upon deep water as dry land, and see the capsizing of a boat like a cart slipping backwards. (*Zhuangzi*, 200; *Liezi*, 43)

An accomplished swimmer or diver is familiar with the behavior of water; the more swiftly and intuitively he or she can respond to turbulent conditions, the more easily he or she can learn to navigate a ferryboat through difficult waters. But new skills can also be acquired through drills and exercise. We may perform exercises in the new skill itself or practice activities that develop the relevant sensitivities. The hunchback who catches cicadas[10] has only a few weeks in the summer to indulge his whims. Before cicada season begins, he must find other ways to cultivate the necessary abilities. He says, somewhat comically, that he practices by balancing balls on top of one another; the more balls he can balance, the more cicadas he will be able to catch. Progress through regulated conditions will enable one to be successful in spontaneous conditions. Now, I am no expert in either balancing balls or catching cicadas, but superficially, it seems unlikely that facility with the former can improve dexterity with the latter. The embodied sensitivity to balance seems quite different in kind from visual sensitivity to the flight patterns of cicadas; the relative stillness that the first activity requires also seems quite different in kind from the agility of movement the second requires. And besides, though it might seem more regulated, in fact the balancing of balls is so unpredictable as to be practically impossible.[11] Nevertheless, the point of the story is not to teach us how to catch cicadas, but to outline some general conditions for the development of a skill. The cicada catcher refers to his practice as his "*dao.*"

In chapter 5 of the *Liezi*, "*Tang Wen*" ("The Questions of Tang"), the apprentice charioteer Zaofu learns to run from his teacher, Taidou, by watching him leap across pegs set into the ground. "Taidou said, '. . . First watch me run. Only after you run like me will you be able to manage six bridles and drive six horses.' . . . Zaofu learned from him and in three days perfected the technique" (113–14). Running is the first stage in learning to steer a chariot. He must reflect on how he controls his own body when running before he can transfer this skill to charioteering. He learns to run as his master does by imitating him. Mimicry is a powerful and fundamental form of embodied knowing: we are hardwired to recognize the bodily movements of others internally, empathetically, as it were. We observe a new posture, a new attitude, a new style of movement, and recognize it from the inside. Different people have different degrees of sensitivity and dexterity, but we are all capable of this kind of embodied internalization. Zaofu thus not only observes the outward movements of Taidao but also senses how he produces those movements. He mimics this and practices until he perfects the technique, but he must also understand what is going on. Taidao explains that it is a process of response in the heart-mind, *xin,* to what he picks up in his feet. His feet and heart-mind are mutually responsive.[12] This sensitivity can now be applied to a more complex skill involving the use of implements: charioteering with horse, bridle, and bit.

> "Applying this to charioteering, you must control the bridle from the point where it meets the bit, and pull tight or slacken from the corners of the lips; correct the measures from within your breast and control the joints from within the palm of your hand. Take it into in your innermost heart-mind and harmonize it outwardly with the horse's intentions . . . then you will see without eyes and urge without a goad. Relaxed in mind and straight in posture, the six bridles unmuddled, twenty-four hooves will fall without fault; swinging around, advancing and returning, none will miss a beat." (114)

The chain of sensitivity and responsiveness continues beyond the biological body. The heart-mind responds to the information provided by the hand; the hand responds to the information provided by the bridle; the bridle responds to the information from the bit. But, we might continue, the bit itself is also responding to the horse's movements, and thereby to its emotions and intentions. Horse, chariot, and reins become extensions of one's body when one cultivates this sensitivity.[13] Then one will be able to move the chariot as intuitively and effortlessly as if moving one's own feet.

REFINEMENT OF PERCEPTION

Since skill depends on responsiveness, increasing skill requires cultivating greater sensitivity. To reach the highest levels of skill, we must become hypersensitive to the subtlest tendencies of things that ordinarily escape our notice. Low levels of skill—technique, method, or procedure—involve ordinary levels of awareness and categorization, and are not responsive to the most subtle levels of natural patterning. Butcher Ding describes the mediocre cook who chops at a carcass oblivious of its inner makeup. In the absence of a subtle understanding of the natural tendencies of things, we will hack at them against the grain, as it were. But we have the natural capacity to increase our sensitivity. This natural capacity is itself a subtle tendency that our ordinary perceptions, concepts, and reflections normally overlook. Only in our quieter, more reflective moments do we become aware of the possibility of greater degrees of sensitivity. And we become aware of corresponding subtle tendencies in the operation of the natural processes we work with.

Thus, training must also include refinement of our perception. The master archer Fei Wei tells his student, Jichang, that he must first learn not to blink. Jichang spends two years in training, with his face directly below the pedal of his wife's loom. Having learned to control his eyes, he then learns to control his vision: "Jichang hung a flea at his window by a hair from a yak's tail, and watched it from a distance with the sun behind it. Within ten days it was growing larger; at the end of three years it was as big as a cartwheel" (112). Through perceptual training, what is ordinarily too minuscule to be noticeable will become evident, and what is faint will become distinct. This might at first seem too fanciful, but people who train with fast-moving objects eventually learn to see them as moving slowly: a juggler sees the balls as though they are simply suspended in the air; a virtuoso pianist does not necessarily perceive his or her own pyrotechnical performance to be particularly fast. We train our perceptions, creating conditions in which we attempt to sense, respond to, and eventually anticipate the slightest changes that escape our ordinary levels of attention. It appears that our bodies even have the capacity to respond to degrees and types of change that do not manifest to conscious awareness. We attend as though watching out for a change and find ourselves anticipating and responding, even though we may not know what we are responding to, and even though what we are responding to may not show up in our conscious awareness. We leap for a speeding ball and somehow find that we have caught it; we know that this was not just blind luck when we discover that we are able to repeat the performance.

In the *Liezi*, the cultivation of skill depends on the cultivation of sensitivity to the innermost subtlest level of things. "Just before the eye grows dim it can discern the tip of a hair; just before the ear goes deaf it can hear the wings of a gnat; just before the palate deteriorates it can discriminate between the waters of the Zi and the Sheng" (84). This is the level that accounts for the way things are: their stuff, their tendencies. This at first might seem comparable to the Greek atomists' conception of the atomic structure of things. But there is an important difference: the Daoist conception, though it talks of the most extremely small, *jixiao* 極小, does not define this as the atomic. Rather, it appears to function more as a limiting concept, perhaps like an asymptote. Phenomenological sensitivity to the innermost subtle tendencies of phenomena enables us to deal successfully with them. But what is infinitesimally subtle is also beyond verbal description.[14] Hence, if we have a capacity that is responsive to this level, it must constitute a kind of knowledge that cannot be put into words.

The question arises, if this kind of sensitivity goes beyond the ordinary limits of our senses, what accounts for its possibility? Is it supposed to be another kind of awareness, another faculty of perception? Butcher Ding says that his senses stop, and instead he encounters the medium with his *shen*, 神, literally "spirit." Zhuangzi, in referring to *shen*, is using the folk psychology[15] of his time. But how are we to make *philosophical* sense of this claim? We could interpret it literally as the claim that he does not use his eyes but some other faculty, or some other entity: a spirit of some sort, without which we would not be able to achieve the highest degrees of subtle skill.

While such an attribution might be appealing to a specialist in comparative religion, it would not be of any interest to a philosopher. Moreover, unless Zhuangzi explicitly requires the distinct existence of such an entity or faculty, there is nothing to prevent us from interpreting it instrumentally:

not all nouns have meaning by referring to entities; some are merely convenient labels for communication of more complex phenomena.[16] In developing a *philosophy* of skill that is of any applicable value, it is more important to understand the role and function of *shen* than to worry about whether the term refers to an existing entity. Butcher Ding, reflecting on his experience while he practices, attempts to describe the phenomenology of skill; he struggles to find the words to convey what he is aware of. "*Shen*," then, refers to *whatever* capacity enables us to understand intuitively and respond immediately to the particular details and individuality of the medium, what enables us to respond to its natural patterning. What Ding describes phenomenologically as *shen* may well turn out to be complex or higher-order functions of the natural capacities of ordinary perception. By projecting from swift changes in ordinary perception, perhaps, our bodies are able to adjust as though aware of more minute changes.

Interpreted this way, "*shen*" may be understood, at least in part, as a reification of the capacity to develop deeper sensitivities that appear to go beyond the ordinary limits of awareness. This is the capacity to sense the empty places, the open spaces; to sense where there is potential for movement, and what kind of movement; to sense the tendencies that underlie and inform things and account for their characteristic textures and qualities. In the *Laozi*, it is the emptiness that makes successful activity possible. In the *Zhuangzi* and *Liezi*, the natural patterns of things are understood through the metaphor of open channels: natural tendencies become possible directions of movement. These are conceived of metaphorically as a thinness, an emptiness, insubstantial channels that we are able somehow to become intuitively familiar with, as we refine our own sensitivities. Ding says that the blade of his knife is so fine that it has no thickness; it is therefore able to enter the empty channels without resistance.

> Perception and understanding stop and spirit-desires work. Depending on the natural striations, I strike through large gaps, guide the knife through the large openings, and adjust according with what is firmly so. I have not yet touched a ligament or tendon, much less a big bone. . . . There are spaces between the joints, and the knife edge has no thickness. When what has no thickness enters such space, then it's wide open! There will certainly be an excess of place for the blade to play. (51)

We need not conceive of these channels as purely physical; they may well be the tendencies or pathways of possibility that arise as we interact with the materials. To be most successful, we must work with these tendencies: anticipate them before they arise, sense them as we encounter them, and respond in anticipation of new directions of possibility that open up as we proceed.

CONDITIONS OF PERFORMANCE

Having attained a level of skill, however, is not sufficient to ensure skillful performance on any occasion. To perform well requires preparation so that one may be wholly invested in the performance. The cicada catcher says that he concentrates his attention so that he is aware only of cicada wings. The rest of the world dissolves away and all his attention is devoted to the presence and movement of the wings. The subtle tendencies of the medium can only be encountered if they are allowed to manifest, that is, when there are no obstacles to our awareness. When aiming to perform well we become self-conscious: thoughts of winning and losing, success and failure, praise and blame, reward and punishment may fill our minds, and thus block our attention. To the extent that they are present, they draw attention away from the medium.

Carpenter Qing, who carved an awe-inspiring bell stand, denies that he has an art, *shu* 術, insisting that he is just a worker. But he described his method of preparation to explain why people are so moved by his artwork:

> When I am going to make a bell stand . . . I must fast in order to still my mind. When I have fasted for three days, I no longer have any thought of congratulations or rewards, of titles or stipends. When I have fasted for five days, I no longer have any thought of praise or blame, of skill or clumsiness. And when I have fasted for seven days, I am so still that I forget I have four limbs and a form and body. . . . My skill is concentrated and all outside distractions fade away. After that, I go into the mountain forest and observe the tendencies of nature (*tian xing* 天性). Only when the form and body are superlative, do I succeed in seeing a bell stand. Only then do I add my own hand to it. Otherwise, it's over. This way I match *tian* with *tian*. (205–6)

He conserves his energy and meditates or fasts in order to still his mind. This is the same as the attenuation of the heart-mind, *xinzhai*, in chapter 4 of the *Zhuangzi*. The process takes several days as he dissolves the hold of external concerns and distractions. Eventually, when he has even forgotten all worldly concerns, he enters the forest and is now able to recognize the natural tendencies of the materials he finds there. Not until he finds wood of consummate quality (or his own form is at its peak) and is able to see the bell stand in its completed form in it does he begin carving. He describes this responsiveness to the natural patterns as harmonizing nature with nature, *yi tian he tian* 以天合天. (Here, "*tian*" seems to be used in the sense of particular natural tendencies, rather than the natural world as a whole.) Thus, he claims it is only the natural tendencies already present that account for the inspiring nature of his artistry. This is perhaps why he denies that *he* has any art.

Now, in chapter 20 of the *Zhuangzi*, "*Shan Mu*," "The Mountain Tree," we are warned against rapt attention: the cicada that had forgotten itself did not see the mantis that was about to strike, but the mantis in its rapt attention on the cicada was unaware that its own life was in danger from the bird that had alighted behind it. The concentrated attention that is criticized there, however, is attention on objects of acquisition, which are obstacles to full presence. When one ties oneself to objects of acquisition, one in turn becomes an object of acquisition. This is, arguably, not the same sort of concentration involved in skill; one is not concerned to gain the object, only to increase mastery over one's actions. One allows the phenomena to manifest so as to respond with fluency, subtlety, and excellence, and this ultimately will have to include contextual phenomena. One may instead thus be released into a fuller presence.

The swimmer at Lüliang Falls also denies having a *dao*. Like Woodcarver Qing, he means that he does not impose himself on his medium but allows it to manifest, follows the way of the water. He cooperates with the water, flows in and out *with*[17] the currents, riptides, and whirlpools, and emerges unharmed. We may try to fight them, following our own intentions and struggling against the flow of the currents. If the currents are weak, we might succeed; if they are too strong, we are more likely to be damaged. This sort of yielding, however, should not be confused with allowing oneself to be thrown around. Consider a bird and a piece of paper in a storm, or a fish and a leaf in the rapids. The bird and fish maintain their balance throughout the turbulence, while the paper and leaf are hurled and tossed in all directions. The bird and fish sense and cooperate with the rapidly and almost randomly shifting currents and so have a chance of maintaining stability while remaining relatively unharmed.

It is not enough, however, to have attenuated one's own heart-mind and forgotten oneself. The subject must lose itself, dissolve itself into the object or the material, which thereby comes to full presence. But, paradoxically, for the highest level of skillful engagement, the object and material must recede as well. The ferryman at Goblet Deeps says that an excellent swimmer can learn quickly because he or she forgets the water. One can forget the water only when thoroughly at home in it. One is thoroughly at home in a medium only when one simply lives through it, oblivious of its presence. When one has forgotten both oneself and the material, subject and object dissolve, and only performance emerges.

DIFFICULTIES

But flawless artistry is not infallible. We can never realistically claim to have completely mastered any skill. For whatever reason, there is always the possibility of some awkward circumstance, uncharacteristically hard and knotty places, unanticipated novelties (51). In these cases, the expert falls back to the stage of apprentice, slows down, applies more conscious methods, acutely aware of nothing but the new formations of the old material. In this way, the artist acquires not only new knowledge about the nature of the material in unusual circumstances, but also new practice in negotiating novelty skillfully. The development of skill itself becomes skillfully developed.

Afterword

A Family of Dao

Is there such a thing as Daoist philosophy? Is there one set of doctrines, an essence, that all forms of Daoism share? Apparently not. Since circumstances can always develop in unexpected ways, and even produce radically opposed consequences, the same is true for beliefs, doctrines, and *daos*. Doctrines and ways transform into opposing views. Just as paths can branch off as they develop, the resulting paths can continue to diverge further. So, as one follows a path, one's practice can manifest in different ways; those differences can multiply over time, eventually giving rise to ways that claim the same ancestry yet oppose each others' interpretations of the way. A single stream follows its tendencies and, according to changes in terrain or amount of rainfall, may end up with branches at opposite ends of the mountain. The author of the *Liezi* gives the example of three students of Confucianism who developed three mutually inconsistent interpretations of the significance of *yi*, rightness (175–76).

Likewise, the *Laozi*, *Zhuangzi*, and *Liezi* present very different approaches to the *dao*. The *Zhuangzi* itself splits into a Zhuangzian mainstream, the Utopians, and the Syncretists, and according to Graham's classification, the Utopians subdivide into the Primitivists and the Yangists. We can nevertheless recognize strong resemblances between the *Laozi* and the Utopians, and between Zhuangzian philosophy and the *Liezi*. Other continuities can also be traced. The critique of Ruism in the *Laozi* is echoed in chapters 1, 4, and 7 of the *Inner Chapters*, and is brought vividly to life in the Utopian chapters. Reflection on the originative potency of the cosmos can be seen in the *Laozi*, Zhuangzian thought, and the *Liezi*. The *Liezi* develops themes from chapters 1, 3, and 6 of the *Inner Chapters* and chapters 17, 19 and 22 of the *Outer Chapters*: the importance of skill, wandering beyond, life and death, waking and dreaming, and not knowing.

Admittedly, the Han dynasty Syncretists are the most distant relatives, but they can be seen to share more than a passing resemblance. Although they adopt the tenets of many schools, core Daoist principles lie at the root of their practice. The importance of cultivation of one's life and potency at the root of political governance, and the metapolitical notion of sageliness within and kingliness without, can both be discerned in the passages of the *Laozi* that refer to rulership of an empire. This is even echoed in chapters 1 and 5 of the *Inner Chapters*, where the potency of the Daoist sage flows effortlessly into a flourishing community. This idea is explicitly articulated in chapter 28, which forms the aikido pivot between utopian anarchism and mystical rule of an empire.

What do we make of a way that diverges into so many paths? How do we identify the right one? *Is* there a single right way, a single correct interpretation of *dao*? The *Liezi* laments the multiplicity of the branches of *dao* and urges that we must trace our path back to the source (176). One might argue that two threads can be found in all these manifestations of Daoist thought: *tian* and *wuwei*. The context to which we must return in order to flourish is the overarching perspective of the cosmos, *tian*. The means by which we engage is diminishing the force of social constructs and imitating the effortless success of natural processes, *wuwei*. How this is to be done is interpreted differently by each group. Perhaps at the root of both of these is a deeper thread, a deeper commonality: a process of reversal, softening, disintegrating, *wu*, that allows natural phenomena to reach their fullest potential.

However, even if these threads can be found in all forms of Daoist thought, it would be a mistake to think of them as the "essence" of Daoism. Rather, the texts form a Daoist family, related members that develop in related ways over time. There is no reason why Daoist thought should stop here, or be confined by these characteristics, or why these characteristics should not continue to be interpreted in new ways. Having followed the paths of Daoist philosophy through their many manifestations, having followed their internal tendencies, we see that all have problems and all have insights. The insistence that there can be only one *dao* seems to be inconsistent with the movement of *dao* itself. Growth and slippage are natural, and it is the nature of an indeterminate path to spread. It should come as no surprise that the same *dao* can manifest in a multiplicity of different ways.

NOTES

1. DAOIST PHILOSOPHIES

1. We might be tempted to insist on a fixed hierarchical ordering of these concepts: perhaps *dao* is more fundamental than *tian*, while *tian* is less fundamental than *wu*, and so on. But we should resist: the texts themselves do not propose a clear and consistent ranking. Rather, they all interrelate to create the web of ideas that is characteristic of the discourse of Daoism.

2. Note the use of the definite article and italicization when referring to the texts: the *Laozi*, the *Zhuangzi*, and the *Liezi*.

3. Other early texts eventually came to be associated to a greater or lesser extent with Daoist traditions. These include the *Huainanzi*, the *Lüshi Chunqiu*, the *He Guanzi*, and the *Guanzi*. They are eclectic anthologies, some containing significant amounts of material that resonate with Confucian, Legalist, and Militarist canons, others containing discussions of economy and agriculture, in addition to passages that echo typically Daoist thought. A philosophical study of the significance of the Daoist passages of these texts and their relation to the strands of thought in the *Laozi*, the *Zhuangzi* and the *Liezi* would undoubtedly be of great value. To that end, Harold Roth's book, *Original Tao: Inward Training* (Nei-yeh) *and the Foundations of Taoist Mysticism*, is a translation and study of the *Neiye* ("Inward Training") chapter of the *Guanzi*. He makes the claim that this neglected text on spiritual cultivation should be considered the source of the Daoist tradition. This intriguing but controversial working hypothesis informs his interpretation of the text, and of the historical development of Daoist traditions.

4. With the notable exception of Legalism, which had no patience with this kind of idealization of the past.

5. See Thomas Nagel, *The View from Nowhere*, for an extended discussion of the conceptual problems with the ideal of a cosmic "perspective."

6. My translations. I use the phrase "flourishing life" throughout this book in a nontechnical sense of a life lived well. In doing so, I am not claiming that it corresponds to any well-defined Chinese philosophical term or phrase.

7. Some commentators refer to such a cosmic *dao* as an "absolute" *dao*, but I prefer to avoid this metaphysically laden term for reasons that will become clear throughout the book. Incidentally, the *Zhong Yong* and the *Yijing*, both Confucian texts, aimed to harmonize the role of the human in the cosmos. However, the shift in *emphasis* from the human to the cosmic appears to be the distinctively Daoist contribution.

8. Harold Roth, in chapter 5 of *Original Tao*, takes this concept of "family" to refer to "lineages" of practice passed down from master to student, and objects to the translation "school" on the grounds that the *jia* were not defined by their self-professed commitment to an unchanging set of doctrines. This objection, however, is based on a misunderstanding of the nature of a philosophical school. The philosophical usage of the term "school" does not in fact require either an explicit self-classification or an unchanging set of doctrines. Philosophical schools can be centered around ethical and political practices and ways of life; members of a single school can, and usually do, disagree with each other; and both doctrines and practices can, and usually do, change over time. I interpret the family metaphor to refer not to ancestral traditions, but simply to the fact that there can be several members of a family who share resemblances but need not look identical. See note 5 to Chapter Four below for more on the concept of family resemblance.

9. Sometimes called the School of Names, or more recently, the Terminologists.

10. See Chapter Five below for further discussion.

11. My translations, from Sima Tan, *Historical Records, 4.70: The Grand Historian's Preface.* Also in Ssu-ma, Ch'ien. *The Grand Scribe's Records, Volume VII, 21–23.*

12. See Chapter Five below.

13. Hans-Georg Moeller refers to this method of grounding political theory in an overarching cosmology and attendant spiritual practice as "metapolitics." In his book, *Daoism Explained*, he uses the term to contrast the Chinese tradition with the metaphysical tendencies of the Greek tradition. While Greek metaphysics sought to ground the natural world in a transcendent realm beyond, the Chinese tradition sought to ground the political in an overarching cosmological context. For the most part, this cosmological context is not conceived of as transcending the natural world altogether.

14. Traditionally, there have also been two recensions of the text, deriving from two commentaries: that of Wang Bi and that attributed to a figure called He Shang Gong. Wang Bi's metaphysically oriented commentary contains conceptual analyses and arguments that were not affiliated with any religious sect. It is therefore not inappropriate to think of it as a philosophical commentary. The He Shang Gong commentary, however, contains no conceptual analyses or arguments, focuses primarily on spiritual practices, and is therefore quite reasonably thought of as religious text. Alan Chan's *Two Visions of the Way* is a comparative analysis of the two.

15. See, for example, Miller on the status of the *Zhuangzi*, in *Daoism: A Short Introduction*, 5.

16. See, for example, Harold Roth's *Original Tao*.

17. Confucianism and Daoism do not involve the worship of God; laypeople do not identify themselves as belonging to a specifically Confucianist or Daoist denomination. The question "What religion are you?" is considered close to meaningless. They make no clear distinction between Confucian and Daoist, or Daoist and Buddhist spirituality.

18. It is sometimes objected that the Hellenistic schools were centrally grounded in logical argument, which makes them radically different from their "antirational" Daoist counterparts. But this exaggerates the differences. It was not just the theories and arguments about the nature of the world that were important to the Hellenistic philosophers, but the actual achievement of tranquility in practice in a world of that nature. Moreover, the Daoists were also concerned to acquire correct insight into the way of the cosmos and how to flourish in it, and gave reasons for rejecting other proposed ways. These reasons did not usually take the form of detailed logical arguments, but it is not correct to insist that rationality plays no role in Daoist texts.

19. Indeed, contrary to what is often claimed, parallels can be found in the West, where there has also been no clear boundary between Western philosophy and Western religion. Plato, Descartes, Spinoza, and Kant, to name just a few major examples, have all philosophized from *within* religious perspectives about matters of religious concern—God, the soul, life after death—but they are not thereby classified as religious leaders and their texts are not treated as scriptures; nor are their philosophies thought of as religions or their students referred to as "disciples." Despite the overlap, the distinction between Western philosophy and Western religion remains meaningful. The insistence that the philosophical and the religious cannot meaningfully be distinguished in China only does a disservice to the complexity of the cultural phenomena on both sides.

20. While there are occasional references to ghosts and spirits, these are not associated with Daoism as such. References to folk beliefs in spirits, mythical creatures, or ritualized codes of behavior for dealing with them, for example, can be found in the *Analects*, the *Yijng*, the *Mozi*, the *Chuci*, the *Shanhaijing*, and the *Guiguzi*. But these beliefs and practices are not identified as belonging to any particular school or lineage, and are certainly not directly associated with Daoism in any sense. They simply reflect the cultural milieu and beliefs of the pre-Qin period.

21. Livia Kohn, while insisting on fluid boundaries between them, nevertheless acknowledges different strands of historical development. She refers to what has come to be known as the Daoist philosophy sometimes as "Lao-Zhuang Daoism" and sometimes as "literati Daoism." See, for example, *Daoism and Chinese Culture*, 5–6.

22. See Shaughnessy, "Western Zhou History," in *Cambridge History of Ancient China*, ed. Loewe and Shaugnhessy.

23. Though one finds dates from 481 to as late as 403 B.C.E. depending on which specific event is chosen to mark its official beginning.

24. They thus appear to be the first pre-Qin thinkers to be concerned with a kind of universality, and the first to articulate a sense of justice, or equitable treatment of all people, *jian'ai* 兼愛, often translated, somewhat misleadingly, as "universal love." "Equitable concern" might be a more accurate translation.

25. I say maximal cohesiveness, because it may well be that some positions are irreconcilable. But the assertion that any two views are irreconcilable should not be our first interpretive option.

26. Wittgenstein, Waismann, Quine, Derrida, and Eco discuss openness of meaning in many forms. Gadamer discusses the historical construction and development of meaning through the fusion of horizons. In chapter 1 of *Zhuangzi and Early Chinese Philosophy*, I explore these issues in detail as they relate to the interpretation of ancient Daoist texts, and explicate and clarify my theoretical and philosophical methodologies.

27. Note that I do not say their "truth." Some philosophers still believe that the goal of philosophy is to discover the truth, in some purely objective and determinate sense. Hermeneutic and pragmatic philosophers see all language and understanding as essentially interpretive, and therefore aim to articulate the best, most plausible interpretations. I prefer to talk of "plausibility" in this sense.

28. Here, I am applying Gadamer's conception of the fusion of historical horizons to cultures that have no prior historical relationship. That is, Gadamer's concept, articulated in *Truth and Method*, applies to the cultural fusion that exists between ancient and modern cultures of the same historical tradition. Ancient China and the modern West do not belong to the same cultural tradition, and so their fusion of horizons must be understood differently. In the former case, it is a fusion that enables the ancient culture to continue living in the present; the latter case, it is an active fusion that creates a new cross-cultural product.

29. Note again, the hermeneutic goal of being persuaded by the plausibility of a view is not to be identified with arguing for the "truth" of a theory in a "realist" sense. Plausible views can be multiple, while realist truth can only be one.

30. Rudolf Wagner engages in a detailed and insightful investigation into the use of parallel structure in the *Laozi*. In his analysis of Wang Bi's edition, he identifies a structure that he calls interlocking parallel style and demonstrates its philosophical significance. See, for example, *A Chinese Reading of the Daodejing*.

31. See *The Philosophy of the Daodejing*, chapter 1.

2. FUNDAMENTAL CONCEPTS OF CHINESE PHILOSOPHY

1. Geoffrey Lloyd and Nathan Sivin, in *The Way and the Word*, identify the dominant tendency of Greek practice and intellectual discourse as dialectical, critical, and analytical,

while the dominant tendency of early Chinese equivalents is rhetorical and synthetic. They find one set of sources for such differences in the social and political conditions that shaped the lives and concerns of people from each culture and were in turn shaped by their thoughts. Though they eschew a label for their approach, it is consistent with the methods of contemporary sociology of knowledge. Francois Jullien, in *Detour and Access*, plots a similar contrast between the cultures in terms of directness and indirection. Ames and Hall, in *Anticipating China*, use the terminology of "first and second problematics" to refer to the cultural tendencies of Chinese and Greek discourse respectively.

2. Ames and Hall, in *Anticipating China,* and *Thinking from the Han,* undertake a thorough investigation of these issues, sensitive to the complexities of each cultural tradition.

3. The walking radical, *chuo*, 辶, in an earlier form, 辵, is composed of *chi*, 彳, having the sense of "footprints," "crossroads," or "path," and *zhi*, 止, a foot stepping.

4. Typical words with this radical have meanings associated directly with movement: to reach, to go, to advance, to be quick, to patrol, to return, to meet; to be distant, to follow, to lead, to hasten, to happen, to stroll, to roam, to delay, to pass through, etc. Other meanings still tend to be primarily verbal (to extend, to greet, to press, etc.) or stative verbs (to be roundabout, to be circuitous, to be close, to be distant, etc.). Finally, nouns with this radical refer usually to paths, ways, or methods.

5. Note, however, that according to Sima Tan, the purpose of the *Mingjia*, the Linguistic School, was also to govern by recognizing the importance of the regulation of terminology. If this is right, then even the philosophers most notorious for their impractical peddling of paradoxes still had a practical purpose behind their obsession with linguistic consistency.

6. "Abduction" is Pierce's term for the most prevalent and important form of reasoning: including interpretation and inference to the best explanation. Typical examples include problem solving, medical diagnosis, and detective sleuthing. In aesthetic terms, one projects an image or a narrative that helps make sense of whatever phenomena are to be understood. Those who have studied deductive logic will recognize it as the "fallacy" of affirming the consequent, though it is only fallacious if intended deductively. For a nontechnical and engaging discussion of abduction, see Eco's anthology *The Sign of Three.*

7. The terminology of "immanence" is problematic insofar as it distinguishes immanent sources from transcendent ones. If one rejects the concept of the transcendent, then the contrast with immanence would seem to become unintelligible. Perhaps adopting the Whiteheadian terminology of "emergence" might circumvent this difficulty.

8. Parmenides, Plato, Plotinus, and Aquinas, for example, give detailed and often extended arguments for the necessity of transcendence.

9. In the *Liezi* and some passages of the *Outer Chapters* of the *Zhuangzi,* we find the beginnings of a movement away from a naturalistic conception of *dao,* but, as we shall see in Chapter Six below, the extent to which that conception becomes fully transcendent is unclear.

10. See the last section of this chapter for a full discussion of complementary contrasts.

11. In the discourse of the academic study of religion, this is sometimes referred to as the Transcendent that is simultaneously Immanent. *Some* of the disagreement over the status of *dao* in academic circles might thus be purely terminological.

12. See Hansen, *A Daoist Theory of Chinese Thought*, 83–85.

13. *Hu xi, huang xi* 恍兮惚兮, *Laozi,* chapter 21.

14. Also, "influence" or "charisma." Traditionally translated as "virtue," "excellence." the traditional translations do not sufficiently emphasize the relational efficacy of *de.*

15. In chapter 29 of the *Zhuangzi.*

16. Again, I use "transcendent" here in the philosophical sense of an independent ground or foundation of existence, entirely separate from and independent of the natural world that is dependent on it. The religious sense of that which is superior to the world it creates need not be metaphysical in the philosophical sense.

17. Often, but not necessarily: on a quantum level, the metaphor of mechanism fails.

18. One find the occasional possible exception, arguably, for example with Spinoza's concept of *"deus sive natura."*

19. An early dictionary, compiled by Xu Shen, dating to the Eastern Han, around the beginning of the second century C.E.

20. 仁 者人也,親親為大. "Humanity is being human; it takes cherishing our close family relations as what is important." *Zhong Yong*, chapter 20, my translation.

21. Confucius himself never raises the issue in this way. While he believes in the human potential for self-improvement, the question of whether this is natural to us or must be imposed on what is natural to us is never articulated.

22. Watson. 252. References to Watson are to his translation, *The Complete Works of Chuang Tzu.*

23. I use the term "enculturation" to refer to the inculcation of a primary culture, to distinguish it from "acculturation" as adaptation to a new culture.

24. Even Mencius, who championed the natural goodness of people, believed that without continuous nurturing and guidance natural goodness cannot flourish.

25. The significance of the distinction between mutually exclusive dichotomies and complementary contrasts will become clear in the last section below.

26. Ames and Hall make a similar point regarding the Daoist critique of Confucianism in *Thinking from the Han*, 174–80. They note that Confucians *also* seek a harmony between the natural and the artificial. The point of contention, however, is where the balance lies: the Confucians never abandon their humanism, while the Daoists see this human-centeredness as a flaw.

27. Further, when we try to control the world, we get trapped in cycles of interference: the more we interfere, the more we have to invent measures to fix the problems created by interference.

28. In simplified characters, 阴阳.

29. For example, chapters 2, 11, 20, 22, 26, 28, 36, 40, 42, 56, and 57 of the *Laozi.*

30. Both characters have the radical for a mountain or hill ß on the left. According to one traditional etymology, on the right side, *yin* has swirling clouds, 侌, denoting the shady side of a mountain, while *yang* has 昜, the sun 日 emitting rays 勿, denoting the sunny side.

31. Compare with *qian* 乾 and *kun* 坤, Confucian terms associated with *yang* and *yin* respectively, but with a stricter hierarchical structure.

32. Hence, in chapter 2 of the *Laozi*, "sound" and "voice" are listed alongside "something" and "nothing," "difficult" and "easy," and so on. The words *sheng* 聲 and *yin* 音 are actually synonyms, and here seem to refer to the way in which contrasting sounds and voices complement and harmonize with one another. A similar point is being made about the other pairings.

33. For more on the relevance of vagueness to Daoist philosophy, see chapter 6 of my book, *Zhuangzi and Early Chinese Philosophy*.

34. *Zhuangzi*, 84, 176, 291; *Liezi*, 66, 67, perhaps also 18.

3. THE *LAOZI*

1. Also known by the Wade-Giles spelling, Lao Tzu.

2. Ssu-ma Ch'ien, *The Grand Scribe's Records, Volume VII: The Memoirs of Pre-Han China*, 21–23. Sima Qian was the son of Sima Tan.

3. "*Er*" means "ears" and is not a personal name; the word "Dan" refers to ears that lack a rim, and seems to be an epithet for a sage rather than a real name.

4. Yuan, Zhouzong, *An Investigation Into the Life and Times of Laozi and His Military Thought*, 54–55.

5. See the Introduction to *Religious and Philosophical Aspects of the* Laozi.

6. For an excellent account of the history of the text, and of recent discoveries and their significance, see the Introduction to Csikszentmihalyi and Ivanoe, *Religious and Philosophical Aspects of the Laozi*.

7. D. C. Lau divides the traditional chapters further into smaller units of coherence.

8. It acquired this sense during the Han dynasty.

9. He was born in 226 C.E. and died when he was only 23 years old, having written two of the most influential commentaries on early Chinese philosophical texts: one on the *Laozi* and the other on the *Yijing, The Classic of Changes*. His name is also associated with the Daoist tradition of *Xuanxue*, or "abstruse learning," a group of intellectuals sometimes called Neo-Daoists, whose philosophical views had striking similarities with Buddhist philosophy.

10. This gives the impression of a text whose parts got reshuffled in large chunks (as might perhaps happen if a scroll of bamboo strips were dropped and picked up again before being transcribed to silk).

11. As noted in Chapter One above, this was an eclectic Han dynasty school of thought tracing its lineage to Huang Di and Laozi and advocating the abstruse political doctrine of

rulership through internal practices of cultivation. See Henricks, *Lao-Tzu Te-Tao Ching*, and Peerenboom's *Law and Morality in Ancient China*.

12. In the introduction to his translation, *Lao Tzu: Tao Te Ching*. See also P. J. Ivanhoe, *The Daodejing of Laozi*.

13. These are discussed in Chapter Five below.

14. See note 16 in Chapter One above.

15. The papers collected in *Religious and Philosophical Aspects of the Laozi*, by Ivanhoe and Csikszentmihalyi, argue for a variety of different interpretations of the *Laozi*.

16. In East Asia, there are scholars, such as Chen Guying (Ch'en Ku-ying), who also adopt an interpretation of Daoist texts consistent with Western metaphysical approaches.

17. See the discussions of "*dao*" and "*tian*" in Chapter Two above for more on the distinction between the cosmological and the metaphysical.

18. Mentioned in chapters 1, 4, 8, 9, 14, 15, 16, 18, 21, 23, 24, 25, 30, 32, 34, 35, 37, 38, 40, 41, 42, 46, 47, 48, 51, 53, 55, 59, 60, 62, 65, 67, 73, 77, 79, 81; the great *dao*: 18, 53; the ancient *dao*: 14; the *dao* of *tian*: 9, 47, 73, 77, 79, 81. Here and in the following, chapter lists are intended to give a thorough sampling of relevant passages for the concepts discussed, but should not be taken to be exhaustive and complete.

19. Chapters where *dao* is explicitly described include: 4, 21, 25, 32, 34, 35, 40, 42, 51, 53, and 62. Chapters 73, 77, 79, and 81 describe the activity of *tiandao*.

20. There is also a doctrine of *buyan*, but this need not be interpreted as asserting that nothing can be said *about dao*. Rather, it means that *dao* does not speak: things follow the way not by being instructed verbally, but by being guided wordlessly. The wise ruler, in the same way, is able to guide without explicit instructions.

21. "*Chang*" did not take on the sense of "eternal" until the introduction of Buddhist philosophy into China several centuries later, when it was adopted to express the concept of "permanence."

22. For example, see chapters 1, 4, 14, 21, and 25. Chapters 10, 15, and 65 attribute these qualities to a sage or sage ruler.

23. See also *wuwei* and *ziran* below.

24. The ancestral, *zong* 宗, 4; beginning, *shi* 始, 1, 14, 52; mother, *mu* 母, 1, 25, 52, 59; root, *gen* 根, 6, 16 ; gateway, doorway, *men* 門, 1, 6. The metaphor *ben* 本, also meaning "root," appears to refer to qualities of a sage ruler: 26, 39.

25. Evolutionary biologists have theorized that all humans must be descended from one female, whom they call "mitochondrial Eve."

26. For want of a better term, I use "creationist" to refer to those who argue that the natural world is the created object of some transcendent origin. This view may also be characterized as a form of metaphysical dualism.

27. As we shall see in Chapter Six below, however, the *Liezi* begins to nudge this concept to its limits: it begins to crystallize the incipient metaphor of a transcendent something that cannot be a thing.

28. Chapter 11.

29. Note that ontologies and cosmologies need not be metaphysical in the strict sense of the word. That is, they need not posit an ultimate Reality that lies beyond the empirical world of Appearance. Empiricists and pragmatists tend to have ontologies that are not metaphysical in this sense.

30. These are the three separate functions of the verb "to be" in Frege, Russell, and Wittgenstein's logically perfect language. "The earth is"—"is" of existence; "Venus is the Morning Star"— "is" of identity; "Iron is a metal"— "is" of predication, or the "copula": any verb used to link a nonverbal predicate to a subject. Surprisingly, although the verb "to be" is taken as synonymous with "to exist," its existential use is so rare as to seem almost ungrammatical: "The earth is," "Santa Claus is not." The sentences sound incomplete, suggesting that the primary functions are identity and predication rather than the assertion of existence. Incidentally, these functions are not conflated in Chinese. There is no one word that merges all three into a single concept. In this regard, the grammar of Chinese, both ancient and modern, reflects the structure of Russell's logically perfect language better than English, German, and Greek.

31. See A. C. Graham's "'Being' in Western Philosophy Compared with *Shih/fei* 是非 and *Yu/wu* 有無 in Chinese Philosophy," in *Studies in Chinese Philosophy and Philosophical Literature*.

32. Chapter 40 says that *you* is produced from *wu*. Indeed, Wang Bi (226–249 B.C.E.), following this chapter, takes *wu* to be a fundamental origin of some kind. According to this view, *wu* attempts to name a primordial Non-being as the origin of all existence. However, chapter 40 is not necessarily inconsistent with chapter 2; it may just be emphasizing one side of a mutually productive process. While Wang Bi's interpretation is intriguing, it is a later development, and I do not pursue it in this text.

33. *Tiandi*: chapters 1, 5, 6, 7, 23, 25, and 32. *Wanwu*: 1, 2, 4, 5, 8, 16, 32, 34, 37, 39, 40, 42, 51, 62, 64.

34. Chapters 16, 25, 39, 59, 67, 68, and 73.

35. *Tiandao*: 47, 79; *Tianzhidao*: 9, 73, 77, 81 (both *tian* and *dao* mentioned: 16, 25, 59, 73).

36. *Tianxia*: 13, 22, 26, 28, 29, 30, 31, 32, 35, 37, 39, 40, 43, 45, 46, 47, 48, 49, 52, 54, 56, 57, 60, 61, 62, 66, 67, 70, 77, 78.

37. Only if the passages date to after the Qin unification.

38. Chapters 2, 25, 32, 67, and 70.

39. Chapters 32, 35, 40, 43, 47, 52, 63, and 78.

40. Confucius makes a similar point: it is only in establishing others that one is able to take one's own stand; *Analects* 6.30.

41. One might attempt to combine these claims into a single theory. For example: *dao* = *wu*; *wu* => *you* (*you* = 1); 1 => 3; 3 => *wanwu*. This is not altogether implausible, though there are problems in working out the details. For example, if *wu* and *you* are mutually producing, as it says in chapter 2, then we should be able to conclude that 3 produces *dao*. Or, if *you* is the same as *yi* 1, why is it not also *wanwu*? Where exactly does *ming* (naming) fit in? Is it in *dao*?

Is it in *you*? Is it between them? Given these sorts of problems, and in the absence of further confirming or disconfirming evidence, I shall refrain from interpreting the text as presupposing a strict etiological hierarchy.

42. Chapters 1, 16, 28, and 52.

43. As noted in the previous chapter, many commentators, under the influence of a long and eminent tradition of Buddhist interpretation, take the term to mean "eternal." In translations of Buddhist sutras the word is used to translate *nicca*, or permanence, and is endowed with a sense of endless endurance of the same. This sense gets read back into the early Daoist texts, which are then interpreted in the light of Buddhist concepts. While there is a complex history of mutual influence between Buddhist and Daoist philosophy, I am here concerned with interpreting the early Daoist tradition prior to this influence, and so will not pursue these Buddhist-influenced readings.

44. Mathematically speaking, an oscillation can be understood as the projection of a circular movement onto a single dimension.

45. This is not to say that all processes are guided *only* by such tendencies. To assert their ubiquity is not to rule out the possibility of other types of patterns.

46. There is an obvious application to consumption of natural resources: continued exploitation (excessive *yang*) vs. the frugal and responsible use and reuse of resources.

47. Chapters 10, 14, 22, 39, and 42.

48. *Analects* 2.3: The master said, "Guide them with enforced regulations, order them with punishments, and the people will be evasive and without shame. Guide them with excellence *de*, order them with propriety *li*, and they will not only have a sense of shame, but will also develop the appropriate disposition."

49. For example, they both promote rulership through potency *de* and noninterference *wuwei* (see below), although their interpretations of each of these is significantly different.

50. Chapter 3, for example, criticizes promoting moral worthiness; 18, 19, and 38 are skeptical of the cultivation of humanity and rightness.

51. See, for example, chapters 19 and 57.

52. A similar problem arises with Nietzsche's transvaluation of values. Nietzsche too rejects traditional virtues, and replaces them with a set of virtues that are motivated more by the cultivation of strength of character than the cultivation of ethical concern for others. Endurance, or a kind of stoic indifference, seems to lie at the heart of such nonhumanistic virtues: the capacity to endure suffering, both our own and that of others, without emotional weakness.

53. According to Mencius, the sprouts of ethical virtue are simply the emotional capacities we are born with, and that must be nurtured. Our natural feelings of compassion will then grow into the virtue of humanity; our natural feelings of respect will grow into the virtue of propriety, and so on. Mencius explicitly identifies the roots of humanistic virtue in our natural tendencies. The *Laozi*, however, lacks any such explicit account of how genuinely ethical virtues might arise from natural propensities alone. We cannot simply supplement the *Laozi* with Mencius' theory of the natural sprouts of humanity and rightness, since the

former explicitly rejects these virtues. The utopian Daoists discussed in Chapter Five below might have the beginnings of a solution to this problem.

54. Straw dogs were ceremonial effigies that were used once and immediately destroyed.

55. See the last section in Chapter Four below on the Zhuangzian attitude toward *shifei* evaluative judgment. Hans-Georg Moeller develops such an amoral outlook in *The Moral Fool*.

56. 1, 3, 19, 34, 37, 46, 57, 64; other relevant chapters that do not explicitly mention *yu*: 9, 12, 44, 80.

57. That is, they involve minimal levels of artifice. Both terms, "needs" and "wants," are ambiguous: they can refer to our psychological or psychophysical state, or they can refer to the *objects* to which those states are directed.

58. 19, 28, 32, 37, 57 make reference to *pu*. Chapters 3, 44, 46, and 80 describe the ideal of a simple life without using the term. The simplified form of the character, *pu* 朴, was originally the name of a type of tree, the Chinese hackberry, and refers also to the kind of wood that it produces. These two words are often taken to be synonymous when interpreting the *Laozi*, and translators often render the philosophical term "uncarved block," thus referring simultaneously to the wood of the tree and to natural simplicity. However, it is unclear to what extent the qualities of the *pu* tree and its timber, 朴, influence the philosophical significance of the Daoist term *pu*, 樸. I suspect none at all.

59. Mozi also complains that social disharmony arises when the clever exploit the foolish. Also, compare *Laozi* chapter 19.

60. Chapter 32 also makes interesting connections between simplicity, minimizing linguistic distinctions, and returning to a natural state of order. See *wuwei* and *ziran* below.

61. *Guo*: chapters 10, 18, 49, 57, 59, 60, 61, 65, 78, and 80.

62. For example, *zhi*: chapters 3, 8, 57, 59 and 65; *min*: 3, 10, 19, 57, 66, 80. Other political terms include "feudal lords and kings" *houwang* 侯王, "ruler" *zhu* 主, and "governing" *zheng* 政.

63. Social libertarian, but not individualistic: the individual is not accorded primacy. In the *Laozi*, flourishing is achieved by mutual nurturing, not the promotion of one's own interests.

64. According to chapter 11 of the *Mozi*, the Emperor could not rule without delegating tasks to the three ministers, who in turn could not rule without further delegating to the feudal lords.

65. See note to *tianxia* in Chapter Two above for references.

66. This is reminiscent of the Confucian text *Da Xue* ("*The Greater Learning*"), and indeed chapter 54 of the *Laozi* uses language that is remarkably similar. Surprisingly, however, unlike the *Da Xue*, chapter 54 does not explicitly find the root of social harmony in cultivating the person.

67. *Wuwei*: 2, 3, 10, 37, 38, 43, 48, 57, 63, 64; also *bukewei*, 29; *buwei*, 47; *wushi* 無事, 48, 57, 63. *Ziran*: 17, 23, 25, 51, 64; chapters 32, 37, and 57 emphasize that the result of governing through minimal artifice is that the people transform themselves, simplify themselves, settle themselves, and rectify themselves (*zihua*, 自化, *zizheng*, 自正, *zipu*, 自朴, *ziding*, 自定).

68. Of course, both "forcing" and "allowing" are drawn from human activity, so neither really applies literally to nature.

69. This should come as no surprise: as Kant argued, the attempt to understand ultimate and all-inclusive phenomena takes us to the limits of rational thought, where we become involved in paradoxes and antinomies. Russell showed that the same sort of logical problem applies to set theory: the attempt to conceive of the set of all sets results in paradox, since the set of all sets cannot itself be conceived as a set. At any rate, if it is a set, it is a set of no ordinary kind.

70. See Liu, Xiaogan, "Naturalness (*Tzu-jan*), the Core Value in Taoism: Its Ancient Meaning and Its Significance Today," in *Lao-tzu and the Tao-te-ching*, ed. Kohn and Lafargue.

71. Chapters that discuss the nature of sagely rule: 3, 7, 12, 17, 22, 27, 28, 29, 48, 49, 57, 58, 59, 60, 61, 63, 64, 65, 66, 67, 72, 77, 78, 80, and 81.

72. Eventually, with the syncretistic tendencies of the Han, the paternalistic and maternalistic models merge in the ideal of the Emperor as both father and mother to the people.

73. Though some do indeed argue for such complete deregulation. Extreme individualists appear to be committed to the dogma that social harmony necessarily arises only from a complete absence of constraints. Faith in such a dogma runs completely contrary to all available evidence. Complete absence of all regulation leaves room for exploitation and manipulation: those interested in benefiting unjustly only have to convince the gullible that they are not being exploited, that this is the best of all possible worlds, and that in it they have the greatest of opportunities.

74. See chapter 53. Here, the *Laozi* seems to be aware of the problem, but does not identify it as a problem that can affect a community run on *laissez-faire* principles. In this, the *Laozi* is mistaken.

4. THE *ZHUANGZI: INNER CHAPTERS* AND ZHUANGZIAN PHILOSOPHY

1. Wade-Giles spelling: Chuang Tzu; personal name, Zhou (Wade-Giles: Chou).

2. See Chapter Five below.

3. There is one very obscure reference to the complete heart in the *Inner Chapters* that Chad Hansen and Lisa Raphals take to be a direct refutation of Mencius. See Hansen's *A Daoist Theory of Chinese Thought*, 77–80, and Raphals' "Skeptical Strategies in the *Zhuangzi* and Thaeatetus." At any rate, it is the concept of human natural tendencies, *renxing* 人性, that Mencius brought to the forefront of philosophical thinking for the first time. Zhuangzi makes no reference to it at all. There is a discussion of *renqing* 人情 in the *Inner Chapters*, but only one reference, and whether to what is "essentially human" or simply to "human emotions" remains a subject of disagreement. In a different vein, Paul Kjellberg sees Zhuangzi's

equalization of social status as a possible response to the social conservatism of Mencius. See his "Sextus Empiricus, Zhuangzi, and Xunzi on 'Why Be Skeptical?'"

4. The last two stories of chapter 1, for example. It is amusing to note that this friendly rivalry echoes suspicions and not-so-friendly criticisms between contemporary Continental and analytical philosophers.

5. Wittgenstein uses the notion of a family to show how several things can be related organically by varying combinations of traits (traits that "crisscross and overlap") without sharing a single unified essence: Sally has her father's eyes and her Aunt Cynthia's nose; her brother Pete has their mother's chin and her grandmother's temperament; there is no single trait or combination of traits that all members share, yet the family resemblance is somehow unmistakable. In a similar way, the philosophies articulated in different parts of the *Zhuangzi* share such family resemblances, even though sometimes the resemblances of distant relatives. For more, see Wittgenstein, *Philosophical Investigations*. Thus, despite the variety of philosophical positions, the various authors of the *Zhuangzi* materials can legitimately be seen to belong to a Daoist "family" *jia*.

6. The one exception is chapter 30, "*Shuo Jian,*" "Discourse on Swords," which appears to have little, if anything, to say that is specifically Daoist.

7. Harold Roth, "Chuang Tzu," in *Early Chinese Texts*, ed. Loewe, 58.

8. David McCraw, in *Stratifying* Zhuangzi, argues that a quantitative analysis of stylistic features of the text, specifically nonstandard rhyme, indicates that the *Inner Chapters* are themselves an anthology of broadly related passages from several different hands. Nevertheless, regardless of who wrote them, the *Inner Chapters* and passages attributed to followers of the *Inner Chapters* express a distinctive worldview and approach to life. Moreover, while there may be problems of consistency, as in any philosophical text, half the pleasure of reading such texts is precisely to come up with a coherent interpretation that plausibly resolves the apparent inconsistencies. See also Esther Klein, "Were There *Inner Chapters* in the Warring States?" *T'oung Pao* 96 (2011), for a new assessment of the available evidence.

9. For example, chapter 3, "*Yang Sheng Zhu,*" is so short that it seems to have been abruptly cut off or edited down. It also contains passages that have greater affinities with other chapters, 5 and 6 for example.

10. Graham refers to them as the "School of Zhuangzi"; Liu Xiaogan calls them the "Transmitter School."

11. The adjective "Zhuangzian" implies philosophies that share a similar outlook or sensibility. I prefer it to "Zhuangist," which has a stronger implication of followers who commit themselves to the teachings of a person.

12. See Chapter One, note 17, above for an explanation of the term "metapolitical."

13. Both philosophies are rooted in an acknowledgment that there are things about the world that escape our control and the limits of our understanding. Joyful tranquility can only be attained by coming to terms with such circumstances. I shall, on occasion, use the term "stoicism" with a lowercase "s" to characterize these aspects of Zhuangzian philosophy. There

are, of course, important differences between the two worldviews. The Stoics, for example, believed in the efficacy of reason and had a dualistic distinction between the perfect freedom of the pure spirit and the causal necessity that governs the physical world. Nevertheless, it is instructive to investigate the degree to which the philosophy of the *Inner Chapters* can be understood as a form of stoicism. For a related and enlightening discussion of the similarities and important differences between ancient Greek Stoicism and the Daoism of the *Liezi*, see May Sim's "Is the *Liezi* an Encheiridion?"

14. Pages 60, 70, 73–74, 80, 91. Also translated as "fate" and "destiny," which, as the following explanation will show, is problematic.

15. See Lecture I of Austin's *How to Do Things with Words*.

16. Note that these are not the same. Indeed, fatalism assumes that determinism is false, insofar as it allows the possibility of different paths to the same final event. Whether, logically, Zhuangzi can avoid fatalism and determinism is a separate issue. I am here concerned only with explicating the meaning of "*ming*" and showing how it differs, at least ostensibly, from "destiny" and "fate."

17. Pages 29, 81, 84–85.

18. See also, Chapter 20, 218; Chapter 21, 225; Chapter 22, 236; Chapter 25, 291.

19. The name "Kun" etymologically has two significant connotations, "roe" and "chaos," both of which imply incipience and indeterminacy. For a thorough investigation into the significance of embryonic metaphors in the *Zhuangzi*, see Girardot, *Myth and Meaning in Early Taoism*.

20. Zhuangzi uses the word to refer not only to the changes themselves but also to their effect on our emotions.

21. In the words of Samuel Beckett, at once comical and horrifying, "They give birth astride of a grave." Spoken by Pozzo in *Waiting for Godot*, Act 2.

22. For example, in the *Phaedo* 78b–84b.

23. From within an entirely different philosophical framework, Wittgenstein phrases the issue with concise elegance: "Death is not an event in life: we do not live to experience death.... Our life has no end in just the way in which our visual field has no limits" (*Tractatus* 6.4311). With decidedly less elegance, Heidegger says, "When Dasein reaches its wholeness in death, it simultaneously loses the Being of its 'there.' By its transition to no-longer-Dasein, it gets lifted right out of the possibility of experiencing this transition" (*Being and Time*, Division Two, chapter I, section 47).

24. The existence of discrete quantum transitions would appear to challenge this claim, if it is understood ontologically. However, since these quantum transitions occur below the threshold of discernibility, the claim might still be preserved phenomenologically. Of course, the very concept of a threshold implies a lower limit and therefore a lack of continuity. Still, the threshold itself may be vague, and from the overlapping of vague thresholds emerges a higher-order continuity.

25. Such conditions, insofar as they have been present in nature from the most distant past, are thought of as ancestral: the productive conditions of existence that are present and that also extend back to ancient times.

26. The phrase *weishi* can also be translated as "never." But translated this way, the repetition of the phrase would then be meaningless, paradoxical, or merely emphatic. My judgment is that these meanings do not yield philosophically productive interpretations of the text.

27. This is, of course, empirically mistaken. The fact that dying is a continuous process does not mean that we can never tell the difference between people who are alive and people who are dead.

28. To apply the words of Heraclitus: "The way up and the way down are one and the same."

29. In the traditional interpretation, there is no significant difference between the beautiful and the ugly. This is because the judgments of beauty and ugliness are relativized: there is always some point of view from which Xi Shi is considered ugly, and someone for whom the most hideous-looking person is beautiful.

30. Note that this is not a radical relativism regarding all values, but an ontological assertion of the identity of life and death and thereby an existential challenge to the manner in which we evaluate them in particular.

31. Pages 31, 47–48, 49, 88–89.

32. Hans-Georg Moeller, in *Daoism Explained*, interprets these transformations in the light of Guo Xiang's commentary and sees them as radical and instantaneous shifts in perspective, *gestalt* shifts between parallel ontologies. I see them as part of the constant and continuous cycles of transformation: one falls slowly into a dream state and wakes up gradually from the dream. Each experiential state dissolves as it reconfigures itself as the other state, but in neither state is there a preserved memory of the other. Thus even though the transformation is continuous, the resulting "identities" (Zhuangzi and the butterfly) remain different.

33. This idealist suggestion, however, was adopted explicitly and developed further, perhaps under Buddhist influence, in the *Liezi*.

34. Pages 29–35, 63–66.

35. Also chapter 17, 175, the Lord of the River says, "In the past, I heard people belittling the learning of Confucius and making light of the righteousness of Boyi, though I never believed them. Now, however, I have seen your unfathomable vastness." Compare also the focus on life that blinds us to the vastness of the absences that surround it, as discussed earlier.

36. This term has been taken from Husserl's phenomenology and adapted to name the world as it appears to us, given our everyday concerns. In this more general sense, our lifeworld includes chairs, tables, computers, traffic, pollution, and so on. It does not appear to us as composed of atoms, as governed by relativistic laws or quantum mechanical probabilities, or as a fleeting dream against a backdrop of emptiness, for example.

37. Mozi, in *Jian'ai*, chapters 14, 15, and 16, identifies the heart of ethics and the root of social harmony precisely in expanding our self-identification. In fact, he advocates expanding

our concerns and loyalties beyond ourselves and our own until we include all people. Only when all people are given equitable concern (*jian'ai* 兼愛) will we have the conditions for social harmony.

38. If this is the ultimate goal, it can never be finitely attained, though it may always be striven for as a regulative ideal. For a multifaceted exploration of this problem, see Nagel, *The View from Nowhere*.

39. See Chapter Seven below on skill in the *Zhuangzi* and *Liezi*.

40. *Laozi*, chapter 64.

41. For a further discussion of the role of focus and field in early Chinese thinking see Ames and Hall, *Thinking from the Han*.

42. Epictetus, in his *Enchiridion*, recommends such exercises in order to cultivate "stoic" tranquility.

43. This line of thinking is taken up explicitly in chapter 17, "Autumn Floods": "Ruo of the North Sea said, 'From the point of view of the Way, things have no nobility or meanness. From the point of view of things themselves, each regards itself as noble and other things as mean. . . . From the point of view of differences, if we regard a thing as big because there is a certain bigness to it, then among all the ten thousand things there are none that are not big. If we regard a thing as small because there is a certain smallness to it, then among the ten thousand things there are none that are not small'" (179).

44. In chapter 1, *Xiao Yao You*, Lianshu criticizes Jianwu, saying that the understanding has its own form of blindness and deafness (33). A little further along, Zhuangzi criticizes Huizi's petty-mindedness in being unable to comprehend what is of value from vaster perspectives (34).

45. Pages 32, 33, 35, 36, 86–87, 93, 94.

46. Also translated as: nonaction, inaction, action without action, noninterference.

47. A shadowy movement is sensed at the periphery of a visual field; for a while, its interpretation remains unspecified. It may be an animal or an object blown by the wind, but it need not be an object at all; perhaps it is the shadow of a bird. Retaining this degree of nonspecificity is probably impossible with experience of everyday things, but we may still actively cultivate the ability to deconstrue and reconstrue what we experience.

48. There will still be success and failure in the cultivation of natural skills, but success as defined by worldly interests is seen to be an artificial and therefore ultimately worthless pursuit.

49. Pages 34, 35, 63–64, 67.

50. The stranger in chapter 1 (34–35) who sold the hand cream to the King of Wu for military purposes and thereby became rich was more imaginative than Huizi, but was still confined by social functions. There is, of course, also room for criticizing the military purposes, which seem inconsistent with Daoist goals, though Zhuangzi does not pursue this line of criticism.

51. Compare what Jian Wu says to Lian Shu on page 33: "I was completely dumbfounded at [the madman of Chu's] words: endless as the Milky Way, vast and wide of the mark, far from the human condition."

52. Pages 64, 65, 66, 156, 209.

53. Harold Roth, *Original Tao*.

54. The assumption is not blind, but based on the results of accumulated practice. Such results should neither be trusted blindly nor dismissed as unscientific. The mere fact that such phenomenological reflection appears to be self-validating (Husserl's *evidenz*, or self-evidentness) does not necessarily mean that it is infallible. By the same token, although the very nature of phenomenological reflection is such that it cannot be reduced in any obvious manner to third-person observable phenomena, this in itself does not invalidate its results. Rather, we should judge the efficacy of such reflection by the extent to which the practice proves successful.

55. Medical science, for example, continues to extend the natural lifespan. This extension is indefinite insofar as we know of no predetermined point beyond which extending life is impossible, but it does not follow that we are capable of extending life infinitely.

56. Pages 57–58, 205.

57. The former attitude leads to utopian tendencies; the latter opens up the possibility of the mystical rule of the syncretists.

58. *Ren Jian Shi* 人間世, literally, "the world of the space between people." The social realm is understood as primarily relational, not merely as a collection of individuals. Relationality is also emphasized in chapter 6, where authentic mutuality, *xiangyu* 相與 (also translatable as "being-with"), is achieved in its own dissolution, *wuxiangyu* 無相與 ("without being-with"). See Lundberg's essay, "A Meditation on Friendship," in *Wandering at Ease in the* Zhuangzi, ed. Ames.

59. Sometimes translated as "virtue," "powers," or "excellence." Pages 35, 66, 69, 70, 71, 73, 74, 75, 134–35, 137.

60. Pages 77–80.

61. Also translated as the "perfect man." Pages 32, 46, 54, 71–72, 74, and also 97, 253–54, 300.

62. Note the similarity to the ancient Stoic ideal of objective tranquility, though without the rationalist epistemology and dualistic metaphysics.

63. The first word of the title, *qi* 齊, is difficult to interpret. Its basic meaning is to even out the collective surface of things of disparate length, so that they appear smooth and tidy. The title thus means something like, "discourse on smoothing out the unevenness in the diversity of things," and has usually been translated as "Discourse on Equalizing Things." This translation follows the popular interpretation of the *Zhuangzi* as espousing a form of radical relativism.

64. *Bian*, written as both 辨 "distinction" and 辯 "disputation": in the "*Qi Wu Lun*" they have a combined technical sense of "disputation over systems of distinctions."

65. The Mohists also associate such distinction making with disputing over alternatives, *bian* 辯. Those who engage in disputes are arguing over whose distinctions or *shifei* judgments are correct, *dang* 當.

66. In the last section of chapter 5, "*De Chong Fu*."

67. Indeed, Graham sometimes translates it as "essence" and sometimes as "identity." However, because "essence" and "identity" are technical terms with precise definitions and ontological implications in Western philosophy, I prefer to steer clear of them, to avoid inappropriately imposing their concomitant ontologies. This is not to deny that the concepts of essence and identity might be found in Chinese philosophy, but simply to avoid presupposing them when translating the term "*qing*."

68. For the purpose of this discussion I use "person" and "human" to translate *ren* and treat them synonymously.

69. Graham and many modern scholars prefer the following interpretation: "*Shifei* judgment is what I mean by *qing* (particular conditions of being human). Being without *qing* means not allowing approval and rejection to harm your person." The important point is that one ought not to make the judgments, but whichever interpretation of *qing* one takes, the question of how deeply this posture affects one's humanity is still an important issue. A sociopath, for example, is defined as person who lacks the capacity to empathize, to be pained by the suffering of other people. There is an important sense in which it is not inappropriate to judge such a person lacking in humanity. It would seem that such reactions are indeed part of what makes us fully human, and Huizi is right to be concerned about the significance of giving up such judgments.

70. Note that the Mohists also use the terms *ren* and *yi*, but unlike the Ruists, provide a utilitarian definition in terms of behavior that brings benefit to the people.

71. In *Chuang-tzu: The Inner Chapters*, 9–14, and *Disputers of the Tao*, 176–83.

72. Graham, *Disputers of the Tao*, 176–83.

73. Graham, *Chuang-tzu: The Inner Chapters*, 9.

74. Affirmative judgment (*shi*) that accords with, adjusts to, accommodates (*yin*) the changing circumstances.

75. In *A Daoist Theory of Chinese Thought*, 265–306.

76. In "Skeptical Strategies in the Zhuangzi and Thaeatetus," in *Essays on Skepticism, Relativism, and Ethics in the Zhuangzi*, ed. Ivanhoe and Kjellberg, 26–42.

77. In "Sextus Empiricus, Zhuangzi, and Xunzi," in *Essays on Skepticism, Relativism, and Ethics in the Zhuangzi*, ed. Ivanhoe and Kjellberg, 1–16.

78. Unlike Hansen's *ming*, the *epoché* does not permit the skeptic to pick and choose among any of the equalized views. Rather, for practical purposes, one acts as though what appears to be the case is the case, though theoretically one remains uncommitted to whether it is in fact the case.

79. Although Zhuangzi praises the tranquility that results from such an attitude, Kjellberg sees this only as a side effect. The real point of Zhuangzian skepticism, according to Kjellberg, is the consummate skill that results when we are free to act spontaneously, without worries about what is right and what is wrong.

80. Radical relativism is the view that no judgment can ever be made between points of view. This is the form of relativism that is usually attributed to Zhuangzi. There are, how-

ever, weaker and more plausible forms of relativism. Pluralism, for example, allows there to be more than one right way, but does not give up the possibility of judging some ways to be wrong.

81. We cannot even say that it *appears* to lead to tranquility, since there are many people for whom not being able to make a decision leads to anxiety.

82. However, as we have seen, relativistic possibilities are taken up more explicitly in chapter 17, for example, on 177–82.

83. For more on the false dichotomy between relativism and absolutism, and for an insightful and timely explanation of the pragmatic middle ground, see Richard Bernstein, *Beyond Objectivism and Relativism*.

84. Translators, unfortunately, take great pains to remove the contradictions under the mistaken belief that they must be reinterpreted. However, though explicit contradictions make a text hard to understand, this does not by itself justify their elimination.

85. For a detailed discussion of the laws of bivalence, contradiction, and excluded middle in the Mohist *Canon* and their relevance to political practice in Mohist philosophy in general, see chapter 5 of my book *Zhuangzi and Early Chinese Philosophy*.

86. Wittgenstein, Waismann, Quine, and Derrida explore the indeterminacy and porosity of language in great depth. I discuss their relevance in *Zhuangzi and Early Chinese Philosophy*. The reader may also wish to explore Wittgenstein's *Philosophical Investigations*, Waismann's essay "Verifiability," and Quine's *From a Logical Point of View*. For the reader who is not already familiar with Derrida, Henry Staten's *Wittgenstein and Derrida* provides a lucid account of Derrida's philosophy of language.

87. The same applies to distinguishing what is so, *ran* 然, from what is not so, *buran* 不然.

88. To do so, we must find the criterion, *yin* 因, that distinguishes horses from non-horses whatever it might be, and make affirmations and denials in accordance with the presence or absence of the criterion.

89. *Porosität*: Waismann's term translated into English as "open texture."

5. THE *OUTER* AND *MISCELLANEOUS CHAPTERS* OF THE *ZHUANGZI*: FROM ANARCHIST UTOPIANISM TO MYSTICAL IMPERIALISM

1. For thorough analyses of the dating and structure of the anthology, see Graham, "How Much of *Chuang-tzu* 莊子 Did Chuang-tzu Write?" in *Studies in Chinese Philosophy and Philosophical Literature*; his introduction to *Chuang-tzu: The Inner Chapters*; Harold Roth, "Who Compiled the *Chuang-tzu*?"; and Liu Xiaogan, *Classifying the* Zhuangzi *Chapters*. Liu Xiaogan has produced a thorough study and evaluation of the results of these analyses, from that of Chen Zhi'an in the Ming dynasty (app. 1632) to Takeuchi Yoshio and A. C. Graham.

2. Graham, however, still sees chapter 30 as Yangist in spirit.

3. These passages are directly influenced by several chapters from the *Laozi*, most notably chapters 18 and 19; chapters 37, 46, 48, 53, 57, 65, 75, and 80 also present a similar critique and utopian vision.

4. Although the social vision expressed in the Primitivist chapters is quite consistent with these chapters, Graham does not attribute the Primitivist chapters to Yangism because they contain explicit criticism of Yang Zhu. Liu Xiaogan, however, does not find a significant reason to differentiate between the two. I agree with Liu that the differences between them do not add up to a significant difference in philosophical position.

5. See, for example, *Hsün Tzu: Basic Writings*, trans. Watson, 157–65.

6. This chapter is also reminiscent of the *Mozi*, which makes a similar argument against aggression. Mozi too is concerned about the ability of the clever to take advantage of those who are less intelligent. According to him, it is our duty to protect the latter from exploitation.

7. Pages 101–2, 105–6.

8. Especially chapter 8; also pages 104–5, 114–17. Watson often translates this as "inborn nature."

9. See the discussion of the swimmer at Lüliang Falls, for example, in Chapter Seven below.

10. The very same phenomena that are understood as law governed by modern science are understood by the Daoists as *ziran*, free and spontaneous. Paradoxically, the advantage of the inappropriately Legalist metaphor is that it encourages discovery and explicit description of the laws that govern things. The metaphor of spontaneity, on the contrary, discourages this sort of construction of explicit scientific theory. The advantage of the metaphor of spontaneity lies in its first-person embodied application to the subtleties of psychophysical functioning and of social interaction.

11. Graham, *Chuang-tzu: The Inner Chapters*, 66–67.

12. The same is true of the "Old Fisherman," chapter 31. These chapters are admired more for their literary merit than the strength of their philosophical argument.

13. A popular candidate is the pleasure one gets from helping others. First, however, one does not always get pleasure from helping others. Second, even when one does, the pleasure itself is a byproduct, not the motivation. The claim that the pleasure was the real motivation cannot simply be stated dogmatically, but must be proven.

14. To deconstruct a view is to show that it could not possibly have the stability, consistency, universality, or necessity that it purports to have.

15. The phenomenon of pianistic "touch," for example: objectively speaking, there is only one factor affecting the sound of a piano string: the faster it is hit by the hammer, the louder it sounds. And yet different musicians seem clearly to have remarkable differences of "touch" on the same piano, not just differences in speed and volume. How this is to be accounted for is a mystery, but those who do not hear the difference simply deny its existence.

16. Hans-Georg Moeller's account of rulership in *The Philosophy of the* Daodejing has deep resonances with the syncretist conception of mystical rule.

17. Or: "The Empire."

18. Indeed, the parallels with Xunzi are so close, it reads like a Daoist response to Xunzi's argument for the superiority of Ruism.

19. Peerenboom, in the introduction to *Law and Morality in Ancient China*.

6. THE *LIEZI*

1. Or Master Lie, also known in the Wade-Giles Romanization as Lieh-tzu; his personal name, "Yukou," means "guard-against-bandits."

2. Yang Bojun believes that, despite the mythologizing of the character, there is sufficient scattered evidence that there probably did exist a real person on whom the stories were based. W. T. Chan places him as early as the fifth century.

3. As noted by A. C. Graham in his introduction to part 5 of *Chuang-tzu: The Inner Chapters*, which deals with what he identifies as the Yangist passages of the *Zhuangzi*.

4. See Graham's "The Date and Composition of the *Lieh-tzu*," in *Studies in Chinese Philosophy and Philosophical Literature*, 216–82.

5. Sometimes, complex philosophical narratives are given abrupt simplistic endings, strongly suggesting that they were tagged on by a storyteller or editor who failed to grasp the philosophical significance of the passage.

6. "Endeavour and Destiny" in Graham's translation.

7. "The Date and Composition of the *Lieh-tzu*," in *Studies in Chinese Philosophy and Philosophical Literature*, 216–82.

8. Zhuang Wanshou, however, points out that the characteristics cited for classifying the text as a forgery—being composed by several authors over several centuries, and drawing from several sources—apply to other philosophical texts that are not dismissed as forgeries, including, for example, the *Analects* and the *Zhuangzi*. Most Western scholars have until recently shared a similar skepticism regarding the classification of the text as a forgery.

9. "The Date and Composition of the *Lieh-tzu*."

10. The editors and contributors to the recent volume, *Riding the Wind with Liezi: New Perspectives on the Daoist Classic*, edited by Ronnie Littlejohn and Jeffrey Dippmann, all share the belief that even though the text is most likely to be a forgery, this does not diminish its scholarly and philosophical interest as a Daoist text.

11. The philosophy of skill in the *Zhuangzi* and *Liezi* will be dealt with in Chapter Seven below.

12. Incidentally, that one of the chapters of the text is named after Confucius should not, by itself, be taken as significant. The chapter is so titled because the name of Confucius appears at the beginning of the first story.

13. See the last section of Chapter One above for explanations of these philosophical methods.

14. While ideas from the *Zhuangzi* are believed to have exerted a significant influence on the interpretation of Buddhism in China, the *Liezi* may constitute a possible converse case of Mahayana Buddhist influence on the development of those Zhuangzian ideas. Stories here and there resonate with some of the tenets of Sanlun (the Chinese form of Madhyamaka) and Weishilun (the Chinese form of Yogacara Idealism). The resonances are highly suggestive, but the evidence is not decisive enough to be sure of any influence, either of Buddhist ideas on the *Liezi* or vice versa. If the conjecture of Buddhist influence is correct, it would also place the relevant passages of the text well into, if not after, the Han dynasty.

15. For example, the new logic of contrasts may have arisen by combining *yinyang* philosophy with the logical resources of Huizi, if Graham's analysis of his paradoxes is correct.

16. Those who insist that texts such as the *Laozi* clearly engage in metaphysics seem to be using the term in a looser sense. The terminological distinction between cosmology and metaphysics is obviously a philosophically significant one, and if my analysis is correct, of fundamental importance in the pursuit of comparative philosophy. We trivialize such a crucial distinction at the risk of falsifying our understanding of early Chinese philosophy.

17. Traditionally known in English as the *Doctrine of the Mean*. Tu Wei-ming translates it as *Centrality and Commonality*, while Roger Ames renders it as *Focusing the Familiar*.

18. Often translated as "sincerity," implying a genuineness that lies at the heart of the cosmos, of humanity, and of ethical behavior; Roger Ames and David Hall, drawing on the philosophy of Whitehead, attempts to draw out deeper significances by translating it as "creativity."

19. Though it is not characteristic of the major trends of thought in the *Zhuangzi*, a similar tendency can be found in a few scattered passages of what appear to be later strata reminiscent of the *Liezi*: pages 198, 242, and 246, for example.

20. Also, the unborn, or nonliving; for ease of translation and commentary, I move freely among the concepts of birth, life, existence, and production. Since the words "birth," "begetting," "life," "living," "born," and "unborn" cannot be applied to nonliving phenomena in English, I use the words "production," "existence," "existing," "unproduced," and "not existing" to refer to the emergence and endurance (and their opposites) of all phenomena, biological and nonbiological. These should not, of course, be identified with the concepts of "being" and "non-being." See "Absence and Presence *Wu You*" in Chapter Two above for the distinction between "existence" and "being."

21. Again, although the unborn and untransformed are articulated separately, and although they are not explicitly identified, it does not seem likely that they are intended to refer to different things.

22. In chapter 3, "King Mu of Zhou," 58–73.

23. Both antirealism and idealism reject realism, but antirealism also rejects the dualistic distinction between the mental and the material that is left unquestioned by idealism. Thus, antirealism cannot be understood as idealism in the traditional sense.

24. See Anacker, *Seven Works of Vasubandhu* (Delhi: Motilal Banarsidass, 1984).

25. Of course, all this depends on accepting the antirealist perspective. I do not go into justifications for antirealism here since none is contained or implied in the *Liezi*.

26. Pages 69–70, for example.

27. One might think of this as using the literary imagination as a skillful means to effect a phenomenological transformation, as Buddhist texts use *upaya* to bring about understanding appropriate to each listener.

28. Page 65; but also relevant are 61–63 and 70–73.

29. Graham translates it as "magic" and "illusion."

30. In the "*Qi Wu Lun,*" 36–37.

31. As Kant argues in the *Critique of Pure Reason*.

32. However, those who develop similar conditions, either through Alzheimer's or through extreme anterograde amnesia, appear to experience some degree of anxiety, albeit short-lived, when they begin to recognize that something is amiss, especially when communicating with people who remember things that they do not.

33. Chapter 5, 94–100.

34. The text says "exhaustible"; it is usually emended to "inexhaustible."

35. Chapter 5, 96, 101–2, 104.

36. Graham translates this word as "the same," but it is more accurately translated as "alike" or "similar." Since similarity and sameness are different, this is philosophically significant.

37. There are places in the *Liezi* where the alternative to cultural chauvinism is not radical relativism. Rather, a certain kind of primitive culture is hailed as superior. These passages are reminiscent of the utopian strands of the *Zhuangzi*.

38. Discussed extensively throughout chapter 6.

39. *Zishou* 自壽, long-lived of itself, *ziyao* 自夭, short-lived of itself, etc., also referred to generally as *ziran* 自然.

40. The difference in timeliness, *shi* 時, for example: we sometimes talk of artists who are born before their time, that is, before their community developed the capacity to appreciate their genius.

41. See, for example, 126, 127, and 129.

42. Though in one incongruous passage, Confucian virtues are listed as the conditions of success (165–66).

7. PHILOSOPHY OF SKILL IN THE *ZHUANGZI* AND *LIEZI*

1. The exception is Mozi, who, like Hobbes, does see antagonism at the root of individual difference. In fact, he seems to be more pessimistic than Hobbes, since he sees this as resulting whether or not resources are limited. See my chapter on Mohism in *Zhuangzi and Early*

Chinese Philosophy. Although Xunzi believed that humans left to follow their natural tendencies will end up in conflict, he did not identify predation or antagonism as the single most salient feature of natural interaction.

2. As I write, I am struck by how difficult it is to find words to describe the workings of nature that are not metaphors drawn from artificial systems: "mechanism," "machinery," even "system," "organization," and "structure" seem to have primary senses of abstract artificial patterns through which the ordering and arrangement of something is understood.

3. A few of these insights are discussed explicitly in the *Laozi* and *Zhuangzi*, but perhaps the majority of them are embodied in practices that were influenced by Daoist philosophy, both directly, and indirectly through its influence on Chinese Buddhism: painting, calligraphy, martial arts, medicine, *taiji*, and *qigong*.

4. Ryle derives his epistemological distinction from Heidegger's phenomenological-ontological distinction in *Being and Time* between *zuhandenheit*, or readiness-to-hand, the mode of being of the tools or *pragmata* that together constitute the web of our social environment, and *vorhandenheit*, presence-at-hand, or the mode of being that we attribute to objectively existing entities. The first is a pragmatic concept; the second is a decontextualized, theoretical construct. *Zuhandenheit* manifests in our successful engagement with our environment (a ball in flight as we reach out to catch it); *vorhandenheit* manifests in a practically decontextualized understanding (a projectile whose parabolic path is interrupted by a moving object).

5. The natural course and tendencies are not "regular," *chang*, not easily understood through the regularities mapped by ordinary language. As the first line of the *Laozi* says, "Ways can be followed, but they are not regular paths." In this vein, the second line might be interpreted as saying that if language can describe these paths, it is not any ordinary form of language.

6. Following directions, for example: "Look out for the red flag; it will look like you have to change lanes, but don't." This is explicit. The road may be such that if you were unprepared, it would simply be too late to correct your mistake.

7. I use the term "knowledge" here in the pragmatic sense of claims that have sufficiently proved their efficacy, even if they should prove in the future to need refinement or revision. There are some sophomoric criticisms of the validity of scientific knowledge from a radically relativistic perspective. Insofar as such criticisms are dogmatically based on radically relativistic presuppositions, and not on any genuine appreciation either of the nature of science and technology or of their *prima facie* successes, they are not strong enough to be taken seriously. There are, however, also political criticisms of scientific knowledge claims from the perspective of the sociology of knowledge. These reveal hidden assumptions and values that cast doubt on the claims to objective neutrality of science and technology. These criticisms are worth taking seriously, but since they have no direct bearing on the point currently being made, I will refrain from engaging with them here.

8. Ronnie Littlejohn, in his contribution to *Riding the Wind with Liezi*, argues that chapter 2 of the *Liezi*, "The Yellow Emperor," in which most of the skill stories occur, may in fact be one of the missing chapters of the *Zhuangzi* edited out by Guo Xiang.

9. In both *Zhuangzi* and *Liezi*.

10. Chapter 19, 199–200. Also in the *Liezi*, chapter 2, 44–45.

11. Each ball is precariously balanced on a point with completely open leeway for random movement; the unpredictability magnifies exponentially from ball to ball, as does the unpredictability of how movement in the hand will affect movement in the balls farther away.

12. We should be careful not to *presuppose* a disconnection here between mind and body. It is tempting to read any reference to a mind and body as presupposing such a separation. Dualisms of this sort, however, are not natural presuppositions, but complex philosophical positions that must be explicitly articulated and argued for. Plato and Descartes, the arch-proponents of mind-body dualism, both go to great length to argue for such a distinction. They both assume that the argument is necessary. Therefore, in the absence of an explicit argument, we have no good reason to impose a metaphysics of dualism.

13. Polanyi discusses the manner in which we utilize a layer of "subsidiary awareness" of sensory information from instruments we manipulate, in the same way as we treat the subsidiary awareness of our own bodies. In this way, we incorporate instruments, and live and act through them as extensions of our bodies. See *Personal Knowledge*.

14. As we have noted, the infinitesimal calculus may succeed, but it is of no use for human skill. Conversely, fuzzy logic, which models human judgment, can be applied successfully to control systems.

15. Contemporary analytical philosophers of mind use this term to refer to concepts that are appealed to in ordinary unscientific explanations of psychological phenomena. The implication is that, while these concepts may be enshrined in ordinary language, they should be rejected in favor of scientific concepts that have proven their worth experimentally and theoretically. It strikes me that some nonscientific concepts prove their worth pragmatically and phenomenologically: that is, although they do not correspond to anything that can be tested in a laboratory, they do correspond to phenomena that are available phenomenologically, and somehow provide powerful explanations of phenomena at a pragmatic level. We might interpret such concepts instrumentally; that is, without worrying about whether they refer to anything that can be explained in terms of current scientific theory, we continue to use them as though they refer to actual things, so long as this results in successful action. Some physicists, because of problems reconciling the wave and particle natures of quanta, interpret subatomic particles in an instrumentalist way: for some purposes, it proves very useful to talk as though they actually exist. We may adopt the same attitude in our interpretation of *shen*, *qi*, and so on.

16. Gilbert Ryle, for example, points out that when we talk about doing something for the "sake" of someone else, we are not required to interpret this as meaning that sakes are a kind of existing thing.

17. Together with, *yu . . . ju,* 與 . . . 俱; in cooperation with, *yu . . . xie,* 與 . . . 偕.

BIBLIOGRAPHY

Ames, Roger, ed. *Wandering at Ease in the* Zhuangzi. Albany: State University of New York Press, 1998.

Ames, Roger and David Hall. *Anticipating China: Thinking Through the Narratives of Chinese and Western Culture.* Albany: State University of New York Press, 1995.

———. *Daodejing: Making This Life Significant.* New York: Ballantine, 2003.

———. *Thinking from the Han: Self, Truth, and Transcendence in Chinese and Western Culture.* Albany: State University of New York Press, 1998.

———. *Thinking Through Confucius.* Albany: State University of New York Press, 1987.

Austin, J. L. *How to Do Things with Words.* Cambridge, Mass.: Harvard University Press, 1962.

Barrett, T. H. "*Lieh Tzu.*" In *Early Chinese Texts: A Bibliographical Guide,* ed. Michael Loewe. Berkeley: Society for the Study of Early China and the Institute of East Asian Studies, University of California, 1993.

Bernstein, Richard. *Beyond Objectivism and Relativism: Science, Hermeneutics, and Praxis.* Philadelphia: University of Pennsylvania Press, 1983.

Chan, Alan. *Two Visions of the Way: A Study of the Wang Pi and the Ho-shang Kung Commentaries on the* Lao-Tzu. Albany: State University of New York Press, 1991.

Chen, Kenneth. *Buddhism in China: A Historical Survey.* Princeton: Princeton University Press, 1964.

Ch'en, Ku-ying. *Lao Tzu: Text, Notes, and Comments.* Trans. Rhett Y. W. Young and Roger Ames. ROC: Chinese Materials Center, 1981.

Ch'ien, Ssu-ma. *The Grand Scribe's Records, Volume VII: The Memoirs of Pre-Han China.* Ed. William H. Nienhauser, Jr. Bloomington: Indiana University Press, 1995.

Chuang Tzu. *Basic Writings.* Trans. Burton Watson. New York: Columbia University Press, 1964.

——. *The Complete Works of Chuang Tzu*. Trans. Burton Watson. New York: Columbia University Press, 1968.

Cook, Scott. *Hiding the World in the World: Uneven Discourses on the* Zhuangzi. Albany: State University of New York Press, 2003.

Coutinho, Steve. *Zhuangzi and Early Chinese Philosophy: Vagueness, Transformation and Paradox*. Aldershot: Ashgate, 2004.

Csikszentmihalyi, Mark and P. J. Ivanhoe. *Religious and Philosophical Aspects of the* Laozi. New York: State University of New York Press, 1999.

de Bary, Theodore. *Sources of Chinese Tradition, Vol. 1*. New York: Columbia University Press, 2000.

Eco, Umberto and Thomas Sebeok. *The Sign of Three: Dupin, Holmes, Pierce*. Bloomington: Indiana University Press, 1988.

Fraser, Chris. "Language and Ontology in Early Chinese Thought." *Philosophy East and West* 57, no. 4.

Fung, Yu-Lan. *Chuang-Tzu: A New Selected Translation with an Exposition of the Philosophy of Kuo Hsiang*. Beijing: Foreign Languages Press, 1991.

Gadamer, Hans Georg. *Truth and Method*. New York: Continuum, 2004.

Girardot, Norman J. *Myth and Meaning in Early Taoism: The Theme of Chaos (Hun-tun)*. Berkeley: University of California Press, 1983.

Graham, Angus Charles. *The Book of Lieh-tzu*. New York: Columbia University Press, 1990.

——. *Chuang-Tzu: The Inner Chapters: A Classic of Tao*. Indianapolis: Hackett, 2001.

——. *Disputers of the Tao: Philosophical Argument in Ancient China*. La Salle: Open Court, 1989.

——. *Later Mohist Logic, Ethics and Science*. London: School of Oriental and African Studies, 1978.

——. *Studies in Chinese Philosophy and Philosophical Literature*. Albany: State University of New York Press, 1990.

——. *Unreason Within Reason*. La Salle, Ill.: Open Court, 1992.

Hansen, Chad. *A Daoist Theory of Chinese Thought: A Philosophical Interpretation*. New York: Oxford University Press, 1992.

——. *Language and Logic in Ancient China*. Ann Arbor: University of Michigan Press, 1983.

Heidegger, Martin. *Being and Time*. Trans. John MacQuarrie and Edward Robinson. New York: Harper and Row, 1962.

Henricks, Robert G. *Lao-Tzu Te-Tao Ching*. New York: Ballantine, 1989.

——. *Lao Tzu's Tao Te Ching*. New York: Columbia University Press, 2000.

Holloway, Kenneth. *Guodian: The Newly Discovered Seeds of Chinese Religious and Political Philosophy*. Oxford: Oxford University Press, 2009.

Hsün Tzu. *Basic Writings*. Trans. Burton Watson. New York: Columbia University Press, 1963.

Ivanhoe, P. J. *The Daodejing of Laozi*. Indianapolis: Hackett, 2003.

Ivanhoe, P. J. and Paul Kjellberg, eds. *Essays on Skepticism, Relativism, and Ethics in the Zhuangzi*. Albany: State University of New York Press, 1996.

Jullien, Francois. *Detour and Access: Strategies of Meaning in China and Greece*. Trans. Sophie Hawkes. Cambridge: MIT Press, 2004.

Kaltenmark, Max. *Lao Tzu and Taoism*. Trans. Roger Greaves. Stanford: Stanford University Press, 1969.

Klein, Esther. "Were There *Inner Chapters* in the Warring States?" *T'oung Pao* 96 (2011): 299–369.

Kohn, L. and Michael Lafargue, eds. *Daoism and Chinese Culture*. Cambridge, Mass.: Three Pines Press, 2001.

Kohn, Livia. *Early Chinese Mysticism: Philosophy and Soteriology in Taoist Tradition*. Princeton: Princeton University Press, 1992.

———. *Introducing Daoism*. Oxford: Routledge, 2009.

———. *Lao-tzu and the* Tao-te-ching. Albany: State University of New York Press, 1998.

LaFargue, Michael. *The Tao of the Tao Te Ching: A Translation and Commentary*. Albany: State University of New York Press, 1992.

Lau, D. C. *Tao Te Ching*. Hong Kong: The Chinese University Press, 1996.

Littlejohn, Ronnie. "The *Liezi*'s Use of the Lost *Zhuangzi*." In *Riding the Wind with Liezi*, ed. Ronnie Littlejohn and Jeffrey Dippmann, 51–74. Albany: State University of New York Press, 1996.

Littlejohn, R. and Jeffrey Dippmann, eds. *Riding the Wind with Liezi: New Perspectives on the Daoist Classic*. Albany: State University of New York Press, 2011.

Liu, Xiaogan. *Classifying the* Zhuangzi *Chapters*. Trans. Donald Munro. Michigan Monographs in Chinese Studies, no. 65. Ann Arbor: University of Michigan, 1994.

Lloyd, Geoffrey and Nathan Sivin. *The Way and the Word: Science and Medicine in Early China and Greece*. New Haven: Yale University Press, 2003.

Loewe, Michael, ed. *Early Chinese Texts: A Bibliographical Guide*. Berkeley: Society for the Study of Early China and the Institute of East Asian Studies, University of California, 1993.

Loewe, Michael and Ed Shaughnessy, eds. *Cambridge History of Ancient China*. Cambridge: Cambridge University Press, 1999.

Mair, Victor H., ed. *Experimental Essays on Chuang-tzu*. Honolulu: University of Hawai'i Press, 1983.

———. *Wandering on the Way: Early Taoist Tales and Parables of Chuang Tzu*. New York: Bantam, 1994.

McCraw, David. *Stratifying* Zhuangzi: *Rhyme and Other Quantitative Evidence*. Language and Linguistics Monograph Series, 41. Taiwan: Institute of Linguistics, Academia Sinica, 2010.

Miller, James. *Daoism: A Short Introduction*. Oxford: Oneworld Publications, 2003.

Moeller, Hans-Georg. *Daoism Explained*. Chicago: Open Court, 2004.

——. *The Philosophy of the Daodejing*. New York: Columbia University Press, 2006.

Mou, Bo. *Polishing the Chinese Mirror: Essays in Honor of Henry Rosemont, Jr.* New York: Global Scholarly Publications, 2008.

Nagel, Thomas. *The View from Nowhere*. Oxford: Oxford University Press, 1989.

Peerenboom, R. P. *Law and Morality in Ancient China: The Silk Manuscripts of Huang-Lao*. New York: State University of New York Press, 1993.

Polanyi, Michael. *Personal Knowledge: Towards a Post-Critical Philosophy*. New York: Harper Torch Books, 1964.

Quine, W. V. O. *From a Logical Point of View*. Cambridge, Mass.: Harvard University Press, 1980.

Raphals, Lisa. "Skeptical Strategies in the *Zhuangzi* and Thaeatetus." In *Essays on Skepticism, Relativism, and Ethics in the Zhuangzi*, ed. P. J. Ivanhoe and Paul Kjellberg, 26–49. Albany: State University of New York Press, 1996.

Rosemont, Henry Jr., ed. *Chinese Texts and Philosophical Contexts: Essays Dedicated to Angus C. Graham*. Vol. I, *Critics and Their Critics*. La Salle, Ill.: Open Court, 1991.

Roth, Harold. "Chuang Tzu." In *Early Chinese Texts: A Bibliographical Guide*, ed. Michael Loewe and Ed Shaughnessy. Berkeley: Society for the Study of Early China and the Institute of East Asian Studies, University of California, 1993.

——. *Original Tao: Inward Training and the Foundations of Taoist Mysticism*. New York: Columbia University Press, 1999.

——. "Who Compiled the Chuang-tzu?" In *Chinese Texts and Philosophical Contexts: Essays Dedicated to Angus C. Graham*, ed. Henry Rosemont, Jr. Vol. I, *Critics and Their Critics*. La Salle, Ill.: Open Court, 1991.

Roth, Harold, ed. "*A Companion to Angus C. Graham's Chuang Tzu: The Inner Chapters*." Monographs of the Society for Asian and Comparative Philosophy. Honolulu: University of Hawai'i Press, 2003.

Ryle, Gilbert. *Collected Papers*. Vols. I and II. New York: Barnes & Noble, 1971.

Sagart, Laurent. *The Roots of Old Chinese*. Amsterdam Studies in the Theory and History of Linguistic Science, Series IV: Current Issues in Linguistic Theory. Amsterdam: John Benjamins, 1999.

Sim, May. "Is the *Liezi* an Encheiridion?" In *Riding the Wind with Liezi*, ed. Ronnie Littlejohn and Jeffrey Dippmann, 51–74. Albany: State University of New York Press, 1996.

Ssu-ma Ch'ien. *The Grand Scribe's Records, Volume VII: The Memoirs of Pre-Han China*. Bloomington: Indiana University Press, 1995.

Staten, Henry. *Wittgenstein and Derrida*. Lincoln: University of Nebraska Press, 1984.

Wagner, Rudolf. *A Chinese Reading of the* Daodejing. Albany: State University of New York Press, 2003.

Waismann, Friedrich. "Verifiability." In *Proceedings of the Aristotelian Society*. XIX (1945): 119–150.

Wittgenstein, Ludwig. *Philosophical Investigations*. Oxford: Blackwell, 2009.

———. *Tractatus Logico-Philosphicus*. London: Routledge and Kegan Paul, 1960.

Yang, Bojun. *Liezi Jishi*. Beijing: Zhonghua Shuju, 1979. 杨伯峻。列子集釋。中华书局, 1979.

Yuan, Zhouzong. *An Investigation Into the Life and Times of Laozi and His Military Thought*. Taibei: Taiwan Shangwu Yinshuguan, 1977, 54–55. 袁宙宗, 老子身世及其兵學思想探賾, 臺灣商務印書館。

Ziporyn, Brook. *Zhuangzi: The Essential Writings: With Selections from Traditional Commentaries*. Indianapolis: Hackett, 2009.

INDEX

abduction, 22–23, 195n6

absence and presence, 55–58, 87

absolute, 191n3

absolutism, 121

action without artifice, 100–2

activity, 34–35

affirmation and denial. *See shifei*

allegory, 79

Ames, Roger, 15

analogy, 13–14

anarchism, 71–73, 128

ancestral, 53–55, 89, 91–92

anomalous cases, 16

anticipation, 74, 76, 184

antirealism, 154–59, 117, 212n23

aporia, 137, 164

appropriateness. *See yi*

approval and disapproval, 34. *See also shifei*

archer, 181

Aristotle, 56, 133

artifice, 33, 34–35, 38–40, 129, 175; Daoist critique, 37

artificial vs. natural, 38–40, 69–70, 123

ataraxia (peace of mind), 118

Austin, J. L., 84

"Autumn Floods," 81, 161, 206n43

awakening, 93

balance, 43–44

bamboo manuscripts, 48

beginning, 90. *See also shi* 始

being, 199n30, 31. *See also you*

ben busheng 本不生 (radically unproduced), 153

benevolence. *See ren* 仁

Bernstein, Richard, 209n83

bian 變 (change, perturbation), 86, 91

biosphere, 28, 88

bivalence, 124, 209n85

Book of the Yellow Emperor, 147

boundaries, 123–24

Brahman, 1–2

Buddhism, 30, 148, 154, 156, 157, 212n14. *See also* Yogacara

buhua 不化 (untransforming), 151

busheng 不生 (unproduced), 150–53

Butcher Ding, 176, 178, 181, 183, 186

butterfly, 92

buyan 不言 (not speaking), 198n20

Cantor, Georg, 162
Carpenter Qing, 184–85
Celestial Masters, 7
center, 43
Chan, Alan, 192n14
chang 常 (constancy, regularity), 30–31,
    198n21, 200n43, 214n5; in the *Laozi*, 50,
    51; in the *Liezi*, 151
charioteer, 180
chu 出 (emerging), 88–89
cicada catcher, 179–80, 184
circumstance, 83–85, 112–14; in the *Liezi*,
    165–67
Communal Daoists, 9
complementary contrasts, 38, 40–44
conditions, 84
Confucianism, 64–65, 66, 140, 141, 196n26
Confucius, 5, 11–12, 21, 32–33, 46, 64; char-
    acter in the *Zhuangzi*, 95, 107–8, 134–
    36
constant. *See chang*
contention (*zheng* 争), 70
contextualism, in the *Liezi*, 167
contradiction, 209n85; in the *Qi Wu Lun*,
    116–17, 122–24
contrast, in the *Liezi*, 148
copula, 35, 56, 199n30
cosmic way, 4, 122
cosmology, 24, 191n1; in the *Laozi*, 60–63
cosmos. *See tian*
craftiness, 68, 70, 131
Creator. *See zaowuzhe*
criterion, problem of, 118
Csikszentmihalyi, Mark, 46
cultivation, 33, 36, 66, 106; of life tenden-
    cies, 105–6
culture, 36–37, 38, 134
cyclical change, 40–44, 61

da 大 (vast): in the *Laozi*, 59; in the
    Zhuangzi, 93–98
dao 道 (way), 2, 21–26; as guiding discourse,
    25; as holistic, 23–24; as immanent
    source, 23–24; as indeterminate, 25–26;
    in the *Laozi*, 50–53; as pragmatic, 21–23;
    as process, 21, 24–25
daodejia, 5
"*Daodejing*," 7, 47
"Daoism," problems with label, 3–10
Daoist thought, unity and diversity of, viii,
    ix, 25–26, 80, 126–28, 187–89
daojia 道家 (school of the way), 5–6; and
    daojiao 道教 (doctrines of the way),
    7–10
daoshu 道樞 (axis of the way), 86–87,
    91–92, 117, 119–20
de 德 (potency), 26–27; in the *Zhuangzi*,
    108–10
deconstruction, 136–37; phenomenological,
    157–59
deformity, 108–10
democracy, 74, 75
depth, 51–52
Descartes, 92, 215n12
desire, 69–70, 131, 167
desirelessness, 70–71
destiny. *See ming* 命
determinism, 84, 204n16; in the *Liezi*, 166
dichotomies. *See opposites*
dichotomous evaluation, 114–25
difference, 162–65
Dippman, Jeffrey, 211n10
discipline, 178–79; psychophysical, 105–6
"Discussion on Smoothing Things Out." *See
    Qi Wu Lun*
distinctions, 25, 65, 115, 123, 207nn64–5
dreaming, 92–93; in the *Liezi*, 153–56

effort, 165–66

egoism, 135–36, 139

emerging, 88–89

empire, in the *Laozi*, 72–73

empirical discourse, 20

emptiness, 57–58, 183

enculturation, 37, 196n23

entering, 88, 89

epoché (suspension of judgment), 118, 119, 208n78

essence, 56, 208n67

eternal. *See chang*

ethical concern, 67–68

ethical problem, ix, 27, 33, 65–69, 103–4, 130; solution, 103–4, 139

ethical virtues, 11, 26, 64–69, 200nn52,53

evaluative judgments, 112

existence, 56. *See also you*

existential significance, 18, 82

expansiveness, cultivation of, 94–96, 122

explanation, 149–50; metaphysical, 23–24; naturalistic, 23–24

fajia (Legalism), 5

fallibilism, 120, 122

family resemblance, 203n5

fan 反 (return, reversal), 61–63

fatalism, 84, 204n16

fate. *See ming* 命

fei 非 (it is not, deny, reject), 115

ferryman, 179, 186

flourishing, 5, 36, 43, 131–34, 169–70

focus and field, 96

forgetting, 157–58, 184–85, 186

formlessness, 51–52

fortune and misfortune, 165–67

free and easy wandering. *See xiaoyaoyou*

friends, 106–7

frog in the well, 94

function, 102. *See also wei* 為

fusion of horizons, viii, 14, 119, 194n28

Gadamer, Hans-Georg, viii, 15, 194n28

genuine, 35

genuine humanity, 110–14

ghosts, 193n20

Girardot, Norman, 204n19

God, 85, 193n17

Gongsun Longzi, 11

governing, 71–73

Graham, 146, 147

Graham, Angus Charles, 81, 82, 116–17, 123, 127, 128–29, 139, 146, 147, 208nn67,69, 209n1

grindstone of nature, 86–87, 91

Guanzi, 191n3

Guo Dian, 48, 79

Guo Xiang (Jin dynasty scholar), 80, 83, 96–97, 116, 205n32

guo 國 (state), 71–73

Hall, David, 15

Hanfeizi, 12

Hansen, Chad, 25, 117, 119, 202–3n3

harm, 66, 68–69, 103–4, 113–14, 131, 136–37, 138

He Shang Gong, 47, 192n14

health, 31, 168–70

heaven, 27–32

heaven and earth, 59

hedonism, 166–67

He Guanzi, 191n3

Heidegger, Martin, 56–57, 204n23, 214n4

Hellenistic schools, 193n18

Heraclitus, 42

hermeneutic discourse, 20

hermeneutic methodology, 13–14, 22–23

Hobbes, 213–14n1

holism, 23–24, 121–12

hua 化 (transformation), 85–92

Huainanzi, 146, 191n3

huan 幻 (phenomenal construct, imaginary, *maya*), 156–59

Huang-Lao, 47, 142, 197–98n11

huan 環 (wheel), 86–87

Hui Shi (Huizi), 11, 22, 80, 103, 113–14, 115, 116

human nature, 33–34

human vs. natural, 32–40, 111

humanism, 11–12; Daoist critique, 37, 64–69, 122

humanity, 40. *See also ren* 人; *ren* 仁

hunchback, 179–80

Hundred Schools, 10–12

Husserl, Edmund, 205n36, 207n54

hypocrisy, 64–65, 134–38

idealism, 154–59, 212n23

identity, 208n67

imagery, 13–14, 17

imitation, 180

impartiality, 95

imperceptibility, 51–52, 97

indeterminacy, 51–52, 54, 57–58, 123–25

ineffability, 2

inexhaustible, 95, 97

infinite, 160–62

infinitesimal, 160–62

inhumane, 33

Inner Chapters, 3, 79, 81

instrumentalist epistemology, 215n15

integration, 54, 88. *See also yi* 一

intermediate phases, 90–92, 124–25

interpretation, 13–18

"In the Realm of Human Interactions," 107–8

Ivanhoe, P. J., 46

jia 家 (school, family), 5, 192n8

journeying: in the *Zhuangzi*; in the *Liezi*, 157–59

kindness. *See ren* 仁

"King Mu of Zhou," 154, 155, 156

Kjellberg, Paul, 117–18

Klein, Esther, 203n8

knowing how, 171

knowing that, 171

knowledge, 120, 130–31, 165, 167, 214n7; verbal vs. embodied, 170–74, 180–81. *See also* craftiness; skepticism

Kohn, Livia, 9–10, 193n21

Kun, 17, 85, 204n19

language, 25, 34, 125, 170–74, 209n86

Lao Dan, 46, 147

Lao-Zhuang, 193n21

Laozi text, 16, 79, 82

large and small, in the *Laozi*, 72–73, 74, 76–77

Lau, D. C., 48

laws, 26, 64

laws of nature, 132

Legalism, 140, 141

li 禮 (ceremony, ritual, propriety), 33, 46

libertarianism, 72–73, 75–77

Liezi text, 16

lifeworld, 205n36

lineage, 192n8

Linguistic school, 5, 195n5

Literati Daoists, 9–10, 193n21

Littlejohn, Ronnie, 211n10, 214n7

Liu Xiang, 74, 128, 146, 202n70, 209n1

living and dying, 87–89, 92–93, 106

Lloyd, Geoffrey, 194–95n1

logocentrism, 136–37

longevity, 170. *See also* natural years

Lundberg, Brian, 207n58

Lüshi Chunqiu, 146, 191n3

Ma Wang Dui, 47, 142

McCraw, David, 203n8

meaning bestowing, 157

memory, 157–58

men 門 (gateway, door), 53

Mencius, 11, 33, 79, 80, 107, 129, 196n24, 200n53, 202–3n3

metaphor, 13–14, 17

metaphysical concepts, 22

metaphysics, 24, 56–57, 192n13

metapolitics, 48, 83, 192n13

methodology, philosophical, viii, 12–18. *See also* textual phenomenology

Miller, James, 193n15

ming 名 (linguistic terminology, names), 34, 70

ming 命 (circumstance, destiny, fate, life), 83–85, 171, 177; in the *Liezi*, 165–67

ming 明 (clarity), 114, 117, 119–20

Mingjia (Linguistic school), 5, 195n5

minimal artifice (*wuwei*), 73–74, 100–2

Miscellaneous Chapters, 81–82, 126–28

modes of discourse, 20

Moeller, Hans-Georg, 16, 48, 192n13, 201n55, 205n32

Mojia (Mohism), 5, 65, 79, 121, 140, 141, 194n24, 208n70

mother, 53–54

Mozi, 11, 21, 162, 205–6n37, 213–14n1

mutuality, 89. *See also* complementary contrasts

myriad things, 59–60

mystery, 51–52

namelessness, 70

names. *See ming* 名

natural abilities, 176–77

natural tendencies, 29, 31–32, 129, 131–34, 176–77

natural years, 104–6, 110, 168

naturalistic concepts, 22, 54–55

nature, 27–32, 73–74, 168–70; as inner tendencies, 29

negation, Daoist, 58

Nei Ye ("Inward Training"), 105

Nietzsche, 95, 200n52

Non-being. *See wu*

nonexistence, 57. *See also wu*

not doing. *See wuwei*

nothing. *See wu*

nurturing, 53, 54, 66, 106; of ruler, 75

one. *See yi*

ontology, 55–58

opposites, 23–24, 42, 123

optimal minimizing, 58

origin, 23–24, 53–55

Original Tao: Inward Training, 191n3

ou 偶 (counterpart), 86

outcasts, 108–10

Outer Chapters, 81–82, 126–28

paradoxes, 82, 202n69; ethical, 66, 68; of action, 73–74; in the *Liezi*, 150; of rulership, 72, 74–75; in the *Zhuangzi*, 116, 122–24

parallel structure, 16

Parmenides, 56, 57

Peerenboom, Randy, 142

Peirce, Charles Sanders, 22, 195n6

"Penetrating Life" ("*Da Sheng*"), 81, 176

Peng, 85, 97, 99

perception, refinement of, 181–84

performance, 184–86

performative utterance, 84

perspective, 4, 67–68, 93–98, 99, 119, 121; cosmic, 93–99, 103, 112

perspectivism, 95, 121–22

phenomenal construct, 156–59

phenomenological discourse, 16–17, 53

philosophy, 8–9

Plato, 87–88, 215n12

pluralism, 164, 121, 122, 208–9n80

Polanyi, 215n13

potency. *See de*

potter's wheel of nature, 86–87, 91

practice, 178, 179, 180

pragmatic discourse, 20, 21–23, 35, 149

pragmatism, 18, 83, 121

Primitivist, 128–29

process, 40, 42, 43, 52, 123–25, 160. *See also* cyclical change; transformation

profit, 135–36

proto-Daoist, 8–9

pu 樸 (simplicity), 70–71, 130, 201n58

Qi Wu Lun, 114–25

qi 氣 (air, breath, energy, mass-energy), 43, 91, 98, 107

qi 齊 (smooth, equalize), 207n63

qing 情 (emotions, circumstances, conditions, nature), 115, 208nn67,69

Quan Zhen, 7

Raphals, Lisa, 117–18, 202–3n3

rational discourse, 20

real. *See zhen*

realism, 154

Reality, 21, 22

regular. *See chang*

relativism, 83, 96–98, 101, 116, 118, 120, 121, 122, 137, 164, 208–9n80

religion, 7–10, 193n17, 193n19

Ren Jian Shi (the realm of human interactions), 207n58

ren 人 (human), 32–33, 34–47

ren 仁 (humanity), 32–33

renqing 人情 (human emotions or circumstances), 115, 130, 202n3

renyi shifei 仁義是非 (virtues and evaluations), 116

returning, 37, 43, 52. *See also fan*

"Rifling Trunks," 130–31

right and wrong. *See shifei*

ritual. *See li*

Robber Zhi, 134–35, 137

root, 53, 54

Roth, Harold, 105, 191n3, 192n8, 209n1

ru 入 (entering), 88, 89

rujia (Ruism, Confucianism), 5

rulership, 71–73; as maternal, 75; reluctant, 138–39

Ru-Mo (Ruists and Mohists), 12, 94–95, 116, 121, 122, 147

Ryle, Gilbert, 171, 214n4, 215n16

sage, in the *Zhuangzi*. *See zhenren; zhiren*

sage ruler: in the *Laozi*, 74–77; in the *Inner Chapters*, 110

sageliness within and kingliness without, 141

sameness and difference, 162–65

school (*jia*), 192n8

School of Names. *See* Linguistic school

school of Zhuangzi, 81, 128

self-governing, 70

shen 神 (spirit), 182–83

sheng 生 (life, birth, produce), 88, 151, 212n20

shengren 聖人 (sage, wise ruler), 74–77

shi 始 (beginning), 53, 90

shi 是 (this, affirm), 86, 115

shifei 是非 (evaluative judgment, right and wrong), 83, 114–25

Shun, 135, 136, 138

silk manuscripts, 47, 142

Sim, May, 203–4n13

Sima Qian (Grand Historian), 45, 46

Sima Tan (Grand Historian, father of Sima Qian), 5–6, 7, 71, 142

similarity, 162

simplicity, 37, 70–71, 130

"Signs of the Fullness of Potency," 108–10

Sivin, Nathan, 194–95n1

Six Schools, 5–6

skepticism, 82, 92, 101, 117, 118, 119, 122

Skepticism, Greek, 117–18, 119

skill, 168–86; acquisition, 179–81; clas-
    sification and terminology, 174–76;
    development, three stages of, 178–79; in
    the *Laozi*, 74, 76

social relations, 71

something. *See you*

source, 23–24, 26, 53–55

space, 160–61

spontaneity, 31–32, 134, 178. *See also ziran*

Spring and Autumn period, 10–12

state (political), 71–73

stoicism, 83, 84, 95, 112–15, 203–4n13

subtle tendencies, 181–85

subtlety, 51–52

swimmer, 185–86

Syncretists, 48, 110, 139–42

Taiping, 7

technology, 35, 38, 174

ten thousand things, 59–60

textual phenomenology, ix, 15, 16–18

that's it which deems. *See weishi* 為是

that's it which goes by circumstance. *See
    yinshi*

"The Mountain Tree," 98

things, 60, 89, 151, 160

this and that, 86

tian 天 (cosmos), 27–32, 84; in the *Laozi*,
    59

"*Tian Dao*," 141–42

tiandi 天地 (cosmos, heaven and earth), 27;
    in the *Laozi*, 59

tianjun 天均 (potter's wheel of nature),
    87

tianni 天倪 (grindstone of nature), 87

tiannian 天年 (natural years), 104–6

tianxia 天下 (the whole world), 59; as
    empire, 72–73

tianxing 天性 (tendencies of nature), 184–85

"*Tian Xia*," 140–41

time, 160–62

tong 同 (same), 162–65

tong wei yi 通為一 (merge continuously),
    86, 91

tranquility, 101, 124–25

transcendence, 1–2, 22, 23–24, 30,
    196nn11,16; in the *Laozi*, 49, 54–55; in
    the *Liezi*, 149–50, 152–53; naturalized,
    30–32

transfinite, 161–62

transformation, 40–44, 61, 85–92; in the
    Liezi, 150, 151, 156–57

transvaluation of values, 66, 200n52

true. *See zhen*

true man. *See genuine humanity*

truth, 21, 194nn27,29

unborn. *See unproduced*

uncarved block. *See pu* 樸

universal claims, vs. generalizations, 16,
    17–18

unproduced, 150–53

use, 58, 102

uselessness, 102–4, 108–10

utopia, in the *Laozi*, 71–72

Utopian strand, 48, 82, 128–39

vagueness, 42, 123–25

vastness, 59, 93–98

Vasubandhu, 154

Vedanta, 1–2

virtue. *See de*

Wagner, Rudolf, 194n30

wai 外 (beyond), 160–61

wandering, 98–100

Wang Bi, 47, 192n14, 197n9, 199n32

wanwu 萬物 (myriad things), 59–60

Warring States, 10–12

way, 4. *See also* dao

way of the ancients, 141

wei 偽 (artifice), 34–35, 111, 129

wei 微 (minuteness), 52

wei 為 (activity), 34–35, 100–101

weishi 未始 (not yet begun), 90, 205n26

weishi 為是 (deeming judgment), 117

wen 文 (culture), 36–37

wheel, 86–87, 91–92

Wheelwright Bian, 171–72, 174

whetstone. *See* grindstone of nature

Wittgenstein, Ludwig, 203n5, 204n23

world, 59

wu 無 (absence, nothing), 55, 57–58, 87, 90,
   99–100

wu 無有 (absence, nothing), 87

wu 物 (things), 60

wuji 無極 (limitless, infinite), 160–62

wujin 無盡 (inexhaustible, infinitesimal),
   160–62

wuwei 無為 (minimal artifice, not doing),
   73–74, 100–2, 140, 141, 142

wuyong 無用 (useless), 102–4

wuyu 無欲 (without desires), 58

wuzhi 無知 (without knowledge), 58

xi 希 (subtlety), 52

xiao 小 (petty, small), 94

xiaoyaoyou 逍遥遊 (wandering beyond),
   98–100. *See also* vastness

xing 性 (natural tendencies), 29, 129,
   131–34, 176–77

xingming zhi qing 性命之情 (conditions of
   natural tendencies and lifespan), 129–30,
   131–34

xinzhai 心齋 (attenuation of the heart-
   mind), 106–8, 184–85

xuan 玄 (mystery, darkness, profundity),
   51–52

Xuanxue (abstruse learning), 197n9

Xunzi, 11, 27, 29, 33, 35, 36, 129, 131, 140, 142,
   167, 213–14n1

Yang Bojun, 211n2

Yang Zhu (Yangzi), 79–80, 139

"*Yang Zhu*" (chapter), 146, 166–67

Yangists, 128–29

Yanhui, 107–8, 113

yao 夭 (untimely death), 104–5

Yao, 135, 136

yi 一 (integration, continuity, one), 63–64,
   91

yi 異 (different), 162–65

yi 義 (rightness, appropriateness), 33, 64

"Yielding the Throne," 138–39

yin 因 (criterion), 209n88

yin 陰, priority of, 43–44, 62, 170

yinshi 因是 (adaptable judgment), 117, 122

yinyang 陰陽, 40–44, 133–34, 197n30

Yinyangjia, 5

Yogacara, 93, 154

you 有 (presence, something), 55–57, 87, 90

youwei 有為 (active governing), 141

yu 欲 (desire), 69–70

zaowuzhe 造物者 (maker of things), 85

Zen (Chan Buddhism), 82

Zhang Ling, 7

Zhang Zhan, 146

zhen 真 (genuine), 110–11

zhenren 真人 (genuine humanity), 110–
   14

zhi 治 (governing), 5–6, 71–73

zhiren 至人 (achieved person), 95, 97–98

Zhou dynasty, 10

Zhuang Wanshou, 211n8

Zhuangzi anthology, 3, 80–82, 126–28

Zhuangzi text, 16

Zhuangzian philosophy, 3, 81–83, 128

Zhuangzian vs. Zhuangist, 203n11

zi 子 (master), 2

ziran 自然 (naturalness, spontaneity), 74, 75. *See also zizheng*

zisheng 自生 (self-producing), 59

zizheng 自正 (self-governing), 70

zong 宗 (ancestral), 53–55

CPSIA information can be obtained
at www.ICGtesting.com
Printed in the USA
LVOW12s2310090318
569348LV00001B/7/P